URBAN LAND REFORM IN CHINA

Urban Land Reform in China

Li Ling Hin
Associate Professor
Department of Real Estate and Construction
University of Hong Kong

First published in Great Britain 1999 by
MACMILLAN PRESS LTD
Houndmills, Basingstoke, Hampshire RG21 6XS and London
Companies and representatives throughout the world

A catalogue record for this book is available from the British Library.

ISBN 0–333–75025–X

First published in the United States of America 1999 by
ST. MARTIN'S PRESS, INC.,
Scholarly and Reference Division,
175 Fifth Avenue, New York, N.Y. 10010

ISBN 0–312–21972–5

Library of Congress Cataloging-in-Publication Data
Li, Ling–hin.
Urban land reform in China / Li Ling Hin.
p. cm.
Includes bibliographical references and index.
ISBN 0–312–21972–5
1. Land reform—China. 2. Land use, Urban—China. 3. Land
tenure—Government policy—China. 4. Land reform—China—Shanghai–
–Case studies. 5. Land reform—China—Hong Kong—Case studies.
I. Title.
HD1333.C6L52   1999
333.3'151—dc21   98–54736
                                                               CIP

This book is printed on paper suitable for recycling and made from fully managed and
sustained forest sources.

10   9   8   7   6   5   4   3   2   1
08   07   06   05   04   03   02   01   00   99

Printed and bound in Great Britain by
Antony Rowe Ltd, Chippenham, Wiltshire

To my son Nicholas

for his smiles change my world

Contents

List of Tables

List of Figures

Preface

China is a huge country in terms of size, population and even economy. When I first started to formulate my ideas for this book I intended to attempt to explain the overall economic reforms as well as the reform of the urban land system. This proved impossible as the interaction between the different subsectors of the economy is so complicated that a reasonable analysis would take years to complete and by then the reforms would have proceeded to another stage. Consequently the analysis focuses on the evolution of the urban land market. There are various reasons for choosing this sector. For example land is an extremely important issue in China as there are so many people to feed, and land reform in rural areas has had important political implications for the ruling class throughout the history of China. However, as China is becoming more and more urbanised the issue of urban land management has yet to be systemised. The main problem with the urban land management system in contemporary China is that it is now intertwined with the property market, which did not exist until the 1990s. The lack of a price system for the allocation of an asset with such an important monetary value in a market system gives a special flavour to this discussion.

Chinese people are addicted to customs, and when any major change is to take place there is always the problem of coordinating this with the prevailing tradition. This was the case with the urban land reform, the tradition in this case being that land ownership should remain firmly in the hands of the government on behalf of the people since the total privatisation of land would mean the creation of a landless class, something considered intolerable in market socialism. Trapped in the dilemma of releasing the government's duty to provide land to users without any monetary consideration and the fear of concentrating land in the hands of those with hard cash and overseas investors, the Chinese authorities adopted a step-by-step approach to the reform. This gradual approach created uncertainty and even chaos at the beginning as no clear signal was given to the market players. However this was the appropriate approach at the time, given the various constraints. The first step forward was difficult and even painful as the market giant had not walked for almost 40 years.

The mere creation of a market is not enough for Chinese urban land reform as more issues are involved than in, say, privatisation of the sugar trade. Chinese cities can now be seen as the biggest construction sites in the world and the implications of this for the socio-political setting are interesting. In addition Premier Zhu Rongji has also made it clear that within his term of office, housing reform, which is being built upon the foundations of the urban land reform, has to be accomplished. For all these reasons part of the focus here will be on the origin of the process, that is, the evolution of the land system in China.

A special feature of this book are two contrasting case-studies: one on the reform of the urban land market in Shanghai, especially the introduction of land use rights as a way of rejuvenating the city; the other on Hong Kong, whose return to mainland China in 1997 added an important dimension to China's transition to a market system within a socialist setting. The irony is that while mainland China is moving towards completion of the market mechanism, Hong Kong is witnessing growing government participation in the land market. The eagerness of the Hong Kong government to rectify the high land and property price situation left behind by the colonial administration has led to it being blamed for the sharp downturn of the economy and the property market. Ironically, the Asian economic crisis at the end of 1997 would have done the same job of adjusting the overheated economy without the same price being paid by the government. The experience of Hong Kong offers an excellent lesson for China on the role and impact of government policies in the urban land market, but that lesson has yet to be learnt.

This book studies the process of urban land reform by looking at the approach taken by China and the results obtained so far. It does not imply that China's approach is the best one as further problems are expected to emerge. What one should remember is that society is so attached to the land that no matter how strong the need for reform, cultural factors should not be disregarded. Reform measures that look good in one society may only be window dressing in others if the implementation constraints are deemed insurmountable.

University of Hong Kong   LI LING HIN

Acknowledgements

The research underpinning this book was supported by the Research Grant Council of Hong Kong. Before starting to write this book I dedicated more than six months to planning its structure and collecting data. The book would not have become a reality had I not been blessed by the assistance of many people. I would like to thank my publisher and project editor Sunder Katwala and copy-editor Keith Povey for their assistance, my student Felix Wong for providing me with ideas on the Hong Kong land market, Dr K. K. Lee in Taiwan for his comments on the ancient Chinese land tenure system, and above all Lisa Incher, my research assistant, for her talented background research and translation. In addition, credit should go to all of my friends in mainland China for their help and assistance in collecting data. Finally, I would like to thank my family, my beloved wife Vivienne and my son Nicholas for supporting me.

LI LING HIN

List of Abbreviations

BMP	Benchmark Price
CIREA	China Institute of Real Estate Appraisers
CLVI	China Land Valuer Institute
CPLD	Committee on Planning and Land Development
CREPR	Certificate of Real Estate Property Rights
DPC	Development Progress Committee
GFA	Gross Floor Area
HDB	Housing Development Bond
LBAC	Land and Building Advisory Committee
LDPC	Land Development Policy Committee
LUR	Land Use Right
MoC	Ministry of Construction
MSLNR	Ministry of State Land and Natural Resources
NPC	National People's Congress
OZP	Outline Zoning Plan
PELB	Planning, Environment and Land Branch
PHRO	Provincial Housing Reform Office
PPCL	Planning Permit for Construction Land
PPCP	Planning Permit for Construction Projects
READ	Real Estate Administration Department
REEC	Real Estate Exchange Centre
SAAB	State Asset Administration Bureau
SAR	Special Administrative Region
SHC	Shanghai Housing Committee
SHLAB	Shanghai Housing and Land Administration Bureau
SLAB	State Land Administration Bureau
SSPDP	Site Selection Proposal for Development Projects
SUPMB	Shanghai Urban Planning Management Bureau
TPB	Town Planning Board
WRB	Wuhan Railway Bureau

Introduction

Since the fall of the Berlin Wall the focus on the socialist system has become more economic than political. The term 'transitional economies' has been used to describe countries engaged in the reform of the socialist system, and research interest in the changes taking place in these countries has been enormous. However most studies concentrate on macroeconomic development and the operation of the price system in the transitional economies (Banuri, 1991; Corbo *et al.*, 1991), and relatively little attention is given to an important aspect of all market economies – the urban land market (an exception is Bertaud and Renaud, 1992).

Hence there is a strong need to investigate the effects of privatisation on the operation of the urban land market in transitional economies. However such an examination requires an active land market with a certain amount of open-market activity, which is not always the case in the ex-Soviet economies. In China the transition process is quite different from that in Eastern Europe. Instead of aiming for a purely capitalist socioeconomic system, China is moving towards 'market socialism'. This means that the socialist/planned economic system in China will not be swept away completely, but will merge with the market mechanism. Hence China's reforms are more complicated than the privatisation programmes underway in Eastern Europe.

This book will examine the Chinese approach to urban land reform from a management and policy perspective rather than provide an economic analysis. This is because the Chinese approach to urban land reform can be regarded as a management approach since the evolving urban land system is a leasehold system and there are more management tools for the state to utilise than in other situations. The other reason for examining the issue from the management viewpoint is to provide a different angle on market reform.

The purpose of discussing the Chinese approach to urban land reform is not to provide other emerging economies with a better solution. Rather it is to highlight an aspect of privatisation that is not found among the economies of Eastern Europe, namely privatisation of the market without an overhaul of the socio-political system.

The book commences with a review of the history of land reform in China in order to explain the cultural factors underlying the current reforms. These cultural factors may be unique to China, but they illustrate the need for all countries to take such matters into account when introducing a new system. Past attempts to develop a proper land tenure system show that it is not a question of whether private or public land ownership is the more superior. In fact these two systems have tended to coexist in China for long periods of time and under various political regimes. The crucial factor is finding the right balance between the two.

The discussion then moves on to the current reforms. The various frameworks are described in turn so that China's urban land reform can be understood in terms of general policy, legal provisions, financial provisions and governmental structure.

Housing reform is one of Premier Zhu Rongji's main priorities. A major aim of this reform is to turn some housing into a tradable commodity that is capable of attracting private investment. The urban land reform is providing a solid foundation for future housing reform as land has to be freely tradable before private developers will start to build houses. The discussion in Chapter 3 of the private housing market, or commodity housing market, serves to illustrate the positive role of a market land system. The need for housing reform in the public sector is even more pressing given the heavy financial burden borne by state enterprises and government units. In this respect, four local initiatives are discussed in detail. A nationwide housing initiative, the *anju* project, is also examined.

Chapter 4 presents the initial outcomes of the reform. Because the urban land system is interlocked with many other aspects of the macroeconomy the reform is producing multiplier effects on the economy as a whole, especially as more internal and foreign investment has been attracted than was initially envisaged. Hence we shall look at the contribution that the urban land market has made to state and local government revenues, as well as to the lives of ordinary people in terms of employment creation and wage increases. Considerable progress has been made towards the creation of a pricing mechanism for urban land. Since land had no monetary value under the communist doctrine, the successful commercialisation of urban real estate has been highly dependent on the establishment of such a mechanism. As the Chinese system involves the leasing rather than the outright sale of land, local government, acting as land owner on behalf of the people, has full control over the purpose to which land is put and the sale of so-called 'land use rights'.

Chapters 5 and 6 are case studies of two of China's major commercial cities. Chapter 5 examines Shanghai, which for most of its existence has been the most prosperous city in China. Numerous pieces of land have been sold in Shanghai since 1992 and the city has been transformed into a modern commercial and financial metropolis that attracts considerable foreign investment. The Hong Kong Special Administrative Region, on the other hand, is the most unique city in China and the subject of Chapter 6. Being a former British colony, a well-developed land tenure system has been in place for many years. The leasehold land system created in what has been one of the freest economies in the world provides the ideal workshop for Chinese reform leaders wishing to examine the effects of government intervention in the urban land market. Since the urban land reform on the mainland also involves the establishment a leasehold system, many lessons can be drawn for the country as a whole.

This examination leads to the conclusion of this review of the Chinese approach to urban land reform. The final chapter looks at the changes the reform has brought to the economy and the factors that have contributed to the initial success of the reform. The problems that need to be tackled before China can act as a successful example for other reforming economies are also listed.

It should be reiterated here that the discussion in this book is aimed at highlighting the special characteristics of the Chinese approach to land issues. Given the existing socio-political environment, this approach has produced satisfactory results. But policies should change with the environment and adjustments must continue to be made, and this depends very much on the willingness of the authorities.

1 Evolution of the Land Tenure System in China

CHINA'S ANCIENT LAND SYSTEM

The current urban land reform in China, which represents a major step towards the market economy, is not a completely new idea in the history of China. In China, and indeed other countries, the evolution of the land tenure system has depended to a certain extent on the historical socio-economic development of society. Hence the substance of an urban land tenure system should change with the environment in question. This evolutionary progression improves the land system by rectifying past mistakes and enhancing the positive aspects. This review of China's ancient land tenure system will show that urban land reform is not a new development, and that the current reform should not be viewed as a new system, superimposed onto the old, deeply rooted one, rather that the past has provided some valuable lessons for the modern age.

Land ownership was not a particularly important issue in ancient times when the population was much smaller. It was obviously unnecessary to attempt to structure any kind of land tenure system when people were free to move about to find a new piece of land for food production. When feudal society began to develop the concept of state land began to emerge. During the Xia Dynasty, land, together with ruling rights, was handed to ministers in fringe areas of the country as a reward for their loyalty as well as to set up a natural defence barrier around the empire. By this time, an embryonic form of state ownership could be observed.

In the Shang Dynasty, which immediately followed the Xia Dynasty, agriculture became much more sophisticated and there was a pressing need to establish a better land management system. State land (mainly agricultural land) was distributed to households for farming and in return their produce was taxed to boost the national reserves. This was the *zhu fa* or help system. Under this system, each household was given 70 mu of agricultural land for their own production (1 mu $\simeq$ 43 560 sq. ft.). Apart from the tax in kind, they also had to farm a communal field. This was the origin of the famous 'well-field' system, discussed below.

During the West Zhou Dynasty society became more sophisticated in terms of both economy and culture. A full feudal society was more or less developed during this period. 'Over the nation, there are only crown lands.

1

Managing these crown lands are the subjects of the King' was the famous cry of the ruling class. At that time the land tenure system was integrated with the political system of *feng di*, or land granting. Under the Zhou feudal system all people were classified into five categories. At the top was the emperor, *tian zi*, or son of heaven. Under him, in descending order, came the royal families, ministers, scholars and the lowest class, the untouchables. As all land belonged to the *tian zi*, he had absolute rights over it and all the people on it. The emperor could bequeath land to members of the royal family, and to ministers who had shown loyalty or contributed significantly to the empire. These people became *de facto* rulers of their alloted land and enjoyed the same rights as the emperor.

An interesting aspect of this system was that the recipients of granted land had the right to bequeath the land to their own ministers or family members. Peasant farmers could rent farmland from the landholders, and the rent was normally in kind. In addition the farmers had to pay a periodic contribution to the landholders according to their means. Such contributions were usually livestock or whatever the farmers could capture in the wild. Finally, farmers also had to perform a certain amount of labour for the landholder, such as maintaining walls and bridges. In this way there developed a hierarchical land tenure system that interlocked with the political structure.

For their part the landholders had to pay taxes in kind to the emperor, the amount and nature of which depended on the size and location of the land. They were also required to provide men for the national army and labour for various infrastructural projects. In this way, the emperor was able to develop and expand his empire with little expenditure of effort on his part.

This new land system prompted a need for an inheritance system for granted land. Consequently the system of *zhong zi* was developed during the West Zhou Dynasty. *Zhong zi* means the eldest son of the first (legitimate) wife – in this society a man could have a wife and a large number of concubines, but the status of the first wife was always supreme. All granted land was inherited by the *zhong zi*, or, if he died before his father, the second son, and so on down the male line. Hence the land remained in the family and a social system, rather than a legal framework, was developed for the protection and preservation of property rights. In a society where legal regulations were not a common way of controlling human behaviour, this cultural custom provided the means to do so and the quasi-private land ownership system was able to be extended.

A distinctive feature of the ancient land management system in China was the coexistence of freehold and leasehold land tenure systems. These were built upon the foundation of the agricultural economy. The well-field or *jin tian* system was a major mechanism in this system. The Chinese character for the word *jin*, which means water well, looks like a grid with nine equal squares. Eight households in the neighbourhood were given a square for their own use, leaving the centre square as public field. The eight outer squares were leasehold farmland whereas the centre square was freehold farmland belonging to the state or the landholder. The lease-holders, apart from paying land rent in the form of farm products to the landlord, were also required to farm the freehold land on a collective basis. Under the Zhou system, each square was about 100 mu in size (unfortunately there are no records of the actual size of a mu during this period).

There are few historical records on the actual operation of the well-field system, but it is known that Mencius, a disciple of Confucius, was a great supporter of the system. The main advantage of the system was that it allowed land to be utilised to its maximum potential by the leaseholders. It is also believed that the well-field system promoted good relations among neighbours as the farming of the public land depended on the coop-eration of the eight leaseholders of the land surrounding it.

From the freeholders' point of view this was the least costly method of developing their land as they had no need to manage their fields or agri-cultural production directly. This economic system was an integral part of the political and social system. From the ruling class's point of view, the system also helped stabilise the migration of citizens as the farming proce-dure of the well-field agricultural land required the leasehold to gather together around the centre freehold land. It more or less confined. The mobility of the leaseholders.

The unification of China established during the Zhou Dynasty was soon eroded after the collapse of the East Zhou Dynasty and the rise of the war-rior states. Due to the loss of credibility of the Zhou *tian zi*, royal family members who had been granted land began to set up independent states and expansionism by military means became the main activity of all the warrior states. As a result, private land ownership was extended and strengthened.

The collapse of the feudal land system, and hence the public ownership of land, at this stage can be attributed to a number of factors, including a change in the urban system. After the collapse of the Zhou Dynasty, warlord landholders created a local government system based on *jun* and *xian* – a *xian* is similar to the modernday county and a *jun* is a much larger *xian*. The warlords appointed their own officials to manage the *juns* and *xians* and the old state land system, whereby all land belonged to the crown, effectively came to an end. In addition migratory trading activities became more and more important economically. Consequently more investment was made in land, especially in urban areas, where markets for trading were created. As a result the well-field system, upon which public land ownership had been based, faced increasing challenges. In 4 BC a minister to the ruler of Wei State pronounced a drive to maximise land utilisation. The 'maximisation of the benefits of land and labour' or *jin di li* was designed to encourage people to engage in agriculture for their livelihood. He also instituted a surplus tax on grain, payable in kind in good harvest years. This grain was stored and redistributed to the people in times of famine and it is thought that the system resulted in Wei State becoming wealthy and powerful.

The *jin di li* system had a lot of supporters, including Gong Sun Yang, or Shang Yang as he was more commonly known. Shang Yang was a famous economist and politician who preferred practical solutions to theoretical hypotheses. He took his ideas to Qin State, where he worked his way up the bureaucratic ladder, initiating policies that would lead to the maximisation of land and labour.

The warrior state era was one of the most chaotic and disruptive eras in ancient Chinese history. It was a period when China was split into separate kingdoms, each trying to conquer the others. Hence territorial expansion was both strategically and practically important. It was against this background that Shang Yang encouraged migration from kingdoms with large populations and little land to Qin State, which was sparsely populated and had an abundance of land. By levying heavy taxes on farmers he forced them to open up virgin land and thus increase agricultural productivity. This was the famous *kai qian mai* ('expand and open up new land') policy, which not only opened up new lands but also guaranteed state revenues and weakened rival states by robbing them of their manpower. In realising his goals Shang Yang changed the pattern of landholding and private ownership came into formal existence. Ironically, it was precisely this privatisation of land – which was considered responsible for the later concentration of land in the hands of wealthy and powerful families – that led to Shang Yang being the subject of harsh criticism.

To increase agricultural productivity, Shang Yang also introduced *yuan tian* (wheel field), a system of field rotation. Fields were graded according to their fertility and the more fertile land was more intensively cultivated than the poorer land, ensuring efficient land use and guarding against overcropping. He also established a cadastral system, which led to the establishment of a large number of small peasant holdings. This allowed the imposition of uniform taxation so that the government could exact the maximum amount of income from the land.

To maximise labour utilisation Shang Yang introduced a system of rewards and punishments. Those who engaged in agriculture were rewarded with tax exemptions, whilst those engaged in non-agricultural occupations were reported and made into government slaves. The tax on households with more than one male was doubled in order to encourage men to go out and till their own fields, thereby doing away with underemployment whilst increasing the amount of land under cultivation. Policies such as these contributed significantly to the success of the Qin Empire.

Eventually Qin Si Huang (*Si Huang* means the first emperor) managed to conquer all the other states and unify the country, by which time private land ownership had been in existence for almost a hundred years. During the Qin Dynasty, land was traded freely and became concentrated among a few families. Since the Qin government regarded trade as more important than agriculture, land trading was not restricted and the landless farming class was plunged into poverty. Under these circumstances the fall of the Qin Empire became inevitable and it was eventually replaced by the strong Han Dynasty.

Under the Han system, although private land ownership continued there was also a revival of the ancient crown land and land-grant system. The main difference between the Han system and the Zhou system was that under the Han system, royal family members and ministers who helped to build the empire were given land based on the number of households living on it. In the other words the highest award of land carried the largest number of household. However, when Emperor Wu separated the administration of the royal family from the government structure, the land-grant system became superfluous.

As a result of financial and monetary reforms during the Han Dynasty the use of currency became more widespread. This caused an expansion of trading activities, including trade in land, which was engaged in by countless people from the *tian zi* down to the lowest untouchables.[1] There is a record to show that a prime minister once purchased a substantial amount of land at a depressed price.[2] This phenomenon of 'land banking' led to royal family members gradually losing administrative power over their land holdings. Furthermore the private land market was developed to a stage where even property rights were recognised. Land conveyance deeds recording the sellers' and vendors' names as well as a description of the land have been found among the historical records.[3]

As this 'land banking' problem became more and more acute, poor people, especially landless farmers, grew ever more dissatisfied, so during Emperor Wu's reign, a scholar who was also a consultant to the *tian zi*, Dong Zhong Shu, advocated a much needed land reform. In line with his

Confucius ideology, Dong proposed a *xian min ming tian* or antimonopoly land system whereby nobody could hold more than 30 hectares of land. In addition to the limitation on land ownership, there was also a limitation on the number of slaves a person could own. However, due to political pressure, especially from the royal family, which was the major landowner, the antimonopoly system collapsed.

The establishment of the Xin Dynasty gave rise to the introduction of a socialist land tenure system. Emperor Wang had been a senior official in the Han government and understood the problem of overconcentration of land ownership. Hence he initiated the *wang tian* or crown field system, which was similar to the well-field system and effectively reestablished the public ownership of land. All households of eight people or fewer who owned more than one square (as in the square in the well-field system) of land had to return the surplus land to the state. This land was then redistributed to the landless for farming purposes. Emperor Wang also nationalised major industries such as salt, wine, iron, forestry, coin minting, clothing and copper in the hope of stabilising supply and prices.

Because of the rapid turnaround of the land tenure system, the crown field system created more problems than it solved, and due to severe opposition from vested interests the system eventually failed. This failure shows how difficult it is to reintroduce public ownership when substantial vested interests are involved. However, this does not necessarily mean that the reverse is true, and the combining of public land ownership with private ownership can produce different results. We shall discuss this later.

The period after the Xin Dynasty was another chaotic time in Chinese history. The 'Era of the Three States' (Wei State, Su State and Wu State) saw the return of war and conflict, which led to a substantial population decrease – by approximately six sevenths according to one historical account.[4] As a result there was plenty of land for all and political rivalry overrode the setting up of a good land tenure system. Hence land concentration continued.

As far as public land was concerned, there were several attempts to rationalise the management system. The population decrease meant that a lot of agricultural land lay fallow and this caused serious food problems. As a result Cao Cao, a powerful minister in Wei State, initiated the *tun tian* or the communal field system. There were two types of *tun tian*: military *tun tian* and civilian *tun tian*. In the military *tun tian*, the army occupied and farmed the land and all produce was the property of the government. In civilian *tun tian*, civilians were invited or sometimes forced to occupy and farm vacant land. Each civilian *tun* was like a commune and was composed of 50 people, each of whom farmed 50 mu of land. Those who borrowed cows from the state government had to give 60 per cent of their products to the state as land rent, or 50 per cent if they did not need state cows. They also had to perform certain labour services on the top of paying the land rent.

After the chaotic Three States era had ended the political rulers of the Jin Dynasty moved to end the trend of land banking by large landlords and the families of former warlords. Under the *zhang tian fa*, or the Possession of Farmland Law, a limit was imposed on the amount of land a government official could hold. For instance a grade one official, the highest rank in the government structure, could hold a maximum of 50 hectares, a grade two official could have no more than 45 hectares, and so on. However, due to the continuing problem of vested interests and unresolved political and military rivalries, this law only paid lip service to the problem.

During the subsequent South and North Dynasties, a protracted period of war and conflict gave rise to a need to increase production and stabilise the society. The *jun tian* or equal distribution of land system was an attempt to revive the public land ownership system. Under this system agricultural land was allocated to citizens according to certain criteria, for example men over the age of 15 received 40 mu of land while women above the age of 20 received 20 mu. Land was also allocated to government staff. Households who had owned land before the *jun tian* system was implemented could keep the land as long as it was less than 20 mu. Any land in excess of this limit had to be sold, although there are no records or other documents showing how this excess land was sold.

The *jun tian* system continued throughout the Xui Dynasty and into the Tang Dynasty. Under the Xui system adult males were allocated 80 mu of agricultural land and women received 40 mu. This was leasehold land and it had to be returned to the state when the leaseholders reached the age of 66. In addition to this, all the male members of households were given 20 mu of freehold land. With regard to land for dwellings, one mu of residential land was given to every three members of the household and one mu was allocated to every five household slaves. The royal family's allocation ranged from 100 hectares to 40 mu, depending on their rank, and all the land was freehold. For the government staff, grade one staff received five hectares and each lower rank received five mu less. This land was treated as part of their salaries and stayed with the job.

The Tang Dynasty's *jun tian* system was very similar to that of the Xui. It was prohibited to sell freehold land except under certain circumstances, such as when poor families needed money for the household or families had been allocated insufficient land and needed to purchase extra. In such cases, prior permission was needed. This system, as with all the previous land ownership systems, depended very much on the political will of the government. At the beginning of the dynasty the government was decent and willing to take care of the poor. Against this background the *jun tian* system achieved its objectives – it combined the social need to allow people to use the land to produce food and the need to keep the land under state control.

However, as the government became more and more corrupt, land acquisition by wealthy individuals became widespread, leading to the concentration of land among the rich. One of the consequences of this was the emergence of the manor system. Manors (*zhuang yuan*, also known as villas) were originally a gift by the emperor to reward those ministers and royal family members who had contributed to the welfare of the country. Manors in the Tang Dynasty were regarded as self-contained systems because a whole set of management structures were attached to them. An ordinary manor contained residential zones for farmers and as well as the mansion house for the master of the manor. The master provided land for agriculture purposes while the farmers provided their labour and rent in kind. At the farmer level there were the basic manor households (*zhuang hu*), together with foster manor households, guests of the manor, guest households and so on. At the management level there were the manor supervisor, the manor staff, the villa staff and the master's representative. It should be emphasised that the manor household staff were not slaves of the master, they too had certain rights to use and occupy the land.

There were different kinds of manor: ministers' manors, which were either a gift from the emperor or were created by enforced merger; crown manors, which were created when land was confiscated from criminals and suchlike; and monastery manors. The Tang Dynasty was a Buddhist and Taoist one and the monasteries enjoyed various privileges, one of which was *jun tian* land (about 20 mu of land per monk). As more and more land was received by them, manors were created for the better management of resources. Finally, civilian manors were created by rich landlords and retired government officials. Hence private land ownership evolved into a new stage in this dynasty.

During the Sung Dynasty a similar system of mixed private and public land ownership was adopted, although there were calls for ancient land tenure systems such as the well-field system or the *xian min ming tian* system to be reestablished. However, due to the weakness of the Sung government, the strong political power of the large landlords and the constant military conflicts with neighbouring countries, this call for land reform was never seriously considered.

When the weak Sung Dynasty was eventually replaced by the strong Yuan Dynasty, the new government at first retained the existing land ownership system. (The Yuan Dynasty was established by Mongolians, the first foreign race, as opposed to the indigenous Han race, to take over China.) Once the new empire was established the new government changed all the government land, including some of the public manors, into public land. Government land was classified into four types. First, rental land, where vacant land was leased to farmers. To encourage more people to farm and thus increase production, land rent/tax became payable only after three or four years from the commencement of the lease. Second, military land or the military *tun tian*. This involved land that was necessary for strategic protection and to provide food for the army, and as such it was normally found along the border. Third, gift land, which, as the name implies, was granted by the emperor to certain ministers, members of the royal family and monasteries (the Mongolians were mostly Buddhists). Fourth, land that was granted to government staff as part of their salary.

When the Yuan Empire was established, most of the private land in the north of the country fell into the hands of the Mongolians landlords, but in the south of the country it remained under a few large Han landlords from the Sung Dynasty. Hence land concentration remained a serious problem. During the next dynasty the Ming government managed to confiscate a considerable amount of private land due to the fall of the powerful royal family and their government staff, the imprisonment of land-owning criminals and the reversal of illegal land mergers. As a result the proportion of government land in the total land stock was extremely high.

On the other hand the private manor system was further developed during the Ming Dynasty. The manors were run by the privileged classes and local government officials could not interfere with their management. There were two principal types of manor: royal manors and government manors for favoured government ministers and staff. Most of the manors were created from confiscated private land and hence the system was not a popular one.

The Qing period was the second time that China had been ruled by a non-Han race. The Manchurian invasion led to a huge loss of human life and this in turn led to vacant land. When the Qing Dynasty had established itself there was a need to accommodate the needs of the Qing people as well as to turn vacant land into productive use. However this land was widely scattered and could pose a security problem to the Qing people. Hence the circling land system was developed. Under this system private land was 'circled' for the use of the Qing people. In theory the former owners of the circled land were given vacant land in exchange, but as circling became more intensive it turned into more of a consfiscation procedure. During the period 1661–9 over 5 per cent of all agricultural land was circled land. This led to serious social unrest and Emperor Kang Xi eventually announced a ban on circling.[5]

The Qing government also carried out a large-scale survey of land that had been acquired illegally during the previous dynasty. Such land was confiscated and some was sold to investors and large landlords. At the same time, in order to preserve the social balance the Qing government promulgated the Transfer of Land Title Law, *gen ming tian fa*. Land surveys were carried out under this law, especially with regard to former manor lands. If the original farmers of the land could be traced, the land was returned to the farmers free of charge. If the farmers could not be traced, other farmers were invited to farm the land.

Although there were calls for the revival of such restrictive measures as the *xian min ming tian* or antimonopoly system, they received little support. In fact Emperor Qian Long was very sceptical about the effectiveness of the system. This reflected the degree of land concentration at this stage of the development of the private land ownership system. Nevertheless the opportunity to try out a public land ownership system arose during the *Tai Ping Tian Guo* (Kingdom of the Peaceful Heaven) rebellion in 1851.

When Hong Xiu Quen, emperor of the *Tai Ping Tian Guo*, and his revolutionary army managed to seize control of an area of land within the Qing empire he declared a set of laws and rules derived from Christian ideology under his *Tian Chao*, or Heaven Dynasty. One such was the *tian chao tian mou ji du*, or land and field system. The basic tenet of this system was that all land belonged to everybody and all had the same right to farm. All land, food, clothing and money would be shared so that inequality would no longer exist.

As the emphasis of the *tian chao tian mou ji du* was on absolute equality, the land and field system differed from those used in the past. In particular, all people, regardless of sex and social status, received the same amount of land. A general land survey was conducted and land within the kingdom was classified into nine grades. This enabled an equal allocation of good, medium and poor land to all households. Hence the equal allocation of state-owned land came into being for the first time in Chinese history.

Throughout ancient China, land management was always a political rather than an economic issue and private land ownership remained an integral part of the evolution of China. Although there were attempts to revive the public land-allocation system, the private market still managed to operate effectively. One of the interesting things that can be observed from this brief discussion of the evolution of land management is that when new dynasties came to power there was an attempt to reintroduce the public land ownership system, but once a dynasty had become establised, state-allocated land tended to return to private hands by one means or another. This caused social unrest, which contributed to the fall of the dynasty. Then the whole process would start all over again.

This illustrates a few important issues concerning proper land management. In a purely agricultural economy, private land ownership must be controlled since land is the sole means of production, and the absence of restrictions on land ownership leads to the overconcentration of land among a powerful landed class. There have been only two periods in China's history when private land ownership has been absent: during the very early stages, when there was more than enough land for everybody; and during the short-lived Kingdom of the Peaceful Heaven, when the state had absolute control over land allocation. However even then it was very difficult to ensure perfectly equal distribution in terms of quality.

Hence the allocation of public land can increase rather than reduce inequality in the absence of fair and simple allocation criteria. If, on the other hand, public and private land ownership are allowed to coexist, there must be a mechanism by which public land (which is normally allocated free of charge) can be transformed into private land in a just and orderly manner without a loss of national resources. This requires a well-developed and independent legal system to safeguard legal land titles, and a good auditing system to monitor the use of public land. In the next section, we shall examine the attempt to create a better land management and tenure system in modern China.

LAND MANAGEMENT IN MODERN CHINA

1911 to 1949

The revolution that broke out in 1911 changed China from a monarchy to a republic. However the land system was basically the same as during the Qing period and land concentration continued. In 1934 the Central Land Commission carried out a large-scale survey with the hope of solving the inequality problem. The Commission found that over 88 per cent of land-owning households in rural areas (or about 73 per cent of the total population) owned less than 30 mu of land each and the total area farmed by these households amounted to just one half of all farmland.[6]

This situation prompted Sun Yat Sen to put forward his ideas on the equalisation of land rights. Sun, who is regarded as the father of the nation, was a highly regarded and respected politician. According to him the best land system was the *jin tian* or well-field system, but because of changing economic and social environment, especially the growth of urban areas, this system could no longer work. Instead he proposed to promote equality in the private land tenure system by imposing a land tax, the value of which was to be assessed by the landowners. In doing so, speculators might have their capital gains taxed away by the land value tax if their speculative activities resulted in substantial rise in land value. On the other hand, if they tried to avoid paying the tax by recording an artificially low land price as the transaction price, the government retained the priority to purchase the land from the landlord at the recorded transaction price level. In addition Sun proposed a capital gains tax on the increased value of land. This was an attempt to nationalise the development potential of all private land without seizing ownership.

Once again, therefore, a private land system was maintained within the framework of public land ownership. Two major aspects of this have to be taken into consideration. First, the equalisation of land rights programme stressed taxation in order to suppress land prices, and this required a team of able and professional government valuers. This was especially important in urban areas. Not only was this team required to be efficient, the team also had to be large enough for an annual review of land values to be carried out – the current practice of *gong gao xian zhi* or government-imposed land values in Taiwan shows the drawbacks of such a system when it is not possible to review land values frequently. Second, a balance must be struck between taxation and the need to encourage real estate investment. Extremely high capital gains taxes deter investors and developers from entering the market, and in such cases it is helpful for the government to purchase all land at low prices. This was the case in the UK in the 1940s when high capital gains taxes were levied.

The equalisation of land rights principle began to be implemented in 1922 when Sun, then president of the newly formed Republic of China, established land bureaux in various counties in Guangdong Province. Four years later a Minister of Land was appointed to the Ministry of the Interior. In 1930 the first Land Law was enacted to deal with land use, land surveys, land taxes, land rights and so on. There were nine basic principles to this law:[7]

1. Land taxes were to be based on land values.
2. The land tax rates were to be based on a progressive rating system.
3. Capital gains tax would be imposed on incremental rises in land value, which was regarded as unearned income.

4. The state could, upon payment of compensation, make compulsory land purchases for national purposes.
5. Land tax would be exempted on land used for government/public purposes.
6. The tax on buildings would be lower than the tax on land.
7. In relation to (6), improved land use would be encouraged.
8. Land administration departments would be established at the provincial and city levels.
9. Prior permission from the government must be sought for the transfer of land rights.

The law clearly stated that all land was state land and belonged to the state on behalf of the people, except in the case of land that had been transferred or conveyed legally, which would remain in private. In recognising the existence of private land ownership, the law stated that under special circumstances, such as to satisfy special local needs, and with respect to types of land and qualities of land, the state could set a limit on the maximum area of each piece of private land.

Part II of the 1930 law was concerned with land registration, which included ownership rights, other rights over land and mortgage rights. The law also stated that any disputes over land rights would be resolved by a land tribunal. Part III dealt with land use problems, particularly in rural areas. Part IV was concerned with taxation. Land taxes included a land price tax and a capital gains tax. The land price tax was based on land value, as calculated by the owners or by government valuers, while capital gains tax was based on profits or unearned income when land was transferred. In urban areas, where the land had been improved through investment the land tax rate was 0.1–0.2 per cent of the assessed value of the land. If the land had not been improved, the rate was 0.15–0.3 per cent, and for vacant land the rate was 0.3–1.0 per cent of the assessed value. In rural areas the rate was 0.1 per cent of the assessed value if improvements had been made and 0.12–0.15 per cent if improvements had not been made. Vacant rural land was subject to a 0.15–1 per cent land price tax. This sliding scale was designed to speed up land development and, most importantly, to discourage land banking and prevent rich landlords from allowing their land to lie idle.

When the value of land in the urban areas increased by 15 per cent and in rural areas by 20 per cent, capital gains tax became payable. The tax rates ranged from 100 per cent when the increse in value was 300 per cent, down to 20 per cent when the increase was 50 per cent. However the tax rate on buildings was much lower – 0.5 per cent.

Once again, the contemporary experience of land management in China showed the need to preserve private land ownership within a framework of more equal land rights. The 'equaliser' chosen by the Guomindang government was a fiscal measure through taxation. This was the first concrete attempt by this state to bring the private and public land systems as close as possible. However, due to the difficulty of coordinating the many provinces and cities the law was ineffective. The law was eventually revised in 1946 after convincing recommendations were received from the Chinese Academy of Land Administration.

With regard to rural land management, there was much talk of agrarian reform after 1927. After the death of Sun Yat Sen, rent reduction was made the most important item on the Guomindang agenda, and at the central political council conference in May 1937 the party decided to revise the land law according to the following principles:

- A minimum area of land for each owner-cultivator should be determined. The further division of these lands should be limited and a maximum debt on the land would be fixed.
- If a peasant had worked his land for more than five years and his landlord was neither feeble, nor an orphan nor a widower depending on the land for income, then the peasant should be able to apply for requisition of the land.
- The maximum rental on the land would be fixed at 8 per cent of the value of the land but remain payable in agricultural products.[8]

The latter principle was referred to as the 'two-five reduction' and later as the 'three-seven-five land rent' because a 25 per cent rent reduction was imposed on the landlords' 50 per cent share of agricultural production, and later the landlords could only ask for 37.5 per cent of agricultural produce as rent. The first province to introduce this policy was Guangdong, although it was most successfully implemented in Zhejiang.

The main hindrance to the rural land reform was that political power in the villages was in the hands of the landlords and gentry, and they regarded the land law as a threat to their interests.

1949 to the 1980s

When the Chinese Communist Party came to power in 1949 it made land reform one of its first tasks. Based on the ideology that all land was common property, the large-scale nationalisation of land was to be carried out. In the northern region land was confiscated from those landlords who rented out their land in order to exploit farmers and surplus land was seized from rich farmers. In addition the personal assets of these two classes of people, who were regarded as residuals of the feudal system, were confiscated. In Henan province, surplus land was defined as land in excess of that owned by the average farmer. Personal assets included farm products, poultry, food and houses, but if any of these were related to the business, no confiscation would be made.

In June 1950 the People's Republic of China Land Reform Law was announced. The law comprised six parts and dealt with issues such as reform policy and its implementation, the confiscation of land, the redistribution of land, policy towards special land use problems, the classification of land in rural areas and land taxes. The 1950 Land Reform Law was soft on rich farmers in that their surplus land would not be confiscated unless the surplus was so great that its confiscation would allow a proper redistribution of land to poor farmers. In such an event the prior approval of the provincial government was required. This was in distinct contrast to the earlier situation, when the much more widescale confiscation of land had taken place.[9] In terms of redistribution, the 1950 Land Reform Law stipulated that all private land that was not regarded as surplus, would not be confiscated for redistribution. Farmers' committees would be set up to manage the confiscated land in order to ensure minimum disturbance and the fair redistribution of the land.

It should be stressed that the 1950 Land Reform Law only applied to rural China. Urban land and urban fringe land came under the 1950 Urban and Urban Fringe Land Reform Regulations. According to the terms of these regulations, all urban and urban fringe land, including agricultural land, was to become state land and would be managed by the people's governments of the various cities. The redistribution of state land to the poor would also be carried out by the people's governments, which would issue special certificates to the farmers in the urban fringe areas to confirm their right to use the land.

The nationalised urban land system remained in force until mid-1980s, when the market system was given a place in the economy. Between the 1950s and the 1980s, the main characteristics of the land tenure system in urban areas were as follows:

1. The administrative allocation of land – this refers to land allocated for purposes determined by the administrative authorities. If the state authorities, armed forces, schools or state enterprises needed land they did not purchase it on the market or lease it. Rather the land was obtained according to specified administrative and political procedures.[10]

First they had to apply to build, and when approval was granted by the relevant agents, they submitted a land use application to the provincial (or higher) level of the people's government. When this was approved they were granted land free of charge.

2. Land use without compensation – this refers to land allocated to state authorities, armed forces, schools and state enterprises free of charge and free of rent and land use fees. The period over which the land could be used was not specified, and if no state construction was planned the users could occupy it for an unlimited time.

3. Limited right to transfer – this refers to limitations on land users' right to sell, lease, mortgage, donate, exchange or perform any other act of land transfer to other departments or individuals. This was in fact written into the national constitution. If land users no longer needed a particular piece of land it had to be returned to the relevant state department or granting agent so that it could be allocated to other users, although this seldom happened.

SUMMARY

The land management systems and land reforms that took place in China over time had many common characteristics. Throughout history, land reform has been used as a political tool to pacify dissatisfied citizens, and it is notable that most land reforms took place almost immediately after the establishment of a new government. This was the case in ancient China, and was also true when the corrupt Qing Dynasty was overthrown by Sun Yat-Sen in 1911 and when the People's Republic was established in 1949. Hence the political need for reform almost entirely outweighed the economic need. When land reform formed part of a package of political reforms, some of the objectives of the land reform programmes, especially in terms of market efficiency, may be outweighed by other political considerations. This is because some sectors in the society may not have the economic resources to gain from market efficiency at the beginning. Land reform in ancient China focused more on property rights and the distribution of such rights than on efficient land use.

A balance therefore had to be sought to suit everybody's interest. This explains the shifting of public and private land ownership systems between regimes, and sometimes within a single regime. Nevertheless, such a focus on property rights rather than economic efficiency was necessary in those times as agriculture lay at the core of the economy. Stability in the rural areas depended on a balanced distribution of property rights over farmland.

The creation of a market mechanism for land was never an issue as there was no need for one.

Since the historical land reforms evolved mainly out of political need, much effort was spent on the redistribution of property rights rather than a proper long-term land use programme. Land reform in ancient China produced positive effects at the beginning, when the central government was powerful and keen, but was often submerged under different political interests and conflicts. Because land reforms was always more political than economical, proper land policies were rare, and management principles such as land use planning and, demand and supply mechanisms were non-existent.

This chapter has provided a very brief history of the development of the land tenure and management system in China from ancient to modern times. The land tenure system at any point in time or in any dynasty could itself form a book, so it has only been possible to provide a very condensed and concise version of the story. The objective has been to show that throughout the history of China there have been experiments with the nationalisation and privatisation of land. However most of these experiments involved rural land as the urban economy was still undeveloped. The historical pattern shows that for social reasons the nationalisation of land was always high on the political agenda when a government first came to power. However, this soon gave way to the need for economic efficiency or was abandoned in times of political struggle. The current reform is different in the sense that the main focus is urban land. The merging of state and private land in urban areas provides a further chapter in China's land reform history, and we now turn to the problems encountered in the final stages of the nationalisation of urban land and the subsequent urban land reform.

2 The Process of Urban Land Reform

Urban land reform did not start with the overall economic reforms of the 1970s because land, is more politically sensitive than other commodities in Chinese society. The urban land reform launched in China in the late 1980s was partly driven by the overall economic reforms and the open door policy advocated by the late leader Deng Xiao Ping, and partly evolved out of the negative consequences of the state land allocation system. The need for urban land reform in the 1990s arose for the pragmatic reason that land had to be used efficiently in order to provide a source of income in the developing market economy. Since the current reforms are very much a top-down affair, the inherent problems of the state land system should be analysed first so that the objectives of the reform can be understood.

The current land system is mainly based on state allocation. In planned economies, the state decides who needs what and how much. Site location is of little importance as enterprises are not competing with each other for profit maximisation or market share, and the acquisition of a prime site is down to luck or the political atmosphere prevailing at the time when an application for land is made. Since land users in planned economies do not need to improve their economic efficiency as much as their counterparts in the market economy, the allocation of land may not accord with efficiency principles. Furthermore there are no allocation criteria other than political variables. Hence land use is not based on economic principles and price mechanisms. Rather land is distributed according to a set of parameters that are subject to social and political pressures. The consequence of this is mismatched land use patterns in urban areas. Bertaud and Renaud (1992) show that in most planned economies, land use patterns are not determined by economic efficiency. Hence location and economic productivity have no direct correlation. The allocation of land for various uses is therefore both accidental and political. According to Bertaud and Renaud, residential land is usually squeezed out in favour of industrial land in urban core areas, which puts pressure on the transportation network.

Table 2.1 shows the 1992 population density of the ten major districts of Shanghai, the largest and most prosperous city in China (excluding the

18

Table 2.1   Area and population density of the major districts of Shanghai, 1992

District	Area (sq. km)	Population	Density/(sq. km)
Huangpu	21.07	703 000	33 363
Nanshi	27.92	801 600	28 712
Luwan	8.05	428 700	53 255
Xuhui	54.76	750 400	13 703
Changning	38.36	595 700	15 530
Jingan	7.62	441 500	57 943
Putuo	54.83	804 500	14 673
Zhabei	28.50	674 100	23 654
Hongkou	23.48	839 300	35 743
Yangpu	59.63	1 096 500	18 388
Total:	281.12	7 077 000	25 174

Source: *Statistical Yearbook of Shanghai* (1993).

Pudong new area). At that time the city centre (Huangpu district) did not possess all the characteristics of central business areas normally found in large cities. The main residential areas form a ring around the centre (Jingan district, Hongkuo district and Luwan district).

Figure 2.1 and Table 2.2 provide a detailed picture of the land use pattern in Shanghai in 1992. The largest category was industrial land, located in the central core, followed by residential land for labourers (together these accounted for 43 per cent of total land in urban Shanghai). China's previous policies required state enterprises to provide housing for their staff, hence labourers' housing was part and parcel of industrial development. Most of the industrial enterprises were state enterprises that were heavily subsidised by the state, and they become the largest housing developers in the nation. When the overall economic reforms started in the 1970s the financial burden of the more inefficient state enterprises soon became obvious, including the problem of loss of revenue from land.

In open economies, different land users bid for properties according to the benefits they can expect from the use of a particular site, and firms that require their business operations to be as near to the best location as possible in order to be profitable will pay the highest rent.[1] At the same time, firms that do not depend on a prime location in order to be profitable will set up in relatively more remote areas and avoid high land prices. The prime area in urban conurbations is the central business area, where the flow of traffic and people creates business opportunities. This land allocation mechanism depends on a common measurement standard – land rent. Without such a standard, and when the occupation of land does

Urban Land Reform in China

Table 2.2   Land use distribution in Shanghai, mid-1992 (sq. km)

Category*	Total area for each use	Luwan (%*)	Jingan (%)	Zhabei (%)	Putuo (%)	Xuhui (%)
R	65.51	3.04 (4.7)	3.60 (5.5)	5.38 (8.2)	7.26 (11.1)	8.57 (13.1)
C	8.78	0.47 (5.4)	0.60 (6.8)	1.04 (11.8)	0.75 (8.5)	1.55 (17.7)
H	1.69	0.16 (9.5)	0.09 (5.3)	0.01 (0.6)	0.012 (0.7)	0.09 (5.3)
B	2.29	0.14 (6.1)	0.29 (12.7)	0.20 (8.7)	0.15 (6.6)	0.26 (11.4)
E	16.87	0.39 (2.3)	0.44 (2.6)	0.80 (4.7)	1.86 (11.0)	4.43 (26.3)
G	7.05	0.14 (2.0)	0.06 (0.9)	0.52 (7.4)	1.21 (17.2)	1.05 (14.9)
M	54.43	1.95 (3.6)	1.26 (2.3)	6.79 (12.5)	6.37 (11.7)	8.66 (15.9)
W	7.08	0.06 (0.8)	0.01 (0.1)	0.60 (8.5)	1.55 (21.9)	1.28 (18.1)
U	3.55	0.14 (3.9)	0.06 (1.7)	0.13 (3.7)	0.30 (8.5)	0.78 (22.0)
T	14.84	0.04 (0.3)	0.02 (0.1)	1.24 (8.4)	1.76 (11.9)	3.24 (21.8)
S	19.56	0.94 (4.8)	0.92 (4.7)	2.22 (11.3)	1.56 (8.0)	2.74 (14.0)
D	3.15	0.01 (0.3)	0.11 (3.5)	0.27 (8.6)	0.05 (1.6)	0.07 (2.2)
L	20.77	0.50 (2.4)	0.04 (0.2)	0.86 (4.1)	1.1 (5.3)	3.02 (14.5)
A	46.70	–	–	7.94 (17.0)	5.23 (11.2)	9.27 (19.9)
O	8.14	0.08 (1.0)	0.11 (1.4)	0.18 (2.2)	0.73 (9.0)	1.72 (21.1)
Total	280.40	8.05 (2.9)	7.62 (2.7)	27.95 (10.0)	29.89 (10.7)	46.63 (16.6)

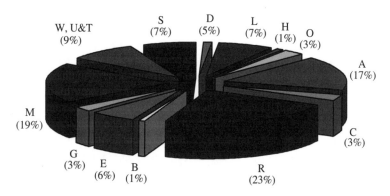

Figure 2.1   Land use distribution in Shanghai, 1992

Hongkou (%)	Changning %	Nanshi (%)	Huangpu (%)	Yangput (%)
7.68 (11.7)	5.97 (9.1)	6.93 (10.6)	5.6 (8.5)	11.47 (17.5)
0.73 (8.3)	0.92 (10.5)	0.56 (6.4)	0.88 (10)	1.51 (17.2)
0.07 (4.1)	1.23 (72.8)	—	0.03 (1.8)	0.01 (0.6)
0.21 (9.2)	0.21 (9.2)	0.24 (10.5)	0.54 (23.6)	0.06 (2.6)
1.34 (7.9)	1.49 (8.8)	0.63 (3.7)	0.93 (5.5)	4.64 (27.5)
0.52 (7.4)	1.32 (18.7)	0.05 (0.7)	0.42 (6.0)	1.76 (25.0)
4.06 (7.5)	4.53 (8.3)	5.59 (10.3)	1.96 (3.6)	13.25 (24.3)
0.26 (3.7)	0.25 (3.5)	0.26 (3.7)	0.32 (4.5)	2.50 (35.3)
0.31 (8.7)	0.40 (11.3)	0.30 (8.5)	0.13 (3.7)	1.00 (28.2)
0.78 (5.3)	4.69 (31.6)	0.57 (3.8)	0.52 (3.5)	1.98 (13.3)
2.21 (11.3)	1.39 (7.1)	2.41 (12.3)	2.01 (10.3)	3.17 (16.2)
1.19 (37.8)	0.20 (6.3)	0.01 (0.3)	0.06 (1.9)	1.18 (37.5)
1.09 (5.2)	0.68 (3.3)	3.55 (17.1)	2.05 (9.9)	7.88 (37.9)
2.46 (5.3)	4.616 (9.9)	5.56 (11.9)	1.63 (3.5)	7.03 (15.1)
0.60 (7.4)	0.92 (11.3)	1.26 (15.5)	0.39 (4.8)	2.15 (26.4)
23.49 (8.4)	28.82 (10.3)	27.92 (10.0)	20.46 (7.3)	59.57 (21.2)

Key:

A: agriculture and animal husbandry
B: commercial, retail and associated housing
C: government buildings, health care premises, places of entertainment, temples, etc.
D: embassies and military use
E: education and research
G: parks and gardens
H: hotels

L: rivers, lakes, etc.
M: industrial and manufacturing
O: vacant land
R: residential
S: roads and public squares
T: railways, port and airport
U: urban services (water, electricity, etc.)
W: warehouses and oil tanks

not involve a financial outlay, rent-bidding activities cease to exist and
urban land is not put to its most efficient use. In China's case the use of
land depended mainly on the priority given by the state authorities to various land uses. One of the consequences of this was that residential land
was lost to industrial projects as they were normally accorded higher priority in the socialist economic planning mechanism.

Research conducted by Yang and Liu (1991) shows that industrial land
accounted for 20.5 per cent of the total city centre area in Shanghai, 30.3
per cent in Guangzhou and 34.15 per cent in Fushun before the land use
reforms. Tang (1989) gives similar figures for Liaoning province, where
84 per cent of the 5000 factories in ten cities were located in the cities
proper and were intermixed with residential buildings.

The misuse of land has resulted in a substantial loss of state revenue.
This became obvious when China began to examine regional land markets
elsewhere. An important guide for the reformists was the case of Hong
Kong. According to Hong Kong government statistics, the proportion of
government revenue from the property and construction industry on average amounted to 33.5 per cent of total revenue between 1983 to 1993. This
revenue was derived from such things as land transactions, property investments by the authorities, rates, property taxes and profit taxes on developers.

The loss of revenue in China was exacerbated by the fact that an active
black market existed within the state land allocation system. Since land
could not legally be transferred between individuals or enterprises, there
was no land title register. Ironically, a direct result of the absence of land
titles was that, because no documents and legal procedures existed,
prospective land users could negotiate transfers with the existing occupiers. Furthermore, when prospective occupiers applied for land through
the administrative system, it was natural for them to request more than they
required (Li, 1996a) and the surplus became a potential source of supply in
the black market. This was heightened by the extreme imbalance of land
use in cities, as examined above.

Another defect in the state land allocation system became evident during the reform of state enterprises. In the march to attract local or overseas
investment, joint ventures were strongly encouraged. In joint ventures, the
local partner, or the poorer partner when both partners were local, normally used the land they occupied as their share of the capital. This posed
a valuation problem as land had no value under the state allocation system.
Because there was no market data for purposes of comparison and no prior
transactions to serve as a reference, it was very tempting for the cash
stakeholder in the joint venture to undervalue the land assets of the other
partner, especially when the land-occupying partner held the right to use

surplus land in a good location. This became a socialist form of asset stripping.

Yang and Liu (1991) highlighted the implications of this problem when they stated that: 'When land is being used without valuable consideration, there will not be a common starting point for different enterprises to compete with each other, hence it is not advantageous to the economy ...' They consider this an important factor in low efficiency and poor land use. This problem is deeply rooted in socialist ideology. According to Article 10 of the constitution of the People's Republic of China (before the 1988 amendments):

Urban land belongs to the state. Land in the countryside and in suburban areas is under collective ownership unless the law stipulates that the land is state-owned. Moreover residential land and family plots belong to the collective. No organisation or individual is allowed to occupy, sell, lease or illegally transfer land in any way.

As a result there were no mechanisms for transferring land between individuals or organisations other than through the administrative channels stipulated by the state. This created the situation where land was neither a factor of production, as there was no need to pay for the use of it, nor an asset, as there was no monetary return to be had from transferring it. There was therefore no need to calculate the appreciation or depreciation of land values.

Because land was regarded as free, wastage arose in the utilisation of land resources. Tang (1989) examines one of the main problems, which he terms 'public squatting': 'the logic of public squatting is that publicly owned firm is automatically entitled to a piece of land for its production...' Tang provides examples of deliberate waste. For instance a research institute in Dalian requested a 50 000 square metre building site when it only required 600 square metres. Moreover, in Shenyang between 1955 and 1963 each 100 million yuan of extra industrial output value corresponded to an 11 hectare increase in demand for industrial land. However between 1964 and 1978 the efficiency rate dropped to 19 hectares for each additional 100 million yuan of industrial output. Discounting the effect of the real need for industrial land, the increase in the hectare/industrial output ratio was still very substantial, suggesting a large-scale waste of land.

One positive aspect of the free land situation was that low-rent housing could be enjoyed by almost all the workforce – state enterprises were responsibile for housing their employees, and the land allocation system made this financially feasible. However it also meant there were no land revenues to fund other housing developments, and because private investors were unwilling to provide housing due to the highly subsidised rents the burden on the state was enormous. As such, the state normally provided a minimal service as far as new housing was concerned.

The seriousness of this can be demonstrated by the problems encountered in the residential market. The rapid increase in the demand for housing was not caused by increases in household income, but was a response to low rents (rent only accounted for about 1 per cent of the average household's income).[2] The high demand in turn created an acute shortage of supply, for instance in Guangzhou about 20 per cent of households occupied an area of 3 square metres or less per person.[3] Meanwhile the low rents meant there was insufficient revenue to meet even the housing maintenance costs, and consequently the supply of new or redeveloped housing fell even lower. This vicious cycle was not unique to China, it also occured in other socialist economies.[4]

The problems arising from the old state land allocation system were more economic and social than political, which made it somewhat easier for the authorities to initiate a reform programme for the urban land market. The main problem was to create a market for an asset whose common ownership was so essential to the socialist ideology in terms of equality among citizens and safeguarding people against exploitative landlords. The authorities had to devise a solution that would conform to the doctrine of state land ownership while improving the market efficiency of the urban land system. The creation of leaseholds was one possible solution, whereby leaseholds would become a market commodity to be traded within the price mechanism. We can examine this within the overall reform framework and the legal, financial and administrative frameworks.

URBAN LAND REFORM: THE REFORM FRAMEWORK

In April 1987 the State Council proposed a new policy for transferable land use rights in the free market. The Special Economic Zones Office was duly charged with testing the scheme in the four open areas of the country, namely Tianjin, Shanghai, Guangzhou and Shenzhen. On 12 April 1988 Clause 4 of Article 10 of the constitution was amended such that 'No organisation or individual may appropriate, buy, sell or unlawfully transfer land in other ways [but] the right of land use can be transferred in accordance with the law ...' With this amendment a leasehold market was created with a similar structure to the land tenure system in Hong Kong (Li, 1997b). Land has not been sacrificed for the sake of economic reform and it still belongs to the state on behalf of the people. This is in line with the socialist doctrine.

The 'Provisional Regulations on the Conveyance, Granting and Transferring of the State Land's Use Rights in Cities and Towns, 1991' (hereafter referred to as the 'Provisional Land Regulations' were enacted by the State Council in May 1991, wherupon land use rights (LURs) were separated from ownership rights and became tradable in the market by private treaty, negotiation or auction. LURs are rights with time limits for different kinds of land use (normally, residential use for 70 years, commercial use for 50 years and so on, but this varies according to local government policies). Moreover LURs can be mortgaged or transferred.

In 1994 Vice Premier Zhou Jia Hua declared that the LUR reform had certain objectives, including the following:[5]

1. To improve land management in the interests of overall economic development. This requires the release of state land into the market system and an end to the practice of occupying land without payment.
2. To reduce the loss and illegal merging of agricultural land. According to Vice Premier Zhou's figures, the loss of agricultural land before 1985 was as high as 100 hectares per year, but this fell to 20–40 hectares between 1986 to 1992.
3. The development of an efficient land use mechanism. As a result of the reforms, land is now regarded as an important financial asset that is exchangeable and tradable in the open market, unlike in the past, when it was seen only in terms of use value.
4. To organise the supply and mangagement of land in such a way as to strengthen the state's macroeconomic control over the market. If the state is both the supplier and the manager of land it can guarantee that land policy will coordinate with other macroeconomic policies. The state can convey land at a lower price to encourage certain uses while undesirable uses can be deterred by higher prices or refusal to supply.
5. To increase state revenues from the land market. Land is an important financial asset that can help bolster the state treasury. This has already been shown in the more popular markets such as Shanghai (a total of more than 10 billion yuan in 1992) and Guangzhou (a total of more than 21 billion yuan in 1992/93). Such income is a very important source of local support, especially with regard to infrastructural development. It reduces the financial burden on the centre on the one hand, and increases the attractiveness of the regional investment environment on the other.

Points 1, 3 and 5 basically echo each other. The essence of the LUR reform, therefore, is to effect the transfer of LURs from the state to commercial land users so that land and eventually buildings will become market commodities and regulated by the price mechanism. This is based on the assumption that commercial land users will use land more efficiently than government units as profit is the major determinant of affordability. Hence the land conveyance system, created under the privatisation of land use rights acted as the gateway to reform.

At present there are several LUR conveyance procedures. State-owned land conveyance, is very straightforward because ownership is clear and the conveyance procedure involves a simple transfer to the buyer. Some problems occur with the second form of conveyance, that is, the conveyance of land under collective ownership. Collectively owned land is usually rural land owned by collectives of farmers. In theory, collectives cannot sell LURs directly to developers, rather the land is sold to the state (as a requisition), which then sells it to the developers. If developers have insufficient knowledge in this area and enter into direct negotiation with village administrations, they face substantial losses when the state authorities refuse to recognise the conveyance.

Finally, there is the case of surplus land previously obtained by state enterprises or government departments. In theory this land cannot be sold to developers without first compensating the state, but many enterprises get round this by entering into a development contract with an overseas investor. Such contracts are not conveyances of LURs but are in the nature of a management contract for the 'land'. This indicates a very weak conception of property rights, not only in the market but in government departments as well.

The methods of selling LURs are more or less the same as in any market economy. There are three main types of selling procedure, namely private negotiations (or agreements), tenders and auctions. However not all the regions allow all three types. For instance Shanghai city permits sale by agreement and tender (although tendering rarely happens) while Zhuhai city in the Pearl River Delta allows tenders and auctions only. Moreover there are no detailed central government guidelines on conveyencing methods and it is up to individual local governments to set their own criteria. For instance the Qingdao city government in Shandong province specifies that sale by agreement can be used in the conveyance of land for non-profit-making use, for special purpose construction activities and for industries that need protection.[6]

In general, sale by agreement is still the most popular way of transferring LURs in the Chinese real estate market, while auction is the least popular.

This is because sale by agreement gives the local authorities maximum control over land prices and development activities. Auctions are regarded by the Chinese authorities as inappropriate because they may push up prices to an unaffordable level for local land users. As price control is always important in socialist economies, a preference for private treaties can be predicted. Nevertheless, there is a call to move towards a complete tendering system for the sale of LURs. This will depend on the political will of the reformers.

As well as the sale and transfer of LURs, the reform also allows for the leasing of LURs. Regulation 28 of the 1988 Land Management Law states that 'the leasing of the land use rights means that a land user leases his land use rights together with any structure on the land to the lessee in return for rental payment'. In theory the duties and rights of the lessor and lessee are more or less the same as in any market economy. For instance lessors are still bound by the LUR conveyance contracts signed between them and the state even after they have leased their properties. However detailed regulations on the leasing procedures for LURs have not been fully formulated in all local markets.

In summary, the urban land reform is aimed at replacing the old land allocation system by a market mechanism. However the changeover is not progressing rapidly and relatively few LURs have been sold on the market. The move towards the market has varied from year to year and from local authority to local authority, as shown in Tables 2.3–2.5.

URBAN LAND REFORM: THE LEGAL FRAMEWORK

The rudimentary legal framework for the urban LUR reform was provided by the Land Management Law of the PRC, 1988[7] (see Appendix 3) and the Provisional Regulations on the Conveyance, Granting and Transfer of State Land Use Rights in Cities and Towns, 1991,[8] both of which were enacted by the State Council. It should be emphasised that these two documents are more like policy statements than legislation, although the regulations are more detailed and specific than the law. Given the fact that central legislation might not be able to take all local variations into consideration, implementation at the provincial and city levels is more relevant to our discussion.

At the provincial level, the general policy and guidelines of this national legislation are often amended according to the special needs of the locality, and in most cases the city government is the driving force behind the implementation of the policy. In general, the lower the level of government, the more detailed the provisions for implementation.

Table 2.3   Comparison of land sold through the market system and
land allocated through the administrative channel, 1994

Region	Market sale of land use rights		Administrative allocation		Ratio of market sale to administrative allocation	
	(no.)	*(ha.)*	*(no.)*	*(ha.)*	*(no.)*	*(ha.)*
National	42076	57338	166690	89750	0.25	0.64
Beijing	135	1196	2754	13026	0.05	0.09
Tianjin	253	1236	3380	389	0.08	3.18
Liaoning	1091	2190	657	472	1.66	4.64
Heilongjiang	1338	827	4436	1429	0.30	0.58
Shanghai	251	4967	3538	11113	0.07	0.45
Jiangsu	832	3544	1600	5912	0.52	0.60
Fujian	1299	1650	4117	2080	0.32	0.80
Shandong	2811	2636	4265	3677	0.66	0.72
Hainan	942	7333	1307	240	0.72	30.60
Guangxi	1950	2388	9048	2398	0.22	0.99
Guangdong	8647	17077	17689	10215	0.49	1.67
Sichuan	935	325	28070	879	0.03	0.37

Source: *China Statistical Yearbook* (1995).

Table 2.4   Comparison of land sold through the market system and land allocated
through the administrative channel, 1995

Region	Market sale of land use rights		Administrative allocation		Ratio of market sale to administrative allocation	
	(no.)	*(ha.)*	*(no.)*	*(ha.)*	*(no.)*	*(ha.)*
National	105473	43092	292285	87608	0.36	0.49
Beijing	419	1219	3147	5006	0.13	0.24
Tianjin	181	613	498	1394	0.36	0.44
Liaoning	1029	1185	509	354	2.02	3.35
Heilongjiang	1980	841	3502	8272	0.57	0.10
Shanghai	276	719	2914	4292	0.10	0.17
Jiangsu	1698	3178	4440	3621	0.38	0.88
Fujian	1661	1272	15749	3267	0.11	0.39
Shandong	5670	2879	22882	5006	0.25	0.58
Guangxi	2511	1015	3250	1958	0.77	0.52
Guangdong	9701	8527	6424	4052	1.50	2.10
Sichuan	9152	845	9354	2911	0.98	0.29

Source: *China Statistical Yearbook* (1996).

Table 2.5   Comparison of land sold through the market system and
land allocated through the administrative channel, 1996

Region	Market sale of land use rights		Administrative allocation		Ratio of market sale to administrative allocation	
	(no.)	*(ha.)*	*(no.)*	*(ha.)*	*(no.)*	*(ha.)*
National	103 921	34 048	289 350	70 266	0.36	0.48
Beijing	340	439	214	207	1.59	2.12
Tianjin	204	364	1 961	1 749	0.10	0.20
Liaoning	1 058	1 190	8 296	3 814	0.13	0.31
Heilongjiang	1 221	535	1 981	3 971	0.62	0.13
Shanghai	617	914	1 786	7 157	0.35	0.13
Jiangsu	2 383	1 450	3 112	2 078	0.77	0.70
Fujian	891	1 079	22 066	6 003	0.04	0.18
Shandong	4 870	3 139	15 195	4 717	0.32	0.67
Guangxi	2 428	494	4 195	1 126	0.58	0.44
Guangdong	6 726	6 236	5 910	3 562	1.15	1.75
Sichuan	8 623	1 463	16 959	2 442	0.51	0.60

Source: *China Statistical Yearbook* (1997).

The Land Management Law deals mainly with the general policy of the LUR reform. It stipulates that the right to use state and collective land can be legally transferred according to methods prescribed by the state. In particular, Article 25 stipulates an approval hierarchy when the area of cultivated land being requisitioned exceeds certain limits (approval from the State Council is needed for all land over 2000 mu). Article 27 defines the compensation criteria that apply to cultivated land users when land is being requisitioned. Such criteria are mainly based on the agricultural output of the land.

The law deals with macro issues of LUR reform rather than setting a concrete legal foundation for the creation of a market system for urban land. As with other major pieces of law, the document does not provide details of how the policy should be implemented. In 1998 the State Council decided that the law should be revised. The main purpose of the revision was to withdraw local authorities' power to grant LURs as local governments below the provincial level had tended to make too many grants of agricultural land. The draft revision of the Land Management Law proposes various changes to land management policies. First, it is proposed to abolish the divisional land granting system. In the past, five levels of local government each had a certain amount of power to grant land for development and construction. This power will be returned to the State Council to enable better control. There is also a possibility that the land administration departments at the village level will be abolished. Second, local governments will have to remit 40 per cent of their land revenues to the central government for reallocation or other purposes. This contrasts greatly with the current 5 per cent.

Article 4 of the revised law is concerned with the establishment of a land use management system. Under this proposal, future land policies will be supported by balanced asset management. Land use planning will be given a higher priority in the future, with definitive plans for different land uses each year, the protection of agricultural land and the rejuvenation of waste land. Based on this management system, land will be generally classified into agricultural land, development and construction land and vacant land. To implement the relevant policies, the revised draft calls for a better bureaucratic structure for land management and better coordination with related ministries and departments.

Premier Zhu made it very clear after his election that greater attention should be given to science and technology, including their application to land management. The revised law stipulates the establishment of a land use database information system. Local governments are to provide accurate land use information and data for the central database. This will assist the formulation of better land policies in the future.

In 1991 the Regulations for the Implementation of the Land Management Law were promulgated. These included the introduction of a system of issuing land use certificates for state land in order to protect property rights. The power to issue such certificates rested with the State Land Administration Bureau (SLAB), which was subsequently combined with other departments to form the Ministry of State Land and Natural Resources, MSLNR. In particular, Regulation 6 states that when it is intended to transfer the right to use and occupy land, or to transfer this right as a result of purchasing, selling and transferring buildings on the land, the user must seek the approval of the State Land Administration Bureau, after which the property rights must be reregistered with the local authority.

The Provisional Regulations on the Conveyance, Granting and Transfer of State Land Use Rights in Cities and Towns, 1991, provide a much more detailed prescription for the transfer of LURs. Regulation 1 states that the purpose of the regulations is to reform the system of state-owned land in urban areas. The principle of the reform is to separate ownership from the right to use and occupy land, which then becomes transferable and tradable. A market for the granting and trading of LURs can then be developed.

Sections 2–4 of the Regulations spell out the legislative procedures for granting, transferring, leasing and mortgaging LURs. Regulation 8 allows the state, as the owner of land, to grant LURs to users in exchange for a fee. This has led the establishment of a price mechanism in the urban land market, but since the state is granting (or selling) LURs rather than ownership, a leasehold system has resulted. For this leasehold system to develop the term of the lease must be clearly defined. Under Regulation 12 the maximum duration of LURs is specified for various uses such as residential, industrial and commercial.

Since the land market is a monopoly market, there has to be provision for transfer between users. This is covered by Regulations 20–27. The transfer of LURs is effected by means of a transfer contract, and all related rights and obligations go with the contract. Since a transfer between land users is in effect a transfer of the lease, the duration of the lease is reduced by the time it was held by the seller. Regulation 23 states that although the ownership of land stays with the state, the transfer of LURs means that the ownership of buildings and other structures on the land is transferred to the purchaser as well. The protection of property rights is ensured by the LUR registration system.

To protect the state from loss of revenue, Regulation 26 stipulates that in the event of LURs being traded at a significantly lower price than the current market price, the city government shall have the right of first refusal.

Despite the significant contribution made by these laws and regulations to the creation of a market for land use rights, the legal framework was still very weak during the early stages of the reform and the period of rapid growth in the real estate and land market was not underpinned by an adequate legal structure.[9] The problems arising from the Oriental Plaza case in Beijing bore testimony to this weakness, especially with respect to the protection of property rights.

Finally, to provide a better legal framework for local governments as well as investors, a more comprehensive and structured piece of legislation was prepared. The Urban Real Estate Administration Law of the PRC, 1995 (Real Estate Law) (see Appendix 2), was adopted at the eighth meeting of the Standing Committee of the Eighth National People's Congress on 5 July 1994 and came into effect on 1 January 1995. The Real Estate Law consists of seven chapters with 72 articles. It sets out general principles on real estate development and land use, real estate transactions, including transfers, mor gages and leasing, property agency services, real estate ownership registration and legal liability.

It should be noted that the Real Estate Law was the first national law to be enacted solely for the purposes of administering urban land and real estate in China. This highlights the importance placed by the central government on a structured legal framework for the process of urban land reform. One of the major objectives of the law was to consolidate the previous legal provisions for the development of an urban real estate market.

Moreover the procedures and administration of urban real estate have been streamlined. Many local authorities, because of the urgent need to create an attractive investment environment, had already formulated their own measures and regulations before the passing of the Real Estate Law, but should any of these provisions conflict with the Real Estate Law, the latter will prevail.[10]

The overall objectives of the Law are contained in Article 1:

1. To strengthen the administration of the urban real estate market.
2. To establish a proper mechanism in the real estate market.
3. To protect the rights and interests of legitimate real estate users.
4. To promote the healthy development of real estate business.

Although the title of this law implies that it is only concerned with urban areas, Article 71 suggests that LUR transfers for real estate development and related issues in rural areas should also be conducted in line with this law.

Article 3 decrees that the state shall adopt a compensatory leasehold system for the use of state-owned land, except where LURs are obtained through the state land allocation system in accordance with this law. This article includes a price mechanism for the allocation of LURs for a defined period of time. Subject to various conditions and the payment of a further land premium, rights can be renewed upon expiry.

The functions and powers of government departments at various levels are defined in Article 6. At the national level, the article defines the duties of the Ministry of Construction (MoC) and the State Land Administration Bureau (SLAB) under the State Council. These two agents act in close coordination and conduct their real estate work in accordance with the division of functions and powers prescribed by the State Council. At the provincial and local levels, administration is handled by real estate and lands departments (in some cities these two departments are combined), which are directly responsible to the local government. It should be noted that the central SLAB and MoC do not have direct administrative control over the local SLABs and real estate administration departments (READs).

Generally speaking, Article 6 allows provincial governments a considerable degree of flexiblity to establish their own administration structures for real estate transactions. However LURs can only be granted by local SLABs after consulting the relevant urban planning and construction committees and READs, and obtaining the approval of the local government.

General Principles of the Legal Framework

Granted Land

Article 7 of the Real Estate Law provides for the state to grant land users the right to use state-owned land for a certain period of time in exchange for a fee. The word 'grant' is the translation used by most law firms in Hong Kong for the Chinese term *chu rang*, which means selling. Hence the legal provisions imply that the state can sell the LURs in the market. Since the state is the owner of all land, it is a vertical conveyance of interest. The law also stipulates that the maximum term for each LUR must be prescribed by the State Council. Moreover the land user has to sign a written contract with the relevant SLAB.

According to Article 12, LURs are granted by the local SLABs through auction, tender or private treaty. With regard to land used for the purposes of commerce, tourism, recreation and luxury development, auctions or tenders can be used when conditions permit. In other circumstances private treaties can be arranged between the two parties (this is the preferred method in almost all the cases in China: see Li, 1996a).

In the case of LURs granted by private treaty, the fees agreed between the two parties must not be lower than the minimum price stipulated by the state, which is normally the benchmark price of land (ibid.). The usual practice is for the local SLAB to provide information on the land and the basic terms upon which the LURs will be granted. Once the terms have been agreed by both parties, the SLAB at the county or municipal level draws up a land grant contract with the prospective land user, with the rights and obligations of both parties defined.

Another way of obtaining LURs is by tender, which generally involves tenders being invited by the local SLAB, which sets the conditions of sale. Interested parties are invited to submit sealed bids and pay a deposit. Usually a bid assessment committee, composed of senior staff in the department, opens the bids and decides which one to accept. The successful party then signs a contract with the department and pays the balance of the land grant fee.

The third way of acquiring LURs is by auction. In this case the land grant is awarded to the party who makes the highest bid. The successful bidder signs a contract with the local SLAB and goes through the usual registration procedures. This is the least popular method of obtaining LURs as it is widely believed that it leads to excessively high prices.

Under Articles 15 and 16, land users must pay the land grant fee in full within a specified period. Failure to do so can result in the local SLAB repealing the contract and claiming damages. Similarly the land user has the right to cancel the contract, claim back the land grant fee and demand compensation for any breach of contract on the part of the SLAB. There have been cases where major international real estate developers have reneged on their commitment upon discovering it was impossible to purchase LURs for neighbouring sites after speculatively purchasing the first one. In such cases local governments may choose to cancel the contract without claiming damages in the interests of long-term goodwill.

If a land user wishes to change the use of the land from that stated in the contract, he must first obtain the consent of the granting party and the relevant urban planning department. In such cases a new contract is concluded and the fee adjusted accordingly (Article 17). This gives both parties the flexibility to change the scale of real estate development when there are major changes in the environment. This is especially important as in most major cities the redevelopment of old areas or the inner city is a major source of land. As mentioned earlier, most socialist economies have unprofitable users occupying prime sites in core urban areas, and removing these occupiers is the best way of realising the full potential of the land. However problems always arise with the resettlement of sitting tenants who obtained the land under the old land use system. This is often the responsibility of the developers themselves and is just one of the variables that can affect a project after the purchase of LURs.

Land users may apply for an extension of their LUR contracts no later than one year prior to the expiry date. Applications are usually approved unless the land is reclaimed by the state for the sake of the 'public interest', (which is not defined). Upon approval of the extension land users enter into a new contract and pay another premium. If land users do not apply for an extension of the term or their applications are not approved in accordance with the law, their land use rights are terminated by the state without compensation (Article 21).

Under the special circumstances stipulated in Article 19, the state may recover a land use right before its term expires. 'Special circumstances' are normally defined as those in the public interest. In such cases the state has to offer appropriate compensation based on the number of years the contract has left to run.

With regard to collectively owned land in urban areas, Article 8 stipulates that before LURs can be transferred the land must first be requisitioned by the state and turned into state-owned land in accordance with the law.

Administratively Allocated Land

Article 22 defines the administrative allocation of LURs as the system by which local government at county level or above allocates land to a user without the latter paying monetary compensation for the use of land. A major difference between this and granted land is that the LURs are held for an indefinite term, unless specified otherwise by laws, administrative rules and regulations. This explains the difficulty of conveyancing land through the administrative channel, as examined earlier. There are at least two problems with this channel. First, when state enterprises plan to transform themselves into public companies and become listed on local and international stock markets, problems arise with the appraisal of their asset value, especially the value of the sites they occupy. The second problem concerns resettlement. As stated above, when land users have obtained their land through the administrative channel the LURs are valid for an indefinite period and cannot be terminated with the passage of time, so in effect they are a form of quasi-ownership. This causes considerable confusion whenever resettlement is involved. As there are no regulations on how these administratively allocated user rights can be 'reallocated' or even terminated, the scale of compensation is always a matter for negotiation.

In general the administrative allocation of LURs applies to the following types of land:

1. Land used by state departments or for military purposes.
2. Land used for urban infrastructure or public facilities.
3. Land used for state-owned projects concerned with energy, communications, water conservation and so on.
4. Land used for other purposes stipulated by laws, administrative rules and regulations.

The Land Conversion Process

Article 26 stipulates that the design and construction of new buildings must comply with the relevant standards and building regulations. All new constructions must be inspected and approved before they can be occupied for use.

Regarding the progress of development of granted land, Article 25 requires the developer to commence construction works on the granted land within a specified time limit, as agreed in the land grant contract. A fine of not more than 25 per cent of the land grant fees is levied on the purchaser if the land lays idle for more than one year. If the site has still not been developed after two years have elapsed, the LURs may be reclaimed without compensation.

To facilitate the process of enterprise reform, whereby state enterprises are gradually being transformed into share issuing companies, Article 27 provides for the market value of LURs to be appraised and then used as capital/shares for real estate development in joint ventures, subject to the provisions of the Real Estate Law and other relevant laws, administrative rules and regulations.

Ordinary Housing Development

One of the key principles of the Real Estate Law is the gradual development of a real estate market. This calls for balanced real estate development with sufficient provision of ordinary housing (as opposed to luxury apartments and so on). In this way the living conditions of the Chinese people can be improved.

Given the low income of most citizens this can only be achieved with the help of preferential measures to encourage and support real estate development enterprises to develop and construct low-cost housing. Although the Real Estate Law does not provide clear details of these preferential measures, such as how they are calculated and under what circumstances they will be granted, they can be expected to include low-priced land grants, a guaranteed profit margin, tax reductions and low-interest loans (as in the case of the affordable housing or *anju* projects). Foreign investors enjoy the same benefits and conditions as their local counterparts, and it is a priority of the central government to attract foreign investment to develop ordinary housing in order to upgrade the living standards of its citizens.

Monitoring Real Estate Development Enterprises

Since commercial real estate development is a completely new concept in China, Article 29 stipulates certain capital and staffing requirements for the establishment of a real estate development enterprise.[11] Each enterprise must:

1. have its own name and organisational structure;
2. have fixed premises for its business operations;
3. have registered capital/assets that comply with the relevant provisions of the State Council;
4. have sufficient professional and technical personnel;
5. adhere to other conditions prescribed by the relevant laws, administrative rules and regulations.

Another new provision established by the Real Estate Law is that real estate development enterprises must be registered with the relevant administrative department in charge of industry and commerce. Upon registration a business license is issued. Development enterprises must, within one month of obtaining their business licenses, report their establishment to the department designated by the local government at or above county level in the place where the registration authority is located. Enterprises also have to report any proposed projects to the relevant department so that they can be recorded (this is called establishing the project, or *lixiang*).

It is also necessary for limited liability companies or joint-stock limited companies engaged in real estate development to comply with the 1994 Company Law.

Private Real Estate Transactions

In the past there were no national laws or regulations governing real estate transactions since commercial transactions did not exist. Therefore the Real Estate Law was a significant step by the central government to control the various kinds of transaction involved in the real estate market. Real estate transactions, for the purposes of this law, are the transfer of real estate, the mortgaging of real estate and the leasing of houses. As stated in Article 2, any real estate transaction involving state-owned land in urban areas must comply with the law.

According to Articles 31 and 35, when real estate is transferred or mortgaged, ownership of the real estate and the LURs must be transferred or mortgaged together. All new owners of real estate and the associated LURs must register their ownership. Moreover a written contract has to be concluded for the transfer, presale, mortgage or leasing of real estate.[12]

In order to ensure a smoothly functioning market mechanism, Articles 33, 34 and 58 stipulate the maintenance of certain standards. Such standards apply to the property appraisal system, the recording and registering system for real estate transaction prices, and authentication of the qualifications of real estate price appraisers (valuers). Article 33 states that the appraisal of real estate values must adhere to the principles of justice, fairness and openness, and be carried out according to the technical standards and appraisal procedures established by the state (although there is no mention of what these are).

In addition the appraisal must be carried out on the basis of a benchmark land price in the case of land and the depreciated replacement cost in the case of old houses, with special reference to the current market prices in the locality in question. The rationale behind this provision was that, in initiating a price system for the land market, the government had to establish a reference point for average land prices in each city for the benefit of the local authority, which acts as the sole landlord on behalf of the people.[13]

This set of benchmark land prices provides local authorities with clear guidelines when selling land to investors.

The benchmark land price is the average price of LURs in a specified time period in a particular neighbourhood, and reflects the overall profitability of the location for different grades of land (Li, 1996a). The state also makes use of this benchmark price when assessing land taxes, distributing land revenue and preventing the granting of LURs at unreasonably low prices.

For the proper recording and registering of real estate transaction prices, Article 34 of the Real Estate Law requires new purchasers of real estate to report the transaction price of the transfer to the relevant department.

The Transfer of Real Estate

The transfer of real estate is defined by Article 36 as the act by which a real estate owner transfers his or her real estate to another person as a gift, a business transaction or any other legally approved purpose. A written transfer contract must be concluded between the transferor and the transferee. The content of the contract may be decided between the two parties, but the original mode of obtaining the LURs must be stated (that is, whether the LURs were originally obtained by a grant from the state, in the open market or through administrative allocation). Upon transfer the rights and obligations of the transferor, as stated in the original land granting contract, are transferred to the new owner.

Article 37 stipulates that real estate must not be transferred when:

1. the LURs are barred by order of the judicial department or the decision of the administrative department;
2. the LURs have been reclaimed by the state in accordance with the law;
3. the written consent of the co-owner has not been obtained in the case of jointly owned real estate;
4. the legal ownership is in dispute;
5. the real estate is not registered and a certificate of ownership has not been obtained;
6. transfer is prohibited according to the provisions of laws and administrative rules.

The Preselling of Real Estate

Due to the shortage of construction finance in China, most developers, especially those engaged in the construction of commodity housing,[14] choose to presell in order to increase their cash flow. Article 44 stipulates the conditions developers must meet if they wish to presell units in their development. First, they must have paid all LUR fees and obtained the relevant land use certificate and construction project planning permit. Second, they must register the presale at the local READ at or above county level and obtain permission to presell the property.

Third, actual expenditure must reach at least 25 per cent of the projected cost of the project before preselling is allowed. This serves to protect the purchaser. The developer should also provide details of the construction schedule and the date of completion of the property. It should be noted that the proceeds from the presale of properties must be used for the relevant construction project. Finally, a presale contract between the seller and the buyer should be filed with the READ and SLAB for registration, and anyone in breach of the presale contract will be penalised.

Real Estate Ownership Registration

As mentioned earlier the administration of land and real estate in China is conducted by the SLAB and the MoC respectively. Although there is a growing trend at the local level for the two institutions to merge, most of the local governments in China have two separate registration systems for LURs and buildings.[15]

In most cases the SLAB is responsible for the registration of granted or allocated LURs while the READ is responsible for the registration of buildings and other constructions on the land. Under Article 60 of the Real Estate Law the registration and certification procedures for LURs and buildings are as follows:

1. Granted and allocated LURs must be registered with the SLAB at or above county level. Upon verification, legitimate land users are issued with an LUR certificate by the people's government.
2. Upon completion of a building the building should be registered with the READ at or above county level. A certificate of ownership is issued to legitimate land users as a title document after verification.
3. Prior approval must be sought for the any transfer or modification of real estate and all instances must be registered with the READ at or above county level. Then an application to register the modification, together with the certificate of ownership of the building, should be submitted to the SLAB. Upon verification a new or a modified certificate is issued.

The Real Estate Law established three types of certificate for real estate ownership registration: the LUR certificate, the certificate of ownership of buildings, and the combined certificate of real estate ownership for those local governments where the READ and SLAB have merged.

The preceding sections have provided a general description of the development of the legal framework for the urban land market system. While most people in the West would point to a general lack of legal provisions in some aspects of the economic reform in China, the discussion does show that an improvement has been made. The learning period is still in its infancy as the first piece of land management law was passed only in 1988. A balance has had to be struck between delegating more powers to the local authorities and strengthening central control so that the reform can be steered in the proper direction. This task has not been easy given the size of China. One tends to overlook this point when examining the central legislature's slow reaction to the changing environment. The 1995 Real Estate Law has provided general guidelines for the real estate and construction industry but the implementation regulations are still not finalised. The central government could have designed a much more detailed piece of legislation, but it would have taken much longer for all the regional particularities to be comprehensively considered. In the absence of proper guidelines it is necessary to take a step-by-step approach and to revise the legal framework as implementation proceeds.

To strengthen the protection of property rights, the Urban Real Estate Property Rights Registration Regulations came into effect on 1 January 1998. These regulations apply to all properties built on urban land. Property rights refer to ownership rights and all other rights connected with ownership, such as mortgage rights. According to Section 4, the legal owners of real estate should register with the local real estate administration department (READ) and obtain a certificate of real estate property rights (CREPR). The CREPR is the only legal document recognised by the state to protect the holders' rights to occupy and use the property. Holder of CREPR therefore has undisputed title against third party. The registration of property rights should fall in line with the interest of the LURs for the same site. In cases where the local government has a joint READ and SLAB department, a unified CREPR is issued. This covers both the land and all structures built upon it.

URBAN LAND REFORM: THE ADMINISTRATIVE FRAMEWORK

The Government Structure

The legal framework described above requires a proper administrative network. At the national level, the State Council administers the whole country via a series of ministries, commissions, administrative units, special agencies and offices. Article 89 of the Chinese constitution specifies 18 State Council functions and powers, including the exercise of any functions and powers assigned to it by the National People's Congress (NPC) or its standing committee.

Under the State Council, the highest administrative authority dealing with land and real property is the State Land Administration Bureau (SLAB), which was established on 1 August 1986 under Article 5 of the Land Management Law. The other authorities involved in real estate administration are the Ministry of Construction (MoC) and the State Asset Administration Bureau (SAAB).

This power structure, however, is to be reorganised as Premier Zhu Rongji, elected in March 1998, has decided to implement a government reform programme whereby some ministries will be merged or closed. The MoC will remain as is but the SLAB will be merged with other bureaus and ministries to become the new Ministry of State Land and Natural Resources (MSLNR). The MSLNR is to be given the tasks of the former Ministries of Geology and Mineral Resources and the former Bureaux of State Land Administration, State Oceanography, Surveying and Cartography. Hence land will be treated more like a natural resource and viewed from a broader perspective. One positive implication of this new structure is that land management policy may come to focus more on socioeconomic and political considerations rather than on purely financial matters.

One of the objectives of Zhu's reform is to transform some of the affiliated government business units into private enterprises. If this also happens within the new Ministry of State Land and Natural Resources, there will probably be more real estate development and related companies with good government connections. This may have two different effects. On the one hand it may open up joint-venture oppurtunities for foreign companies with well-connected local partners. This would bring in more foreign investment. On the other hand it could act as a barrier to new companies that do not have such connections. What actually happens will depend on the development of the market mechanism. If the market becomes more and more open, then positive competition will encourage the first scenario.

The following sections provide a brief description of the structure and roles of the MoC, SLAB and SAAB.

The Ministry of Construction
The Ministry of Construction (MoC) is made up of 13 departments (Figure 2.2) and is responsible for all activities in the construction sector, such as engineering construction, urban construction, the construction of villages and townships, the building industry, the real estate industry,

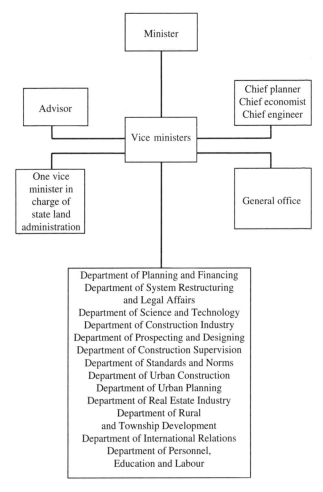

Figure 2.2   Organisation of the Ministry of Construction
Source: Ministry of Construction, The People's Republic of China.

public utilities and so on. The various activities are shared among the 13 departments. The MoC also has 93 affiliated institutions, which can be divided into five categories:

1. Affiliated enterprises.
2. Affiliated scientific research and design units.
3. Affiliated universities, colleges and research centres.

4. Affiliated newspaper and press.
5. Affiliated social associations.

The main functions of the MoC are as follows:

1. To formulate principles, policies and regulations for engineering construction, urban construction, the construction of villages and townships, the building industry, the real estate industry and municipal engineering, and the relevant development strategies, industrial policies, reform schemes and medium to long-term plans related to construction; and to provide guidance for their implementation.

2. To set (a) national standards and norms for engineering and civil construction at the implementation stages, (b) unified national norms and (c) standards for industries administered by the Ministry and to issue national standards jointly with the State Administration of Technological Supervision. In collaboration with the State Planning Commission and other relevant agencies, to approve and promulgate economic evaluation methods for feasibility studies on construction projects, economic parameters, construction standards, an index of investment estimates, construction time limits, construction land use surveys and construction cost management regulations.

3. To develop regulations for tender preparation and the design and construction of engineering projects. To undertake project management in construction works. To regulate the construction market. To manage geotechnical surveys and the construction prices. To supervise and inspect engineering quality and construction safety.

4. To direct national urban planning, urban geological investigations and surveys for civil engineering. To examine and approve city master plans assigned by the State Council. To protect cities that are of historical and cultural importance (this jointly with the State Bureau of Relics). To participate in national and regional land planning. To direct the management of urban construction sites.

5. To provide guidance at the national level for urban water supplies, gas supplies, district heating, public transport, municipal utilities, parks and gardens, city landscaping and sanitation. To take charge of national parks and beauty spots. To be responsible for the comprehensive administration of the water supply and conservation, and the development, utilisation and protection of underground water in urban areas. To direct the renovation of the urban environment, and to supervise urban construction, urban flood prevention and drainage.

6. To take charge of the industrial management of the real estate industry. To provide guidance on the transfer of land use rights, the development

and operation of real estate and the commercialisation of housing. To guide and promote urban housing construction. To participate in and guide housing reform.

7. To direct the planning and construction of villages and market towns. To promote the development of towns and villages.

8. To formulate scientific and technological development plans and technical and economic policies for the building industry. To organise research on key scientific and technological items. To publicise and popularise scientific and technological research achievements. To direct and administer major technological introductions.

9. To work out training programmes for professionals in the construction industry. To guide the training and continued education of staff. To set the standards for architectural and urban construction education in universities and colleges throughout the country. To manage all universities and colleges affiliated to the MoC.

10. To oversee the protection of national urban developments and industrial and residential buildings, and the construction of civil defence facilities attached to buildings.

11. To engage in foreign economic and technological cooperation and other foreign affairs in the field of construction. To help enterprises to develop building markets and real estate markets overseas, and to carry out subcontracted projects.

The State Land Administration Bureau

The State Land Administration Bureau (SLAB), established in 1986, is a functional and executive department of the State Council and is responsible for the overall management of urban and rural land and land policy in the country as a whole. The SLAB has nine departments and five institutional units (Figure 2.3). A land management bureau system has been set up at the provincial, county and township levels in 30 provinces (Figure 2.4). As mentioned earlier, the SLAB has recently been merged into the new Ministry of State Land Resources and its future structure is still not known.

The main responsibilities of the SLAB are as follows:[16]

1. To formulate land policy principles and regulations and to organise, supervise and inspect their implementation.

2. To speed up the construction of a land information system. To research and devise a national strategy for land management development. To forecast the medium- and long-term demand for land for various uses in order to achieve a balance between demand and supply.

Figure 2.3   Departments and institutional units under the SLAB
Source: State Land Administration Bureau, People's Republic of China, 1996.

3. To devise and standardise a management policy and system for land in both urban and rural areas. To carry out cadastral surveys and settle land ownership disputes. To be responsible for nationwide land surveys, statistics, classification, registration and certification. To carry out land appraisal jointly with the other organisations concerned. To work out criteria for land classification and appraisal and plans for a nationwide land survey. To establish a land statistics system and a land information monitoring system. To draw up technical regulations on cadastral management.
4. On the basis of the national economic and social development plan, to plan land use and the development of land resources. To monitor the implementation of planning and plans.
5. To be responsible for land requisition, allocation and granting. To convert rural collective land into state land. To undertake the examination and verification of land for construction use approved by the

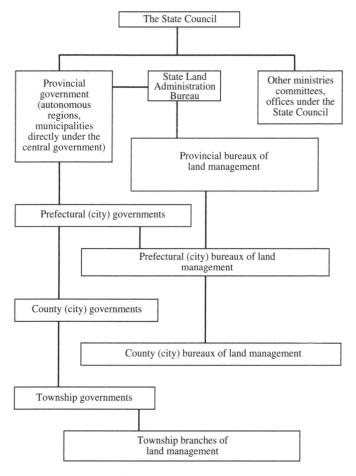

Figure 2.4   The land management bureau system
Source: State Land Administration Bureau, People's Republic of China, 1996.

State Council. To be responsible for the organisation, coordination, examination, verification and implementation of the granting of land use rights. To draft a supply policy for various types of land for different constru tion uses.

6. To undertake the administrative management of the land market and formulate regulations and rules for land market management jointly with the other organisations concerned. To inspect and supervise the

transfer, leasing, mortgaging and so on of land use rights. To assist the financial and tax departments to collect land use fees and taxes.
7. To design a programme to deepen the reform of the land management and land use systems. To monitor the progress of the reforms and improve reform measures when necessary.
8. To take responsibility for the work of science and technology in land management. To provide publicity and education on land management and to organise and guide the training of the staff of the various land management bureaux.
9. To be responsible for the foreign affairs of the SLAB and the land management bureaux. To guide and coordinate international exchanges and cooperative ventures through the land management bureaux system.
10. To be responsible for matters pertaining to the personnel of the SLAB and the land management bureaux and to guide personnel management.
11. To undertake other tasks dictated by the State Council.

The State Assets Administration Bureau (SAAB)
The State Assets Administration Bureau (SAAB) is responsible for structuring and managing all state assets. Unlike the SLAB and the MoC it is not directly responsible to the State Council, rather it is part of the financial management hierarchy. Since the inception of the LUR reform it has had the important task of valuing these assets for purposes such as listing on the stock market. It has the following duties:

1. To cooperate with other government branches in the formulation of policies, regulations and legistation. To manage, monitor the use of and publicise the misuse of state assets.
2. To audit and clarify property rights, arbitrate disputes and register all rights to state assets.
3. To improve the information flow on state assets and create an efficient market for the sale or transfer of such assets.
4. In coordination with other departments, to approve the establishment, management, merger, separation, termination or auction of state enterprises. To act as administrator of the assets of dissolved state enterprises.
5. To give advice on and monitor state investments.
6. To conduct research on the allocation of after-tax profits and the shareholding benefits of state enterprises.
7. Together with other departments, to devise ways of improving the value of state assets. To draw up regulations on the auditing and valuation of the assets of state enterprises. To examine the financial status of state enterprises.

With regard to administrative structure, the SAAB has six functional departments:

1. The General Office Department: this is the central administrative unit, which deals with all kinds of administration such as record keeping, publicity, external affairs, finance, personnel and coordination with other departments and units.
2. The policy and Regulations Department: this is responsible for the drafting of all legislation and regulations concerning the management and auditing of state assets. It also conducts research on future policies and arbitrates disputes among departments over state assets.
3. The Registration and Statistics Department: this deals with the clarification and registration of property rights. It also keeps records of state assets and produces reports on the distribution, management, auditing and profitability of these assets. When major investment decisions about state assets are being planned, this department offers opinions and advice. In the age of economic reform, this department also has the task of promoting or establishing open markets for state assets.
4. The Enterprises Department: in coordination with other relevant departments, this department audits the assets of state enterprises within and outside China. It is also involved in the creation of share-issuing state enterprises as well as the leasing and joint-venture arrangements of these enterprises. In addition it handles disputes among state enterprises over property rights and issues guidelines on the improvement of asset values.
5. The Administrative Units Resources Department: this department, in coordination with other relevant departments, formulate the management of state assets owned by various governmental units. In case there is dispute over property rights, it coordinates with central administrative departments to clarify.
6. The Local Authority Department: this department forms a bridge between the central policies unit and local representative offices of SAAB. It helps local SAAB departments to inspect local state enterprises on their management of state assets and carry out central asset management policies.

The Assets Appraisal Centre of the SAAB has the task of improving valuation standards in the real estate market. Its job is to:

1. study the administrative regulations and devise a set of laws covering the appraisal of asset values;
2. manage the nation's asset valuations, including at the local level;

3. certify valuation reports on the value of state assets and issue certificates for them.

In this brief discussion of the three major institutions, it is not difficult to detect a certain overlapping of functions. First of all, it is very difficult to draw a sharp line between the responsibilities for land and built structures, especially in the urban context. Furthermore, having a separate management structure for land and property invariably increases the administrative burden shouldered by the government and the developers. An obvious example here is the registration of interests. In most Chinese cities, separate registration of LUR certificates and real estate ownership certificates is required for every transaction, which serves to prolong the development process, especially in the case of preselling. This problem is now being tackled at the local level as some local governments are combining the SLAB and the READ into a single entity so that a combined LUR–property ownership certificate can be issued.

A further problem arising from this blurring of responsibilies involves appraisal. The evaluation of real estate is a very new concept in China and it has a very important role to play in the urban land reform. However, due to the separation of responsibilities it is proving difficult to develop a proper real estate appraisal system, not to mention a body of well-trained real estate professionals. One underlying cause of the problem is that land administration in China has been historically related to rural or agricultural land management while construction has been very much an urban concept. Given the potential power offered by the development of the real estate market, it is not difficult to imagine that competition exists among the various institutional bodies concerned.

Personnel Development

Two major professional bodies are being developed to address the problem of real estate appraisal: the China Institute of Real Estate Appraisers (CIREA) and the China Land Valuer Institute (CLVI). The CIREA has a relatively closer relationship with the MoC while the CLVI is allied with the SLAB.

Under the terms of the Registration Regulations of Societies and Associations of China, the activities of all registered societies must be controlled and supervised by a relevant government department. Hence in the constitution of the CIREA there is a clause stating that the institute is under the supervision of the MoC. By the same token the CLVI is supervised by the SLAB. Before anyone can become a member of the CIREA they have to obtain a 'Certificate of Real Estate Valuer', which is issued by the institute upon the successful completion of qualifying examinations. A similar requirement exists for the CLVI.

Because of their supervisory role the MoC and SLAB have access to a constant supply of trained personnel for their divisions, but the MoC has an advantage in this respect because the central government National Personnel Office only recognises membership of the CIREA as a valid qualification.

A guidebook on the CIREA's qualifying examinations is jointly edited by the MoC and the National Personnel Office. A similar guidebook is available for the CLVI examination, and both contain a mock examination section for the readers. A look at the contents of the mock examinations reveals the difference in focus between the two institutes. The questions in the CIREA guidebook are divided into four main subject areas: the real estate market mechanism, real estate investment and management, real estate appraisal, and case studies. In the CLVI guidebook, on the other hand, there are questions on the land management system, the conveyance of land use rights, the development of land by foreign investors, the taxation of agricultural land, the classification of land grades and the registration of land titles. Hence the CLVI examination covers everything to do with land but little about the property market. Obviously a large amount of effort has been made to avoid an overlap with the CIREA examinations and the market interests of these two institutes is obvious.

Both the MoC and the SLAVB have drawn up regulations to strengthen their own systems. According to a joint document by the MoC and the National Personnel Office – Provisional Regulations on the Qualifying Mechanism for Practicing as a Real Estate Valuer, – all real estate appraisal practices must employ a certain number of qualified, MoC-approved valuers in their companies, and the regulations list the duties and rights of these valuers, in particular, only MoC-approved valuers are allowed to work in appraisal practices 'whose nature of trade, scope of business and working procedures are regulated by the MoC in accordance with the relevant regulations of the state'. In the appendix of the regulations real estate business is defined as activities relating to property as well as land.

For its part the SLAB insists that at least 25 per cent of employees of companies specialising in land value appraisal should be qualified land valuers, where qualified means successful completion of the CLVI examination described above. All qualified land valuers working for private practices have the right to examine land titles and collect information on land prices and land transactions in the local land management departments.

URBAN LAND REFORM: THE MORTGAGE AND
FINANCE FRAMEWORK

Despite the fact that the central government is very keen to develop a market system for land and real estate, there is still no national law on the mortgaging of real estate and increasing the flexibility of property finance. The 1995 Real Estate Law only stipulates the basic requirements and legal formalities for mortgaging activities.

Under Article 46 of the Real Estate Law the words 'mortgage of real estate' refer to a mortgagee providing finance to a mortgagor, with the real estate acting as collateral or security against the non-payment of debt. Until the debt is repaid the real estate in question cannot be disposed of. If the mortgagor is not able to fulfill his obligation to repay the debt to the mortgagee, the Real Estate Law states that the mortgaged property may be auctioned and the mortgagee has the first right to the sale proceeds as compensation. This definition clearly reflects the concept of real estate as non-disposable collateral against debt.

It should be noted that Article 50 allows the mortgaging of real estate where the land use right has been obtained by administrative allocation. However, in the event of non-payment of the debt the mortgagee is only compensated when an amount equal to the land grant fee has been paid to the state from the proceeds of the sale of the mortgaged real estate.

There are two ways in which a mortgage may be obtained (Article 57): by mortgaging a lawfully obtained house and the associated LUR, and by mortgaging an LUR obtained through the granting system – both require a valid LUR certificate and a certificate of ownership of the property.

The mortgagor and the mortgagee enter into a written contract and register the same with a department designated by the local government at or above county level. When the LUR and the house have been obtained as a result of the sale of mortgaged real estate, the change of ownership of the LUR and the house must be registered in accordance with the relevant provisions in the Real Estate Law (Articles 49 and 61).

Another principle established by the Real Estate Law (Article 51) is that any new buildings on mortgaged land are not regarded as mortgaged assets if they were built after the mortgage contract had been concluded. If the mortgaged land is disposed of by auction the buildings may also be auctioned, but in this case the mortgagee does not have first claim on the sale proceeds of the buildings.

In 1997 the Regulations on the Mortgaging of Urban Real Estate, were promulgated by the MoC, as of June 1997. These regulations apply to all mortgage activities on state-owned land in urban areas, but not to the mortgaging of LURs for state-owned land that contains no built structures.

The regulations define a mortgage as a transaction where a mortgagor offers legally obtained real estate as collateral in exchange for a loan, without having to transfer the legal title to the mortgagee. In the event of loan default the mortgagee can arrange to auction the mortgaged property and extract the money owed, including interest, from the sale proceeds. Article 3 of the regulations specifies two types of mortgage. The first concerns commodity properties traded on the open market. The purchaser pays the developer a down payment for the property and the balance is financed by a mortgage from a bank. The property becomes collateral for the loan and the bank is the mortgagee. The second type is concerned with the construction process. Developers can mortgage to a bank their legally obtained LURs together with all fixed capital investments and other structures on the site. This is similar to the practice in market economies in that the right to use the land on which the property stands is mortgaged as well.

Chapter 2 of the mortgage regulations defines mortgage rights and related issues. It stipulates that certain properties may not be mortgaged, such as properties whose legal right is in dispute, properties belonging to educational, medical and social services institutions, properties subject to preservation orders, properties that are to be redeveloped and illegal properties. Chapter 2 also stipulates that if the value of a mortgaged property exceeds the mortgaged sum, a second mortgage is allowed, provided the value of the second mortgage does not exceed the difference between the value of the property and the value of the first mortgage. When a second or subsequent mortgage is arranged, the first mortgagee must be notified.

Prior approval from the relevant bodies or institutions is required when a mortgage involves real estate belonging to farmers' collectives, joint-venture companies and limited liability companies. Furthermore, the term of the mortgage must not exceed the term of the associated LURs, minus the number of years that elapsed prior to the creation of the mortgage.

Chapter 4 of the mortgage regulations specifies the registration requirements. Both mortgagee and mortgagor must register their rights with the local READ within 30 days of signing the mortgage contract, and the contract only becomes effective when it has been properly registered. If there are changes to the mortgage arrangements, such as full repayment of the loan, reregistration is required within 15 days of the change.

Chapter 6 details the duties and responsibilities of the two parties. In the following situations a mortgagee can take legal action against the mortgagor:

- When the mortgagor fails to repay the loan and does not seek an extension of the term of the loan from the mortgagee.
- When the mortgagor dies leaving no successor, or his or her successor refuses to repay the loan.
- When the mortgagor is declared bankrupt.
- When the mortgagor is in breach of any of the conditions laid down in the mortgage contract.

Under most of these circumstances the mortgagee can negotiate with the mortgagor to auction the property. If the negotiations fail the mortgagee has the right to approach the court for judgement. When auctioning the mortgaged real estate, any property built after the start of the contract is also auctioned. However the mortgagee receives no share of the proceeds from such structures. When properties built on land obtained through administrative allocation are mortgaged and later auctioned because of loan default, the state is entitled to reimbursement of the LUR fee before the mortgagee can reclaim the outstanding debt.

In addition to these regualtions, the financial institutions have taken steps to improve the loan finance situation in the housing market. The 1997 Trial Regulations on the Management of Individual Housing Loans with Collateral provides an interesting example as this mortgage arrangement was initiated by a bank and not by the local government, although banks can be classified as state enterprises. The Housing Loan Regulations, which were issued by the People's Bank (the *de facto* central bank) on 28 April 1997, apply to housing loans, and the property itself (or any financial assets or third party guarantees) is used as collateral. Applicants for housing loans must fulfill the following requirements:

1. The applicant must be a legal householder in the city in question.
2. The applicant must have a valid home purchase contract or agreement issued by the city government.
3. The applicant must have a valid 'Permit for the Sale of Commodity Housing' in the case of newly built commodity housing or an approved 'Sale of Public Housing' proposal, certified by the relevant local department.
4. The applicant must have savings or deposits in a housing provident fund of at least 30 per cent of the price of the property to act as the down payment for the property.
5. The applicant must be able to prove his or her ability to repay the loan.

6. The applicant must possess approved assets as collateral, or the personal guarantee of a financially secured third party.

Chapter 3 stipulates that the loan given to an applicant must not exceed the appraised value of the property, as certified by the local appraisal institute. If an applicant is using his or her housing provident fund to purchase a dwelling, the loan must not be more than double the amount that will have been contributed to the fund by the household members upon reaching the age of retirement. Chapter 4 deals with loan terms and interest rates. Although it states that it is up to individual commercial banks to decide the term of a loan, it advises that this should not be more than 20 years. Those using their housing provident fund to purchase a dwelling pay interest at a fixed rate based on the current saving interest rate. Those using personal loans pay interest at a three-year fixed rate if the loan term is five years, and a five-year fixed rate if the loan term is between five and ten years.

Chapter 5 lists the various conditions for the loan guarantee. In general, assets used as collateral must comply with those listed in Sections 34 and 37 of the PRC Guarantee Law. The rest of the Housing Loan Regulations relate to the liabilities and duties of the mortgagee, mortgagor and guarantor.

At the local level, an interesting example of mortgage regulations initiated by a bank rather than the local government are the 1997 Trial Regulations on Housing Loan with Collateral and Guarantee issued by the Beijing branch of the Construction Bank. The Construction Bank is the largest of the banks that deal with property and construction finance. The regulations apply to housing loans using the property itself, or other financial assets such as bonds, debentures or third party guarantees, as collateral. Chapter 2 of the regulations lists the criteria that applicants for housing loans must satisfy before a loan can be considered. These are the same as those listed above in connection with the People's Bank. Chapter 5 deals with the terms of the loan. A housing loan must not exceed 70 per cent of the appraised value of the property (although it does not stipulate which organisation shall be responsible for the appraisal). Except under very special circumstances, the loan period cannot exceed 10 years. With regard to the loan guarantee, in general, when using the property as collateral, the mortgagor and mortgagee have to register the mortgage after a proper valuation has been carried out. Before the loan can be granted a personal guarantee has to be signed by a third party. Furthermore, the mortgagor must arrange proper insurance cover for the property with an approved insurance company.

When using a third party guarantee only, the third party (which must be a legal entity such as an enterprise) must be able to prove that it is properly registered with the relevant commerce department. It must also submit its accounts for examination and have a standard Construction Bank account in good standing. The regulations also allow citizen to use financial assets such as savings, bonds or debentures as collateral. In such cases all documents are kept by the bank until the loan is repaid.

Chapter 6 relates to the repayment formula. The monthly repayment mainly consists of interest at the beginning, and later repayment of the principal. The formula used to calculate the monthly repayment amount is:

$$A = \frac{PI(1+I)^n}{(1+I)^n - 1}$$

where A is the monthly repayment, P is the principal, n is the number of monthly repayments and I is the current interest rate on the loan, as specified by the People's Bank.

This set of trial regulations provides much more detailed arrangements for the mortgage financing of residential property, especially with regard to technical matters than the Housing Loan Regulations issued by the People's Bank of China.

CONCLUSIONS

The old state land allocation system instilled in people the idea that land should be available free of charge. This is true today only to the extent that some land uses, by their nature, can not generate sufficient income to cover the land rent. The obvious examples are public housing for the poor, schools and hospitals. Under such circumstances land should be made directly available to the user and not involve the open market. The social element should override economic element in this land use consideration.

In the majority of cases, if land is not allocated according to the economic efficiency of the user but to a certain set of political criteria, it will distort the whole supply and demand system. The key issue here is that once land has been put to a particular use, that use is difficult to revoke and any undesirable effects created by the user can only be addressed by compulsorily state purchase. However when the land use system has no price mechanism, the standard against which to measure property rights disappears. A direct result of this is the state tends not to take action against undesirable land use as the social and political consequences of resettlement are huge.

Furthermore, with state-allocated land prospective users tend to apply for more land than they really need in order to avoid application problems in the future, as the political criteria for allocation can change at any time. This land 'banking' reduces the overall supply of land, especially in core urban areas. However this risk avoidance behaviour, in fact and in substance, is little different from the activities of investors in market economies, except that the latter use money as the medium for their activities. Hence it is human greed that erodes the system.

We have seen above that the LUR reform, launched in late 1980s, was aimed at rectifing the inherent problems of the state land allocation system. As mentioned, an administrative allocation system is not wrong in itself, it is the extent to which it is taken that matters. The LUR reformists in China wished to combine political ideology with economic reality, and they have been successful in this respect in that the new leasehold system seperates the right to use land from ownership of the land, which in the socialist ideology belongs to all the people.

However, this success will be shortlived if administrative allocation is not reduced to the bare minimum. In some regions a much larger proportion of land is handed out via the administrative channel than sold on the market. An obvious example is Shanghai, which had a smaller market-to-allocation ratio than the national average in both 1994 and 1995, when the land market was booming in that city (Li, 1996a). Furthermore the degree to which the market structure has been established varies considerably among the provinces. Hence it is local effort that determines the success of efforts to transform planned allocation into a more efficient market structure.

The slow learning curve in the legal provisions for land management is evidenced by the fact that it has taken ten years to revise the Land Management Law. However this has a lot to do with the size of the country and its cultural heritage. One should also bear in mind the necessity of gaining general acceptance of the market mechanism and the associated legal framework. In this respect the length of the learning curve seems acceptable. The new provisions laid down in the revised draft are admirable. Land should be treated as an important national asset and managed in the simplest and most efficient way with as little red tape as possible. The revised draft represents a positive step towards a centralised land granting mechanism with a network of information systems.

Urban land reform in China has followed a top-down approach. It was prompted by the need for economic efficiency and was not a by-product of China's political reforms. It is a gradual approach as the reform is proceeding within the framework of socialist economic, or in Chinese terminology, market socialism.

Because of this gradual approach there is no comprehensive reform package to activate the market mechanism in all aspects of the macro economy that intermittently affect the urban land market. Hence there is still no proper legal framework for the protection of property rights, developers are finding it difficult to arrange financing as the mortgage regulations are weak, and policy makers are finding it difficult to commercialise the housing market as this depends on the reform of state enterprises and wage policies. However the authorities have had the opportunity to gain step-by-step experiences of the urban land market and to learn from their mistakes. Since this is a top-down reform, the messages given out by the reformers need to be very clear if they are to be effective. The gradual pace of the reform is allowing time for the new measures to gain social acceptance, which is important as no one in present-day China has had prior experience of the operations of the urban land market.

3 The Housing Market

INTRODUCTION

The problems caused by of the state land allocation system are also reflected in the housing supply. As private land and real estate ownership were banned under the earlier socialist doctrine, private real estate development was almost non-existent and the provision of housing was the responsibility of the state. This imposed a substantial financial burden on the state, as shown in Figure 3.1.

As can be seen, the total expenditure on housing between 1949 and the prereform period was almost nine times greater than on the food industry and substantially higher than on most of the income-earning industries. As rents on housing were and still are extremely low, most of this expenditure went on maintenance and management costs. Basic economic theory dictates that the direct result of this kind of overinvestment/overexpenditure without a reasonable return is dilapidation. The solution to this is to make the provision of housing a self-financing process by creating a market value for land and property in order to generate sufficient revenue to fund further real estate development.

Despite continued efforts to build residential units since 1949, housing shortages in urban areas, deteriorating housing conditions and overcrowding still exist. Many urban residents have to tolerate cramped living space, inadequate facilities and shared living arrangements. The housing conditions vary among cities and are worse in the larger cities. Before 1952 the

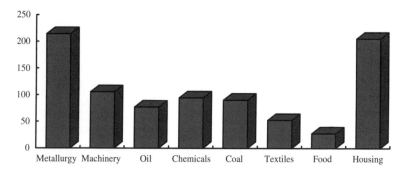

Figure 3.1   Accumulative state investment in various industries since 1949
(billion yuan)
Source: *China Statistical Yearbook* (1990).

58

average living area was about 45 square metres per person.[1] Since housing was viewed as non-productive and had a low development priority, less and less state money was spent on urban housing. As a result the average amount of living space per person gradually decreased to 3.6 square metres in 1978. However, from 1979 the government began to invest more in housing and by 1990 the average living space per person had increased to 6.7 square metres. In the mean time the housing shortage persisted and in 1982 more than 1.83 million families resided permanently in warehouses, workshops, classrooms or cellars. It was very common in urban areas for a typical family of three or four to reside in just one room, sharing a communal kitchen and toilet with up to eight other families because bathrooms and kitchens were costly to install. According to a government survey carried out between July 1985 and July 1986, the average per capita living space was 6.1 square metres. Only about 40 per cent of dwellings had indoor toilets and just 12 per cent were supplied with gas. It was also very common for three-generation families to occupy a single flat with two to three rooms – in 1982 the number of families with three generations sharing a unit reached 1.89 million.

As stated above, the Chinese government began to invest more in urban housing from 1979, and around 12 million apartments have been built since then at the rate of almost two million units a year.[2] Even though this massive programme has accounted for 20 per cent of the nation's capital investments the housing shortage is still acute. An additional 2.7 billion units need to be constructed each year until 2000, at which point 40 million apartments will be required to house China's urban population.[3]

China's urban housing shortage is the result not only of the factors discussed above, but also the population increase and the increasing number of marriages. China's urban population grew from 57.65 million in 1949 to 130.73 million in 1960 and 382.44 million in 1985. The population density was much higher in the larger cities, for example in Shanghai in 1992–93 it was 2043 people a square kilometre, which was three to four times higher than in other cities.[4] Furthermore, the growth rate was much higher in the large cities, partly because of the return of people from the countryside. During the Cultural Revolution a considerable effort was made to control the growth of urban centres by sending people to small cities and rural areas. The return of these people significantly boosted the demand for housing since a large proportion of them were young and seeking to form their own families. Added to this was the constant influx of peasants looking for work. Hence the failure to raise housing standards was not only due to an inability to meet the planned housing targets, but also to the higher than expected growth rate of the urban population.

As stated above, the increase in the number of marriages has added to the demand for housing. Economic development and changes to the traditional way of life have resulted in young people wishing to set up separate households after marriage and hence to a rapid increase in the number of individual families. In China, finding a house has become a major concern of the entire family when children are about to marry. The number of marriages increased from 7.2 million in 1980 to 9.5 million in 1992, and several hundred thousand newly married couples could not find their own accommodation.[5] Instead they had to share their parrents' already cramped quarters and their living conditions became intolerable. Even though the government was attempting to resolve the housing shortage, the accumulated shortfall was just too great to overcome.

Investment in housing has been hindered by lack of capital, which is parlty the result of artificially low rents. In urban areas of China, cheap subsidised housing has been regarded as a fringe benefit offered by work units to their workers. Housing is a welfare good and in effect a wage in kind. In the early 1950s rents were set at about 8 per cent of household income, and even though the government subsequently made several major upward adjustments to wages, rents remained more or less unchanged. Indeed the average monthly rent in 1987 was 0.13 yuan a square metre. With an average floor space of 6.1 square metres a person, each household was paying an average of 0.793 yuan a month for their living space, or about 1–2 per cent of household income. (In Western countries the figure was in the range of 10–30 per cent for public housing.) So while the rent levels remained consistently low, the state was facing high and increasing construction costs. According to one source, in 1985 the annual gross return on a residential building was 0.92 yuan while the construction cost to the state was 177 yuan for every square metre of floor space.[6] This illustrates the degree to which housing is subsidised by the state, and if lack of capital continues to constrain investment in urban housing, rents will have to rise.

Furthermore low rents mean that workers have no incentive to invest in their own housing and move out of their allocated units. Because of this lack of mobility, new housing stock is contantly required to meet new demands. This heavy burden should be borne by the work unit. In addition the rents charged are not related to the quality of the housing provided. Rather, rents are based on the amount of floor space provided, regardless of facilities, location and quality, factors that are usually taken into account when setting rents in capitalist societies. The fixed rent policy has created inequality in resource distribution as people who live in lower-quality houses pay the same rent as those with better houses. Nor is rent related to the means of the tenants. In 1992 the ratio of rent to total living expenditure was 0.88 per cent for the lowest-income families but 0.65 per cent for the highest-income families. The average rent to total expenditure was just 0.73 per cent, which was extremely low by Western standards.[7]

Needless to say, this low rent structure means that land costs, construction costs and accumulated interest can never be recovered and no allowance can be made for maintenance, repairs and depreciation. It has been found that the average maintenance cost is about 2 yuan per square metre per month, which is 1.3 times the average monthly rent of 0.13 yuan per square metre.[8] Almost no maintenance work has been carried out on urban housing, and the rapid deterioration of the housing stock resulted in about 11 million square metres of housing being demolished in 1982 alone.[9] If this situation continues the supply will never be able to meet the demand.

Fundamental, practical property management principals will have to be introduced if any impact is to be made on China's housing problems. Today in China, even three-year-old buildings may have rusting windows, broken glass, minimum landscaping and so on. The appearance of urban housing is not attended to because of the absence of an adequate management system. Housing programmes will fail if these problems are not solved, even if rents are increased to support the costs. There are also insufficient management personnel in China.[10] Chinese officials acknowledge this, but stress that the solution will cost money. It cannot be denied that the failure to provide trained management personnel and the deferral of maintenance will have a huge negative impact on China's urban housing reform.

THE PRIVATE HOUSING MARKET

One of the main objectives of the urban land reform has been to convert state-built housing into marketable properties and encourage private real estate development, in particular housing. This required the introduction of private property ownership, and the introduction of commodity housing (residential properties built by private developers or state enterprises for sale in the open market) created a market channel for the exchange of these private property rights. Consequently, private home ownership increased quite substantially after the launch of the reform, and individual purchasers of commodity houses doubled after 1993.

Residential properties have been a major element in market reform. A mature real estate market should contain a substantial residential element. This is because a well-developed residential market provides inherent demand for properities in the new supply as well as in the secondary market. When there is general economic and population growth in the society, there will be a trade-up effect such that every level of citizens would trade up to better housing. This becomes a constant source of demand. In case of office and commercial sectors in the property market, this flow of demand is not constant and to a certain extent in the case of emerging economies, depends on the investment decision of multinational corporations.

Private home ownership did not grow as rapidly as expected between 1987 and 1991. Most properties were bought by enterprises, either to house their employees or for resale. Given the subsidised rents in the public sector and the relatively small secondary market for commodity real estate, before 1992 individuals had little incentive to spend their savings on real estate. However in 1992 Deng Xiaoping publicly reasserted that economic reform was the only solution to China's problems. This was regarded as confirming the continuation of the open door policy and an indication of the government's long-term economic policy. As a reslt, confidence in the reforms grew and the total floor area sold in the open market increased by 50 per cent. In particular the proportion of individual purchasers of residential properties increased from 14 per cent in 1986, when the urban housing reform was about to be launched, to an average of 50 per cent in 1994 (Table 3.1). This eagerness to purchase commodity housing subsided in 1994 when the government launched austerity measures to damper down the overheated economy. Despite this fall in interest there was a rise in the prices fetched. This was because the high-value sector of the property market was governed more by foreign investment interests than local demand, and immense interest was being shown by Chinese investors from Hong Kong, Taiwan and Singapore because of the relatively low property prices.

However in the longer term foreign investors too were affected by market confidence and became more selective in their choice of investment location (Table 3.2). In addition, overdependence on foreign demand polarised the market and limited investment in the ordinary residential market. This could have defeated the purpose of the urban land reform – to create a healthy real estate market – but fortunately the problem of overdependence was spotted by some real estate developers and investors who started to look at local housing projects with a state-guaranteed return. We shall discuss this in more detail later on.

Table 3.3 presents some interesting findings. Investment in the residential sector accounted for about 56 per cent of all investment in commodity real estate in 1996 and 1997 and about three times more than in commercial properties. Likewise the sales volume and area sold were both much higher in the residential sector than other sectors. In terms of the value of

Table 3.1 Sale of commodity properties, 1986–96

	Floor space sold per year (10 000 sq. m)	Percentage change	Residential content (10 000 sq. m and % of total)	Percentage change	Amount purchased by private individuals (10 000 sq. m)	Percentage change	Sales value (100 million yuan)	Percentage change	Residential content	Percentage change
1986	–	–	1834.95	–	256.11	–	–	–	–	–
1987	2697.24	–	2376.72 (88)	29.53	426.66	66.59	1 100 967	–	–	–
1988	2927.33	8.53	2549.12 (87)	7.25	722.56	69.35	1 472 164	33.72	–	–
1989	2855.36	–2.46	2491.38 (87)	–2.27	805.49	11.48	1 637 542	11.23	–	–
1990	2871.54	0.57	2544.61 (89)	2.14	730.85	–9.27	2 018 263	23.25	–	–
1991	3025.46	5.36	2745.17 (91)	7.88	926.55	26.78	2 378 597	17.85	2 075 979	–
1992	4288.86	41.76	3812.21 (89)	38.87	1456.01	57.14	4 265 938	79.35	3 798 493	82.97
1993	6687.91	55.94	6035.19 (90)	58.31	2943.39	102.15	8 637 141	102.47	7 291 913	91.97
1994	7230.35	8.11	6118.03 (85)	1.37	3344.53	13.63	10 184 950	17.92	7 305 208	0.18
1995	7905.94	9.34	6787.03 (86)	10.93	3344.81	0.01	12 577 269	23.49	10 240 705	40.18
1996	7900.41	–0.07	6898.46 (87)	1.64	3666.82	9.6	14 271 292	13.5	11 069 006	8.09

Source: China Statistical Yearbook (1995, 1996, 1997).

Table 3.2   Investment in real estate, 1994–96

	State-owned companies	Collectively owned companies	Foreign-funded companies	Companies funded from Hong Kong, Taiwan and Macao
Nationwide				
1994	11 939	5478	1231	3456
1995	9 869	5589	2542	2255
1996	8 676	4755	2202	2135
Beijing				
1994	77	1	0	0
1995	183	18	160	48
1996	175	13	115	59
Shanghai				
1994	1 453	152	95	296
1995	759	309	152	64
1996	793	379	163	93
Tianjin				
1994	359	120	86	144
1995	198	75	46	45
1996	193	67	41	39
Fujian				
1994	430	272	203	274
1995	314	214	306	311
1996	293	198	267	284
Guangdong				
1994	1 483	1579	146	562
1995	1 703	1710	303	631
1996	1 326	1305	293	546

the real estate sold, the residential sector brought in about nine times more than the office sector and eight times more than commercial properties. In terms of floor area sold the difference was even higher. This shows that although most developers find the office sector more attractive at the beginning of market reforms in transitional economies, the importance of the residential market should not be overlooked.

The growth of the private housing market in urban areas was not mirrored in rural areas. Table 3.4 shows that although private investment in buildings increased from 70 per cent to 85 per cent total fixed investments between 1996 and 1998, the residential proportion of this fell from 90 per cent to 79 per cent. However this does not mean that the overall proportion of residential development decreased, just that private investors were more interested in other types of property. As can be seen in the last

Table 3.3 Performance of the various sectors in the commodity property market, 1996–98[1]

	Total			Residential			Office			Commercial/retail			Other		
	1996 (January–September)[2]	1997	1998 (January–May)[2]	1996 (January–September)[2]	1997	1998 (January–May)[2]	1996 (January–September)[2]	1997	1998 (January–May)[2]	1996 (January–September)[2]	1997	1998 (January–May)[2]	1996 (January–September)[2]	1997	1998 (January–May)[2]
Investment amount (0.1 billion yuan)	1622.71	3106.40	749.93	912.27 (56.22)	1707.33 (54.96)	443.78 (59.18)	247.48 (15.25)	469.89 (15.13)	101.53 (13.54)	236.16 (14.55)	448.23 (14.43)	98.92 (13.19)	226.81 (13.98)	480.95 (15.48)	105.69 (14.01)
Sales value (0.1 billion yuan)	474.03	1563.52	411	387.47 (81.74)	1216.71 (77.82)	326.77 (79.51)	35.52 (7.49)	140.33 (8.98)	n.a.	41.97 (8.85)	475.45 (11.22)	n.a.	9.07 (1.91)	31.02 (1.98)	n.a.
Area under construction (10000 sq. m)	34295.90	43467.55	27320	22932.04 (66.87)	28642.48 (65.89)	18239.26 (66.76)	4226.92 (12.32)	5576.16 (12.83)	n.a.	4945.43 (14.42)	6446.71 (14.83)	n.a.	2191.51 (6.39)	2802.20 (6.45)	n.a.
Area completed (10 000 sq. m)	4049.36	13787.24	1689	3255.23 (80.39)	10886.27 (78.96)	1350.55 (79.96)	235.30 (5.81)	883.81 (6.41)	n.a.	394.23 (9.74)	1454.35 (10.55)	n.a.	164.60 (4.06)	562.81 (4.08)	n.a.
Areas sold (10 000 sq. m)	2714.88	7911.91	1816	2375.79 (87.51)	6888.23 (87.06)	1621.72 (89.3)	102.56 (3.78)	316.02 (3.99)	n.a.	185.70 (6.84)	561.06 (7.09)	n.a.	50.83 (1.87)	146.60 (1.85)	n.a.

Notes:
1. The figures in brackets are percentages of the total.
2. Data for the whole year are not available.
Source: China Statistical Yearbook (1995, 1996, 1997).

Table 3.4 Private investment in construction in rural areas, 1984–96

Year	Total investment (10⁸ yuan)	% change	Investment in construction				Floor space under construction (10000 sq. m)	% change	Floor space completed (10000 sq. m)			
			Total investment	% change	Residential content	% change			Total	% change	Residential content	% change
1984	379.11	–	265.83	–	239.38	–	–	–	66 854	–	57 838	–
1985	478.43	26.20	350.13	31.71	313.15	30.82		–	78 973	18.13	69 542	20.24
1986	574.82	20.15	503.00	43.66	388.56	24.08	109 622	–	103 225	30.71	94 468	35.84
1987	695.35	20.97	603.17	19.91	487.21	25.39	100 923	–7.94	96 477	–6.54	85 524	–9.47
1988	865.23	24.43	741.22	22.89	580.97	19.24	92 781	–8.07	89 092	–7.65	80 799	–5.52
1989	892.03	3.10	794.15	7.14	641.68	10.45	74 906	–19.27	71 026	–20.28	66 134	–18.15
1990	876.47	–1.74	777.14	–2.14	649.78	1.26	76 819	2.55	71 136	0.15	67 812	2.54
1991	1042.56	18.95	912.48	17.42	759.25	16.85	85 405	11.18	79 501	11.76	74 193	9.41
1992	1005.52	–3.55	937.51	2.74	678.52	–10.63	83 392	–2.36	65 338	–17.81	60 442	–18.53
1993	1137.73	13.15	1015.37	8.30	760.26	12.05	57 432	–31.13	56 012	–14.27	46 129	–23.68
1994	1519.24	33.53	1315.92	29.60	1002.73	31.89	72 283	25.86	65 390	16.74	57 646	24.97
1995	2007.85	32.16	1709.41	29.90	1349.85	34.62	78 192	8.17	73 522	12.44	66 230	14.89
1996	2544.03	26.70	2250.87	31.70	1766.40	30.90	96 115	22.9	87 277	18.70	79 531	20.10

Source: China Statistical Yearbook (1995, 1996, 1997).

few columns of Table 3.4, the amount of residential floor space completed each year remained very high and on average accounted for 90 per cent of total floor space. A possible explanation of the increased private interest in commercial/industrial properties is that some rural enterprises expanded during these years.

In addition to this, private real estate development in rural areas is handicapped by property rights. As mentioned earlier, land in rural areas belongs to farmers' collectives, and collectively owned land cannot be sold for private development without it first being requisitioned and converted into state land. The potential problems surrounding compensation, resettlement and legal procedures are much greater than the profit, to be gained by individual investors. Hence the urban land reform is not mirrored in the countryside, which is perhaps fortunate given the scale of the reforms the state would have to take care of.

THE PRIVATISATION OF PUBLIC SECTOR HOUSING

As in other socialist economies, the Chinese state and its enterprises have been burdened with the task of prividing public housing. Premier Zhu Rongji has made it clear that public sector housing reform will be one of the five priority reform programmes during his term of office (1998–2003). In order to establish a balanced and healthy public sector housing market, there should be a mechanism whereby the housing stock that is currently provided and managed by state enterprises and non-housing-oriented institutions can be released to the market. The urban land reform allows LURs to be traded so that the ownership of houses built on the land can be transferred. Since land rights must be combined with property ownership rights in order to make the transfer of property sensible, the tranformation of LURs into a commodity will assist the development of a more rational public sector housing market and smooth the transformation of part of the public sector housing stock into market stock.

In 1980 the State Council announced that state employees and individuals could build and sell residential units. In addition the state would start to build what was called 'commodity housing' (housing for sale on the open market) and state employees would be able to purchase such housing by instalment. In 1982 the State Council approved the subsidised sale of public housing in Changzhou, Zhengzhou, Siping and Shashi – subsidised because each purchaser only needed to pay one third of the construction price of the unit (approximately 150–200 yuan per square metre), the rest being equally shared between the state enterprise to which the purchaser belonged and the state. Of course this meant that housing would continue to impose a financial burden on the state, but the widespread sale of public housing remained one of the chief objectives of the reform programme. Table 3.5 shows the terms of sale for public housing in a number of localities.

The most effective method of privatisation was thought to be the complete commercialisation of housing. To achieve this, rents on housing had to reflect market forces. Consequently in 1986 four cities – Yantai, Shanghai, Tangshan and Bangbu – were selected to test the second round of housing reforms. The objective was to raise rents so that housing could become a self-financing operation. Table 3.6 shows that state enterprises and state units contributed significantly to the construction of residential properties (about 50 per cent of all construction works). From 1987, when the housing reform pilot scheme was launched, the proportion of housing for employees dropped gradually to an average of 40 per cent of all ongoing construction works. The following sections briefly describe the efforts of a number of provinces and cities and one state enterprise to reform the housing supply system and how this paved the way for a more effective urban land reform.

The Yantai Model

Yantai's plan for the commercialisation of housing was approved by the State Council in October 1986 and went into effect in August 1987.[11] The Yantai plan was notable in three respects: it dealt with rent as a central component of housing reform; it introduced the use of housing vouchers as a form of subsidy; and it was designed to encourage home buyers to pay 100 per cent for their purchase.

The Yantai reform was based on the following principles. First, although money was spent on subsidised housing for workers, this was compensated by increased rent. Second, it was believed that people who occupied better housing and had more living space should pay higher rents. Third, the objective was to raise rents to a level close to that of the market in order to encourage private investment in housing.

The Yantai authorities realised that if rent remained as low as 1–2 per cent of household income there would be no incentive for tenants to purchase homes and the commercialisation of housing could not be achieved. As a consequence rents were raised to a minimum of 1.28 yuan per square metre, which was much higher than the national average of 0.13 yuan per square metre. This new minimum rent reflected the cost of depreciation and maintenance, management, property taxes and interest

Table 3.5 Terms of sale of public housing, 1997

	Shanghai	Tianjin	Beijing	Guangzhou	Fuzhou	Nanjing	Wuhan	Hangzhou	Shenyang	Shenzhen	Zhengzhou
Unit cost (yuan/sq. m)	1198	1050	1450	1273	935	795	800	850	880	1300	920
Price differential (each grade)	10% difference per grade	0–30% for 4 grades	6% difference per grade	1% difference per grade	300 yuan/sq. m per grade	0–15% for 4 grades	15% per grade	15% per grade	44 yuan per grade	2% per grade	–
Annual depreciation (%)	2	2	2	2	2	2	2	2	2	2	2
Length of service discount (per year)	15.3 yuan/sq. m per year	4 yuan/sq. m per year	12 yuan/sq. m per year	9.42 yuan/sq. m per year	0.6% per year	1.2% per year	3.43 yuan/sq. m per year	0.6% per year	3.2 yuan/sq. m per year	–	4.57 yuan/sq. m per year
One-off payment discount (%)	20	15	Nil	Nil	20	14	20	20	20	15	20
Maximum loan term (years)	–	15	25	–	10	10	15	5	5	–	5
Preferential interest rate (%)	–	5.976	4.68–6.3	Nil	–	5.22	6.444	6.66	Nil	–	–
% sold	50	61	28	56.8	–	–	40	62	46	95	56.7

Sources: Local housing reform departments.

Table 3.6 Floor area built by state-owned units/enterprises, 1985–96

	Under construction (10000 sq. m)	% change	Residential content (10000 sq. m) (%)	% change	Annual completion (10000 sq. m)	% change	Residential contents (10000 sq. m) (%)	% change
1985	37029.20	–	18893.90 (51)	–	17161.20	–	9565.10 (56)	–
1986	33086.20	−10.65	15940.40 (48)	−15.63	16650.50	−2.98	8915.50 (54)	−6.79
1987	29435.70	−11.03	11990.10 (41)	−24.78	14359.00	−13.76	6452.80 (45)	−27.62
1988	28413.79	−3.47	11334.02 (40)	−5.47	13307.84	−7.32	6008.99 (45)	−6.88
1989	24744.18	−12.91	9749.94 (40)	−13.98	11611.55	−12.75	5064.20 (44)	−15.72
1990	23236.54	−6.09	9259.90 (40)	−5.03	11245.93	−3.15	4824.78 (43)	−4.73
1991	27262.61	17.33	11309.23 (41)	22.13	12604.48	12.08	5687.92 (45)	17.89
1992	32709.19	19.98	13399.25 (41)	18.48	15133.72	20.07	6919.15 (46)	21.65
1993	39535.76	20.87	15016.40 (38)	12.07	17070.05	12.79	7993.44 (47)	15.53
1994	42749.88	8.13	16981.97 (40)	13.09	18644.05	9.22	8955.12 (48)	12.03
1995	41948.29	−1.88	16739.06 (40)	−1.43	19929.32	6.89	9249.25 (46)	3.28
1996	43661.23	4.08	17269.40 (40)	3.17	21256.63	6.66	9824.79 (46)	6.22

on investment. The unit construction cost per square metre of living space in Yantai at that time was 203.34 yuan. The new rent of 1.28 yuan would therefore cover 83.7 per cent of this cost, which was estimated to be 1.53 yuan per month, and 53 per cent of the market rent (2.4 yuan per month). Under this rent reform, rents also varied according to the location, size and quality of each dwelling.[12]

Since the upward rent adjustments were substantial it was necessary to increase the tenant's wages. This increase was offered in the form of housing vouchers for an amount not exceeding 25 per cent of each worker's wage. The subsidy rate was calculated as follows: [(average rent per sq. m × average living area) − original monthly rent]/average monthly salary × 100 per cent. The value of the housing vouchers was then established by multiplying the montly salary by the subsidy rate. If a household's rent was greater than the value of their housing voucher they had to pay the difference themselves. On the other hand, if their rent was lower than the value of the voucher they could retain the surplus and deposit it in an interest-earning bank account. The amount in the bank could be used to pay repair costs or construct or buy a new dwelling unit as the household wished, but it could not be spent on anything other than housing.

The new rent structure and use of the housing voucher system meant that people who occupied large flats now had to pay more than those occupying inferior housing. In effect the rent reform penalised those deemed to have too much room by imposing a certain fee per excess square metre of floor space. It was expected that this heavy financial penalty would force most of these people to move to smaller housing units, thus making the space available larger families currently residing in very small quarters or substandard accommodation.

With regard to the sale of housing, the authorities proposed to sell its public housing stock to sitting tenants at preferential prices. The price was set at 25 yuan per square metre, which was much lower than the current market level. Upon full payment purchasers would have full ownership rights, including inheritance rights and the right to earn income from the property in whatever way they liked. Thus they could lease, resell or transfer the property to others in the future. Alternatively individuals could choose to pay only 70 per cent of the price and the remainder would be contributed by their work units, but in this case they would have more limited ownership rights and could not transfer or, lease the property without prior permission. If they wished to resell, it must be to the work unit concerned.[13] It was also stipulated that urban residents could only purchase one unit on preferential terms during their lifetime.

Workers who wanted to buy houses had to pay a minimum of 30 per cent of the price, but those who could pay more than 30 per cent in one payment were entitled to a discount. Most urban workers had few if any savings, so banks were authorised to make low-interest loans of up to 70 per cent of the sales price of a dwelling, with a repayment period of 10–20 years. The repayment of mortgage loans was made from the purchasers' wages or housing vouchers and was paid to the banks by the purchaser's work units on a monthly basis.[14]

Under the urban housing reform in Yantai, the financial resources for housing came from established housing funds at three levels, namely the city, the work unit and the individual. In addition there was support from two savings banks, one in Yantai and the other in Bengbu city in Anhui province.[15] As well as reforming the housing financial system, it was also proposed to set up independent management companies for the future maintenance and management of residential units, which, it was hoped, would increase the incentive for tenants to purchase their own homes.[16]

The Shanghai Model

Shanghai's plan for comprehensive reform of the housing system was formally introduced on 1 May 1991 with the approval of the State Council. As in Yantai, the plan included rent increases, housing subsidies and private investment. The most significant difference from the Yantai model was the introduction of a provident fund system. The Shanghai reform has been considered as success as it focused on an overall package rather than tackling the reform bit by bit. We shall examine five aspects of the reform package namely the provident fund system, rent increases and subsidies, housing allocation bonds, the preferential pricing of houses and the establishment of a housing committee.

Provident Funds

An experimental provident fund was set up in Shanghai and it was expected that all other cities in China would eventually follow suit. The provident fund was based on the Singapore model,[17] whereby all workers contribute a certain proportion of their wages (5 per cent in 1991). An equal amount is contributed by the work units and the government. The percentage of wages paid into the fund is to be adjusted according to economic growth and any changes in the workers' income. The banks act as agents for the fund and the bank savings rate is used as a benchmark for the rate of return on the fund.

Tenants can use their accumulated provident funds as a downpayment on a flat or house, but in the event of subsequent resale the same amount of money must be put back into the fund. Provident funds can only be used to purchase, construct or rebuild houses, or for major repairs. Any decoration daily maintenance and rental payments are the responsibility of the householder. The employees of state enterprises can mobilise both their own and their family's provident funds to purchase a home, and if they have not accumulated a sufficient amount they can borrow the difference from the fund.

Housing Development Bonds
Citizens in Shanghai are able to buy housing development bonds (HDBs) to supplement their housing development funds. Work units can also use their workers' HDBs to construct new residential buildings for those workers. HDBs are issued once a year and interest is calculated twice yearly (March and September). The redemption period is five years. When they were first issued the interest rate was set at 3.6 per cent.

Whenever there is a new allocation of public housing (newly built houses or old ones), the households in question are required to purchase HDBs in a quantity established by the following formula: newly allocated living area × HDBs subscription rate × subscription rate factor. The HDB subscription rate depends on the type of housing involved. For instance in 1991 the highest rate was for apartment-type housing, which had a subscription rate of 80 yuan per square metre. Newly built alley-type housing was 60 yuan per square metre and old alley-type (block) housing was 30 yuan per square metre. At the bottom was slum housing, with a rate of 20 yuan per square metre. The subscritption rate factor depends on the location of the housing. The best location (the urban core area), had a subscription rate factor of 1.1 in 1991. For second-grade, third-grade, fourth-grade and rural locations the subscription rate factors were 1.0, 0.9, 0.8 and 0.7 respectively.

Rent Increases and Subsidies
Part of the Shanghai reform was the doubling of rent on all public housing. To compensate for this dramatic increase a monthly housing subsidy was introduced. This amounts to 2 per cent of a worker's salary. All other housing allowances were cancelled. When a tenant changes job the subsidy is paid by the new employer, but if a tenant moves to private housing or purchases a flat or house the subsidy is cancelled.

The Preferential Pricing of Houses
Under the terms of the 1991 Shanghai City Housing Reform, enterprises and institutions may sell up to 20 per cent of their housing stock to individual

employees at a preferential price. New stock may be sold to those who would have been eligible for the old-type, administratively allocated housing. Occupied housing can only be sold to the sitting tenants. The sales-price formula is the preferential base price multiplied by the variation factor. For new housing the base price is the construction cost of the unit, and the base price for old housing is assessed on a replacement-cost basis, that is, by estimating the construction cost of a similar flat and multiplying it by the depreciation rate. The variation factor is composed of three elements: location (graded from 0.7 to 1.3, depending on the desirability of the location), orientation (north, south, east or west) and storey level in the case of flats.

Tenants who purchase the homes they have been renting from their employers are given a 10 per cent discount, subject to a minimum price (in 1991 this was 120 yuan per square metre). Those who pay the full amount upon purchase receive a 20 per cent discount. Those who pay by instalment have to repay within ten years.

Housing sold at preferential prices may be resold or passed on to successors. However if not all instalments have been paid, or if the purchaser has occupied the unit for less than five years, the unit must be transferred back to the enterprise that sold it. Those who have occupied their homes for more than five years can sell them on the open market, but a percentage of the realised price has to be paid to the eneterprise and the vendor is not allowed to buy on preferential terms again.

The Shanghai Housing Committee
The Shanghai Housing Committee (SHC) was established to monitor all the above measures and to formulate long-term policy on housing reform. The SHC is directly responsible to the city government and the committee members serve for a term of five years. As well as formulating long-term planning and policy the SHC initiates housing research, is involved in housing development and management, monitors housing finance and determines the various aspects of housing development bonds and preferential pricing.

The Wuhan Railway Bureau Model

In China most people work for state enterprises and institutions, which have traditionally provided their workers with housing. When this was recognised as a financial burden in the early 1970s there were calls for reform. The Wuhan Railway Bureau (WRB) tackled this from two main directions, namely finance and sale.

One of the first steps was the introduction of the 'user pays' principle, whereby the employees' department, the employees and the WRB each contribute one third of the construction cost of new housing. The actual construction is handled by the individual departments. The standard type of housing is two-storey apartment buildings. Upon completion, employees who have contributed to the financing of the project are entitled to occupy the flats and the money they have contributed is treated as prepaid rent. At the end of the designated prepayment period rents are charged at the standard WRB housing rate.

Alternatively employees may choose to purchase their flats, and again the financial contribution they have made is to be regarded as a prepayment. The rest can be paid either in instalments or as a lump sum. The purchase price depends on the base prices set in 1988: 200 yuan per square metre in the Wuhan area, 180 yuan per square metre in rural areas and 150–180 yuan in other areas. The prices are then adjusted according to four major factors: structure, location, storey level and view. The sum of these four adjustment factors becomes a percentage increment to the base price. This sum must lie between 15 per cent and 22 per cent. Accordingly, the selling price of the new units is base price × (1 + the sum of the four adjustment factors) × size.

In the case of payment by instalment, the ownership rights stay with the WRB until all instalments are paid. Upon full payment the purchaser can sell the flat back to the WRB at a price based on the cost of similar properties built the previous year. Any financial gain is shared between the vendor and the WRB at a preset ratio.

Following the widespread acceptance of the need for housing reform in urban areas, the Wuhan state authorities resolved to move towards the comprehensive commercialisation of real estate, which would also provide important support for the urban and reform. The 'Decision on Deepening Urban and Township Housing Reform by the State Council' was promulgated in 1994 (hereafter referred to as the State Council Decision 1994) to serve as a guideline for the local authorities.

The State Council Decision 1994 is aimed at deepening the housing reform and promoting the commercialisation of residential properties and housing development. This involves converting the old system of 'investment by the state and distribution by the working unit' to a fair distribution of responsibility between the state, the working unit and the employee. The State Council has also established a price system for the distribution of housing, as opposed to the old welfare system, and aims to create a housing market for the middle- to low-income groups. Together with this supply system, there is a housing provident fund, housing finance and an insurance system. The reform is intended to be a gradual and phased one.

The Housing Provident Fund

All employees have a personal account with the housing provident fund, whose purpose is to finance the purchase construction and repair of housing. Upon retirement all contributions, plus interest, are repaid to the employee. The current contribution is 5 per cent from employee's salary by the individual and the employing unit together. For any enterprise using a higher rate, the proportion of contribution from each party can remain unchanged. For foreign firms based in China, the employees' contribution is determined by the relevant local government, which is also responsible for regulating the fund.

Rent Reform

It is hoped that by the year 2000 the average family will spend about 15 per cent (which represents the five basic costs of housing, namely depreciation, maintenance, management, bank interest and real estate taxes) of their household income on rent. In the meantime some rents have been set at a higher level than the current standard rent for new housing.

The Gradual Sale of Public Housing

All new housing units and vacant old ones must be offered for sale before they can be rented out, and families without decent housing are given first refusal. The prices set for public housing vary according to the financial means of the purchaser. For high-income families, the price is set at the market level. For the middle to low-income groups, the price is based on cost. This includes the cost of requisitioning land, resettlement costs, housing development fees, infrastructure fees, management fees, bank interest and taxes. For old housing it is based on the cost of similar new housing but discounted for depreciation.

In cities and counties where it is proving difficult to sell even at cost, a standard price is set. This is calculated from two elements. The first is a multiplier of the average annual salary of a working couple, which varies from city to city – the average in 1994 was 3. The second part is 80 per cent of a total contribution of 65 years (assuming 35 years of contribution for the husband and 30 years of contribution for the wife) made to the housing provident fund by the relevant working units. The first element is subject to a 5 per cent discount when a tenant buys his or her rented accommodation. The standard price is a transitional arrangement, and the ultimate objective in the long run is to price housing on a cost basis.

Those who purchase their homes at the market price enjoy full property rights. They can sell their properties on the open market or use them as a source of income provided they have paid the relevant taxes. Those who purchase on a cost basis have ownership rights but they cannot sell the property until they have occupied it for at least five years. They also have to pay the premium for the land use rights and the relevant taxes before they can derive any income from the property. People who pay the standard price only enjoy partial property rights, including occupation right, use right and a limited right to receive income. These rights are inheritable. The ultimate objective in the long run is to price the housing on cost basis property cannot be put on the open market unless five years of occupation have lapsed, and the organisation or department that sold the property in the first place has first right of refusal. After payment of the land premium and taxes, the vendor and previous owner share the income from the sale of the property.

It is stated in State Decision 1994 that the provisions contained therein take precedence over all other reform packages on regulations that diverge in any way from these provisions. This is aimed at preventing local authorities from deviating from the central policy on housing privatisation.

The Jilin Province Model

According to the 1995 Provisional Regulations on the Sale of Public Housing in Jilin Province, state enterprises (which account for a very large proportion of the economic units in China) can sell their housing stock (which were originally built as staff housing) to their employees. Before doing so they must submit the following documents to the Provincial Housing Reform Office (PHRO):

1. Details of the privatisation programme.
2. Application form.
3. Certificate of ownership and of user's right.
4. Documents showing payments to a housing fund.
5. Documents showing the purchase of a housing development debenture by the sitting tenants.
6. Other relevant documents.

If the PHRO is satisfied with the submission, a Notification of Approval of the Sale of Public Housing by a State Enterprise (Notification) is issued.

The enterprise then applies, together with this Notification, for a Certificate of Real Estate Property Rights (CREPR) from the local Real Estate Administration Department. This certificate and an appraisal of the property is handed to the PHRO, which, with the help of other departments, evaluates all details of the privatisation programme, and in particular the pricing policy. Upon receipt of approval the enterprise obtains a sales permit and applies to the local Real Estate Management Department for a transfer of ownership and the associated rights.

All legally registered citizens in the city where the selling enterprise is located are entitled to purchase housing units. Each household can purchase not more than once the public housing unit at the cost level accordingly to the housing control standard or the standard selling price. However, where the enterprise does not have an established housing provident fund, they cannot sell the flats at these preferential price levels. Households below the poverty level have first option to purchase at this price.

Individuals wishing to purchase a public housing unit have to submit the following documents to the vendor:

1. Written application.
2. Proof of age and wages.
3. Statement on current living conditions.
4. Other relevant documents.

Even if a housing unit is not fully paid for it can be passed on to legitimate heirs should the purchaser die or migrate overseas, but if a purchaser or his legitimate heir fails to keep up with the payments the selling enterprise is entitled to repossess the unit.

All state enterprises with housing units can sell them to their employees, except in the following circumstances:

1. If there is no valid certificate of ownership or a certificate of user's right, or if the legal status of these certificates is in dispute.
2. If the units lie within a recently designated urban renewal area.
3. If the units are dilapidated.
4. If the units are located on a main street containing retail stores.
5. If the units have historical value.
6. If the units are built in the traditional courtyard style.

Pricing Policy
The sales price of individual public housing units is based on gross floor area (GFA), which is calculated as follows: usable floor space occupied by

each household multiplied by the GFA of the whole building and divided by the useable area of the whole building. In addition, prices vary according to the status of the purchasers:

1. Households with an average annual income of 10 000 yuan or more are required to pay the market price.
2. Households with an income of less than 10 000 yuan a year pay either the cost price or the standard price. In 1995 the cost price of newly built public housing units was set at 860 yuan per square metre and the standard price at 526 yuan per square metre. Those who purchase old public housing units at cost receive an annual depreciation rate of 2 per cent whereas those who purchase at the standard level receive 1.5 per cent.

When an employee purchases a housing unit at the standard price the property rights are shared by the employee and the selling enterprise. The employee enjoys the right to occupy the unit and a limited right to obtain an income from the property. The distribution of the property rights between the selling enterprise and the employee depends on the proportion of the standard price in the cost price. Should the purchaser decide to sell or lease out the unit, the selling enterprise has first option to buy or rent. The sales or rental income is shared between the two parties according to their share of the property rights.

The Jilin model is an example of local implementation and extension of one of the target goals of the 1994 state decision. Given the vast differences among provinces and cities, local authorities are allowed the room to adapt the terms of the policy to meet special local conditions. In turn this serves to inform future central policy for nationwide implementation and partly explains why new laws are first announced in general policy terms rather than concrete regulations.

The housing reform programmes on rental adjustment and sale of existing public housing stock in most cities will only become effective when a wider scale of programme is launched to induce more private ownership of housing. When private ownership becomes more popular, the burden of providing housing of staff on the state enterprises and government units will be released.

The Guangdong Province Housing Subsidy Programme

In coordination with the overall privatisation of housing in china, in March 1998 Guangzhou city introduced housing subsidies for those who joined state enterprises or government departments after 29 September 1997 without any housing benefits, and for those who joined their work units before this date but voluntarily opted for this subsidy (including retirees). The level of the subsidies is directly linked to the price of *anju* housing (see below for details of the *anju* project). The current price of *anju* housing is set at 3500 yuan per square metre. This amount is then multiplied by the standard living area (gross floor area) for each grade of staff (Table 3.7). Eighty per cent of the figure obtained becomes the housing subsidy granted to the applicant, who is responsible for the remaining 20 per cent, paid monthly.

In Doumeng country in Zhuhai city, since March 1997 lump-sum housing subsidies have been given to staff instead of allocated housing. Married people who have worked in a department for at least three years, single people aged 30 or older who have worked in the country for at least 10 years and those living in substandard private housing can apply for this subsidy. The amount paid is the difference between the price of ordinary commodity housing and privatised public housing plus a length of service subsidy. These three elements are defined by the government, and the maximum amount payable is 33 000 yuan for department heads, 28 000 yuan for those of officer grade and 25 000 yuan for ordinary clerks.

Table 3.7   Housing benefit in Guangzhou city, 1998

Staff grade	Monthly subsidy per person (yuan)	Total housing subsidy for 25 years (10 000 yuan)		Standard living area for each staff grade (sq. m)	
		Single	Married	Single	Married
Clerical	233	6.99	13.98	25	50
Officer	280	8.40	16.80	30	60
Deputy chief officer	327	9.81	19.62	35	70
Officer	373	11.19	22.38	40	80
Deputy department head	420	12.60	25.20	45	90
Department head	467	14.01	28.02	50	100
Deputy bureau chief	513	15.39	30.78	55	110
Bureau chief	607	18.21	36.42	65	130
Deputy city govt head	747	22.41	44.82	80	160
City govt head	933	27.99	55.98	100	200

Source: Zhongda Real Estate Information, no. 8 (1998).

THE NATIONWIDE *ANJU* PROJECT

The *anju* project (or comfortable housing project), launched in 1995, is a massive house-building project that is expectated to provide an additional 0.15 billion square metres of housing space by the year 2000 in medium to large cities. The target for the first year was 12.5 million square metres at an estimated cost of 12.5 billion yuan, 5.0 billion of which was loaned by the state and the rest arranged by the local governments. The targets are adjusted annually. The state-loan funds are paid to designated *anju* project contractors by the relevant banks and instiutions. To reduce production costs, development land is administratively allocated free of charge.

The aim of the *anju* project is to create private-sector housing for middle- to low-income families. The units are sold at cost to such families, especially those with inadequate or no accommodation or who are living in a dangerous environment. Local governments are not allowed to profit from the project. The cost of each unit is based on land requisition and resettlement fees, site preparation fees, construction and decoration fees, infrastructure fees, management fees, bank interest and taxes.

Local governments participating in the project must arrange the provision of mortgages, to a maximum of 60 per cent, payable over ten years. To be eligible for state loans, local governments must first establish a housing provident fund, carry out a proper rent reform and begin the sale of public housing. The housing provident fund should cover at least 60 per cent of employees in the city. In addition to this, they must be able to show that they have requisitioned all the land required for the project and drawn up clearly defined construction. In terms of finance, they should also have accumulated at least 50 per cent of the city infrastructure fund. Generally, applications to participate in the project are submitted by provincial governments for approval by the central authorities, including the Housing Reform Group, the Ministry of Construction, the State Planning Commission, the People's Bank of China and the Ministry of Finance.

Tables 3.8 and 3.9 show that the *anju* project will substantially increase the housing supply in most of the participating cities. Chongquing city is the major beneficiary of the project due to the fact that it has just been upgraded and is now the fourth directly administered municipality in China.

By the first quarter of 1997 a total of 10 136 300 square metres of residential floor space had been under construction, and 3 383 200 square metres of this had been completed. A total of 6 211 000 square metres of *anju* floor space has been sold out of the 9 781 300 square metres available, an absorption rate of 63 per cent.

Table 3.8 Investment plan for the *anju* project, selected cities, 1996–97

City	Gross floor area (10 000 sq. m)		Investment planned (100 million yuan)		Bank loan proportion of planned investment (100 million yuan)						Funds raised by cities (100 million yuan)	
					Total loan planned		With Construction Bank		With other banks			
	1996	1997	1996	1997	1996	1997	1996	1997	1996	1997	1996	1997
National total	1578.9	2800	125.5	250.00	50.2	100.0	26.1	58.7	24.1	41.4	75.3	150.0
Beijing	50.0	83	7.5	15.00	3.0	6.0	3.0	3.5	–	2.5	4.5	9.0
Shanghai	68.0	94	7.0	15.00	3.0	6.0	3.0	6.0	–	–	4.5	9.0
Tianjin	67.0	135	8.0	16.25	3.2	6.5	3.2	4.5	–	2.0	4.8	9.75
Chongqing	25.0	125	2.5	12.50	1.0	5.0	0.2	1.8	0.8	3.2	1.5	7.5
Fuzhou	20.0	28	2.0	2.50	0.8	1.0	0.8	0.5	–	0.5	1.2	1.5
Guangzhou	25.0	25	2.5	2.50	1.0	1.0	1.0	1.0	–	–	1.5	1.5
Nanjing	12.5	40	1.0	3.75	0.4	1.5	0.2	1.0	0.2	0.5	0.6	2.3
Wuhan	41.6	50	3.8	5.00	1.5	2.0	1.0	0.9	0.5	1.1	2.3	3.0
Haikou	16.0	22	1.5	2.00	0.6	0.8	0.3	0.3	0.3	0.5	0.9	1.2
Xian	21.0	43	2.0	4.25	0.8	1.7	0.4	0.9	0.4	0.9	1.2	2.6

Source: Ministry of Construction.

Table 3.9 Investment performance of the overall *anju* project, 1997

	Cumulative sum in 1997	Comparison with previous year
(A) Funding (100 million years)		
Total investment planned	364.00	–
B/f from previous year of which	113.45	–
self-raised	68.57	–
bank loans	44.88	–
Investment planned this year of which	250.70	–
self-raised	150.65	–
bank loans	100.05	–
Actual funding met	325.25	+321.18
B/f from previous year of which	95.02	+8.36
self-raised	63.38	+4.31
bank loans	31.64	+4.05
Investment planned this year of which	230.23	+49.38
self-raised	155.85	+26.05
bank loans	74.38	+23.33
Actual investment made	281.86	+83.63
B/f from previous year	87.26	+21.45
This year	194.60	+62.18
(B) Construction (10 000 sq. m)		
Planned floor area	4245.47	
B/f from previous year	1428.97	
This year	2816.50	
Floor space actually under construction	4057.86	+716.59
B/f from previous year	1309.27	+164.40
This year	2748.59	+552.19
Floor space completed	2665.09	+1618.32
B/f from previous year	992.62	+435.11
This year	1672.47	+1183.21
(C) Sales performance		
Floor area available for preselling (10 000 sq. m)	3012.82	+899.78
Number of units	425 981	+127 652
Actual floor area presold (10 000 sq. m)	2654.54	+858.99
B/f from previous year	1136.11	+267.65
This year	1518.43	+591.34
Number of units presold	378 562	+124 195
B/f from previous year	168 246	+44 100
This year	210 316	+80 095
Unsold floor area (10 000 sq. m)	358.28	+40.79
B/f from previous year	155.67	−42.87
This year	202.61	+83.66
Number of units unsold	47 419	+6457
B/f from previous year	19 120	−7 660
This year	28 299	+11 117

Table 3.9   (*Continued*)

	Cumulative sum in 1997	Compared with last year
Total sales revenue (100 million yuan)	183.80	+70.73
B/f from previous year	62.74	–
This year	121.06	+55.62
(D) Repayment of fund (100 million yuan)		
Amount repaid	71.71	+27.89
of which		
self-raised funds	40.80	+18.10
bank loans	30.91	+9.79
Unpaid arrears	9.22	+0.79
of which		
self-raised funds	4.63	+3.13
bank loans	4.59	−2.34
Bad debts	0.06	+0.05

Source: Real Estate Branch, Ministry of Construction.

SUMMARY

No discussion of Chinese urban land reform is complete without at least a brief look at urban housing reform. Housing reform received early attention in China because the privatisation of housing was ideologically less contentious than that of land. The successful housing reform programme has provided the basis for the authorities to set up the urban land market, as the value of urban land in a market system depends on the market value of real estate. Urban housing reform should therefore be viewed as an important step in rationalising the urban land market, which should also encourage private housing initiatives and enhance the housing market structure. Thus housing reform and urban land reform can be seen as complementary rather than individual reform programmes.

4 Urban Land Reform in China: the Initial Outcomes

In the ten years since the first draft of the Land Management Law 1988 was passed, the scale at which urban land markets have been created has been breathtaking. Not only has land in most major cities been granted by the state to private developers and individuals as a market product, but land usage has also been rationalised by the market price mechanism. The government has obtained an additional source of revenue to finance other long-overdue projects, such as the development of social and physical infrastructure, and individuals now have an extra vehicle for investing their personal wealth or developing their talents. This chapter will discuss the changes that the reform has brought to the economy, to institutional standards and to local environments.

THE GENERAL ECONOMY

State Revenue

One of the reasons for initiating the urban land reform was to provide an additional source of revenue for the state treasury. The old system of administratively distributing land to all users proved detrimental to state income, and the enormous interest shown in urban land development by international and overseas Chinese investors has provided a means to recover some of the losses.

Table 4.1 shows the three main types of land income that have been generated since privatisation began: land requisition fees, which are paid by developers to the state in the case of collective land and other types of land where resettlement costs are incurred; development fees, which are site preparation costs incurred by the state on behalf of developers; and fees paid for land use rights. The table shows that the total income received from the sale of state land has decreased since the State Statistical Bureau first began to keep records of such transactions (1994). This is mainly due to the austerity programme launched in 1994, which was designed to cool down the overheated economy. However, Sichuan and

86

Table 4.1 Land revenues, selected areas, 1994–96 (10000 yuam)

Region	Land requisition fees			Development fees			Sale of land use rights and other incomes		
	1994	1995	1996	1994	1995	1996	1994	1995	1996
National	1665248	818848	625963	740630	487555	452103	3241465	2570817	2238725
Beijing	–	619	2201	–	1039	86	13317	368749	318090
Tianjin	–	–	3433	–	–	10170	82574	131431	65233
Liaoning	58583	13779	55018	18148	8385	67289	117247	117681	24687
Shanghai	–	–	6720	–	–	19356	1977701	645102	514009
Jiangsu	151843	100119	–	238909	56340	–	49848	57460	173811
Fujian	60449	15782	27658	32175	9610	13390	46614	55076	37905
Guangdong	271415	59731	54902	119184	103379	78743	378417	326391	337529
Sichuan	16469	24194	19766	8790	5719	19630	13283	37427	26484

Source: China Statistical Yearbook (1995, 1996, 1997).

Jiangsu have enjoyed some growth in income from the sale of land use rights (LURs). This reflects the advantage of having a relatively large geographical market, as investors to were able to switch to subregional markets during the experimental stage of the economic reforms.

Table 4.2 shows that the average annual growth rate of the revenue generated by the urban land and real estate markets (both private and public) rose by 32 per cent a year between 1988 and 1996, compared with the average annual GNP growth rate (in nominal terms) of 18.27 per cent. A further breakdown of urban land and real estate revenue shows that the average annual growth rates for income from the market transfer of LURs, the sale of commodity real estate and rental activities were 35.4 per cent, 29.7 per cent and 48 per cent respectively, all of which exceeded the average GNP growth rate. Thus the reform of the urban land and real estate system has brought more revenue to the government and enhanced overall economic growth.

Table 4.3 shows that the profits made by construction enterprises in some areas rose considerably in the 1994–96 period. The construction and related sectors have had an average income growth rate of 24.8 per cent, which is substantially higher than the average growth rate of state revenue. Interestingly the proportion of state income coming from the construction and related sectors was negative in the early 1970s and did not start to shoot up until 1986. Although the contribution made by this sector to state revenues is numerically small (Table 4.4), the magnitude of its increase (from −0.1 per cent in 1975 to 1.9 per cent of total state revenue in 1995) speaks of its growing importance.

Local Government Revenue

Table 4.5 illustrates the importance of land revenues to the local authorities, especially in major cities such as Beijing, Shanghai and Tianjin. In addition to direct income from the land market there are various business taxes on land and real estate development, and a particularly important source of revenue is the profit tax levied on land development companies, which is currently set at 33 per cent. The contribution of land sale proceeds and related taxes in the local context varies among cities and regions – as high as 43 per cent in Beijing in 1995 but just 6 per cent in Sichuan province in the same year. In general, the better developed cities and regions enjoy a larger contribution from the urban land and real estate market. However, as can be seen in Table 4.5, these sources of local government revenue are not steady and may vary quite substantially from year to year, depending on the local land sale programme and investors'

Table 4.2 Total income generated from the urban land and real estate market, 1988–96 (10 000 yuan)

	Total revenue	Transfer of land	Sale of commodity real estate	Rental income	Other	Business taxes and charges
1988	1 621 234	78 573	1 472 164	8 826	61 671	–
1989	1 795 114	74 680	1 637 541	10 970	71 923	–
1990	2 187 081	87 145	2 018 263	22 610	59 063	–
1991	2 840 325	153 810	2 378 597	39 221	268 697	205 551
1992	5 285 565	427 420	4 265 938	59 617	532 590	414 435
1993	11 359 074	839 281	8 637 141	106 348	1 776 304	965 917
1994	12 881 866	959 357	10 184 950	172 817	1 564 742	951 029
1995	17 316 624	1 943 981	12 582 817	257 927	2 531 899	903 047
1996	19 687 850	1 203 378	15 337 647	299 899	2 846 926	927 779

Source: China Statistical Yearbook (1995, 1996, 1997).

Table 4.3 Annual profits of construction enterprises, selected areas, 1994–96 (1 million yuan)

Region	Total			State-owned			Collective-owned			Joint-owned and shareholding			Foreign and overseas Chinese investment including Hong Kong and Taiwan			Other units		
	1994	1995	1996	1994	1995	1996	1994	1995	1996	1994	1995	1996	1994	1995	1996	1994	1995	1996
National	7 252	7 420	10 935	3 466	3 089	2 071	3 379	3 660	7 766	279	555	827	128	116	213.2	0.26	0.85	7.59
Beijing	944	779	889	376	405	488	535	323	352	10	12	22	23	40	28	−0.01	−0.98	−0.02
Tianjin	65	103	137	32	45	58	26	52	72	1	−0.1	0.1	7	5	72	–	–	–
Liaoning	634	185	284	72	−263	−125	504	409	356	32	32	31	25	5	15	–	1.32	0.44
Shanghai	799	853	818	339	360	406	398	419	322	31	46	75	31	28	16	–	–	0.15
Fujian	3	250	235	2	87	87	2	157	110	1	6	38	–	1	0.6	–	–	–
Guangdong	1 289	1 906	1 433	679	969	797	503	724	523	95	197	66	12	16	44	–	0.41	–
Hainan	36	11	8	9	−4	−1	21	15	11	1	1	1	5	−0.3	−2	–	0.07	−0.02
Sichuan	219	195	606	96	107	45	110	78	494	12	12	61	0.3	−4	−0.7	–	–	0.79

Source: China Statistical Yearbook (1995, 1996, 1997).

Table 4.4 State revenue from construction enterprises, selected areas, 1994–96 (10 millian yuan)

Region	Total			State-owned			Collective-owned			Joint-owned and shareholding			Foreign and overseas Chinese investment including Hong Kong and Taiwan			Other units		
	1994	1995	1996	1994	1995	1996	1994	1995	1996	1994	1995	1996	1994	1995	1996	1994	1995	1996
National	44 966	54 809	75 874	30 974	37 041	41 689	13 011	15 713	30 313	592	1 467	2 632	379	558	966	3.0	6.0	44
Beijing	3 083	3 551	4 648	2 272	2 610	3 421	747	793	974	17	63	114	46	83	137	0.2	1.0	1
Tianjin	1 190	1 518	1 727	1 064	1 352	1 502	105	142	207	11	8	8	10	16	11	–	–	–
Liaoning	3 750	3 900	4 054	2 097	2 196	2 294	1 588	1 625	1 655	41	53	58	24	22	36	–	2.0	2
Shanghai	3 278	3 997	4 283	1 994	2 523	2 714	1 046	1 193	1 136	104	112	232	134	168	196	–	–	2
Fujian	1 214	1 556	1 977	753	981	1 069	430	526	752	14	21	98	16	18	46	–	2.0	–
Guangdong	4 608	6 082	5 976	2 598	3 206	3 378	1 817	2 540	2 358	144	284	141	49	83	91	0.1	0.2	0.4
Hainan	179	145	139	99	73	98	69	65	41	8	–	0.4	3	0.1	0.3	–	–	–
Sichuan	2 658	3 250	5 691	1 953	2 401	2 755	683	806	2 699	13	29	192	9	12	13	–	–	8

Source: China Statistical Yearbook (1995, 1996, 1997).

Table 4.5 Contribution of land revenue to local government revenue, selected areas, 1995–96 (10000 yuan)

Region	Total land revenue (% of total revenue)		Total land revenue plus business taxes (% of total revenue)		Total local government revenue	
	1995	1996	1995	1996	1995	1996
Beijing	370 407 (32.0)	320 377 (21.2)	495 518 (43.0)	390 017 (25.9)	1 152 614	1 509 030
Tianjin	131 431 (21.2)	78 836 (10.0)	144 372 (23.3)	91 561 (11.6)	618 977	790 403
Liaoning	139 845 (7.6)	146 994 (7.0)	190 601 (10.3)	184 086 (8.7)	1 843 660	2 116 883
Shanghai	645 102 (29.4)	540 085 (19.3)	759 669 (34.6)	721 064 (25.7)	2 195,645	2 804 733
Jiangsu	213 919 (12.4)	173 811 (7.8)	273 863 (15.9)	239 964 (10.8)	1 726 399	2 231 711
Fujian	80 468 (6.9)	78 953 (5.6)	117 014 (10.0)	106 457 (7.5)	1 173 692	1 421 160
Guangdong	489 501 (12.8)	471 174 (9.8)	689 198 (18.0)	708 144 (14.8)	3 823 449	4 794 470
Sichuan	67 340 (4.03)	65 880 (3.2)	99 293 (5.9)	138 199 (6.6)	1 670 728	2 090 094

Source: China Statistical Yearbook (1996, 1997).

perception of the land and real estate market. For instance in Beijing and Tianjin the share of land and real estate revenue in total local government revenue halved in 1996, while in Sichuan it increased slightly.

The reforms have not only financially benefited government departments, they have also allowed state and private construction enterprises to flourish, as can be seen in Table 4.3. Construction enterprises are usually the major beneficiaries of an active real estate market as they are necessary not only for real estate development, but also for the development of physical infrastructure and urban redevelopment projects. However it should be noted that not all construction enterprises benefit from urban land reform – when the market mechanism is operating it is only efficient companies that enjoy the competitive edge. In China, joint-owned, shareholding (which usually have foreign management partners) and foreign-owned construction enterprises are outperforming the state enterprises. This effect would produce direct impact on the less efficient enterprises and eventually will work as a catalyst for the overall enterprise reform since these inefficient enterprises might be forced to close down or taken over by the efficient ones. However, discussion of this is beyond the scope of this book. In any case, the urban land reform does allow a wider expansion frontier for commercial enterprises and hence increases the scope of enterprise reform.

In addition to the above, urban land reform benefits the so-called 'secondary markets' (Table 4.6). For example in the less prosperous cities are also receiving attention from foreign investors (including investors from Hong Kong and Taiwan) in the urban land and real estate market, and there has been an increase in local and, in some cases, individual investment. This is a positive sign for the development of a proper urban land market as internal demand provides a much longer-term guarantee of growth.

Employment Creation

The privatisation of the urban land market has given citizens the opportunity to improve their living standards by providing new jobs with higher wages. The creation of the urban land and real estate market has produced a new category of workers known as professionals. Some of these professionals work for government institutions, but more work for private companies or even own their own firms. Because of their specialist knowledge and skills they are able to command a higher income, which has a multiplier effect on the macro economy.

Table 4.7 shows the changes that have taken place in the wages of staff in state-owned and collectively-owned enterprises, joint venture companies, shareholding companies and companies owned by overseas Chinese

Table 4.6 Investment in urban land in the secondary markets

City	Year	Foreign investment		Local investment		Investment by individuals	
		land area (sq. m)	Number of sites	land area (sq. m)	Number of sites	land area (sq. m)	Number of sites
Shenyang	1992	5 497	1	68 453	8	190	1
Dalian	1993	23 298	3	532 400	97	–	–
Jinzhou	1992	3 300	1	153 182	9	–	–
Xiamen	1990–93	44 444	8	97 527.9	22	18 727.6	5

Source: China Statistical Yearbook (1995, 1996, 1997).

Table 4.7   Average yearly wages by sector, state-owned and private enterprises 1978–96 (yuan)

	National average	Farming, forestry, fishery, etc	Percentage of national average	Transport, storage and communi-cations	Percentage of national average	Manu-facturing	Percentage of national average	Financial services and insurance	Percentage of national average
1978	615	470	76.42	694	112.85	597	97.07	610	99.19
1980	762	616	80.84	832	109.19	752	98.69	720	94.49
1985	1148	878	76.48	1275	111.06	1112	96.86	1154	100.52
1986	1329	1048	78.86	1476	111.06	1275	95.94	1353	101.81
1987	1459	1143	78.34	1621	111.10	1418	97.19	1458	99.93
1988	1747	1280	73.27	1941	111.10	1710	97.88	1739	99.54
1989	1935	1389	71.78	2197	113.54	1900	98.19	1867	96.49
1990	2140	1541	72.01	2426	113.36	2073	96.87	2097	97.99
1991	2340	1652	70.60	2686	114.79	2289	97.82	2255	96.37
1992	2711	1828	67.43	3114	114.87	2635	97.20	2829	104.35
1993	3371	2042	60.58	4273	126.76	3348	99.32	3740	110.95
1994	4538	2819	62.12	5690	125.39	4283	94.38	6712	147.91
1995	5500	3522	64.04	6948	126.33	5169	93.98	7376	134.11
1996	6210	4050	65.22	7870	126.73	5642	90.85	8406	135.36

Wholesale retail trade and catering	Percentage of national average	Govt and party agencies, social institutes	Percentage of national average	Scientific research services	Percentage of national average	Real estate activities	Percentage of national average	Construction	Percentage of national average
551	89.59	655	106.50	669	108.78	548	89.11	714	116.10
692	90.81	800	104.99	851	111.68	694	91.08	855	112.20
1 007	87.72	1127	98.17	1272	110.80	1028	89.55	1362	118.64
1 148	86.38	1356	102.03	1492	112.26	1216	91.50	1536	115.58
1 270	87.05	1468	100.62	1620	111.03	1327	90.95	1684	115.42
1 556	89.07	1707	97.71	1931	110.53	1715	98.17	1959	112.14
1 660	85.79	1874	96.85	2118	109.46	1925	99.48	2166	111.94
1 818	84.95	2113	98.74	2403	112.29	2243	104.81	2384	111.40
1 981	84.66	2275	97.22	2573	109.96	2507	107.14	2649	113.21
2 204	81.30	2768	102.10	3115	114.90	3106	114.57	3066	113.09
2 679	79.47	3505	103.98	3904	115.81	4320	128.15	3779	112.10
3 537	77.94	4962	109.34	6162	135.79	6288	138.56	4894	107.84
4 248	77.24	5526	100.47	6846	124.47	7330	133.27	5785	105.18
4 661	75.06	6340	102.1	8048	129.47	8337	134.25	6249	100.63

Source: China Statistical Yearbook (1995, 1996, 1997).

and Chinese from Hong Kong, Macau and Taiwan. It can be seen that the average wages of those engaged in real estate activities were below the national average until 1990, when the urban land reform became more formalised, but after 1990 they increased annually. In general this growth was not accompanied by similar wage growth in the other major employment sectors, except in financial services (which was predictable given the opening up of the economy) and scientific research. Interestingly, the wage increases in the construction sector did not match those in the real estate sector, and even fell as a percentage of the national average. This shows that the development of the urban land and real estate market has benefited professionals more than manual labourers working in the real estate sector.

Thus from 1990–96 the real estate sector enjoyed the highest average annual growth in wages, followed by financial services and scientific research. We can further qualify this by looking at wage growth in the 'private sector' alone. Table 4.8 shows the changes in nominal wage levels in joint-venture enterprises, shareholding companies, foreign-owned companies and companies owned by overseas Chinese investors (since there are no separate statistics for private enterprises, these types of company are taken as a proxy for the private sector). Here financial services workers enjoy the highest nominal wages of all the selected sectors. However Figure 4.1 shows that this sector is not the fasting growing one. While the average national wage growth rate was 15.8 per cent for all 'private sector' companies between 1992 and 1996, wages in the real estate sector rose by 16.24 per cent a year but in the financial services sector they only rose by 10.14 per cent. Once again, construction workers had the lowest growth in wages.

With regard to changing employment patterns, Table 4.9 provides a sectoral comparison of workforce size. Between 1978 and 1996 the real estate and construction sectors witnessed a higher than average employee growth rate, although not as great as in the financial sector. An extrapolation of the data in this table provides an estimate of the workforce in the 'private sector' (Table 4.10). As can be seen, employment growth in the private real estate enterprises has been substantial, second only to the private scientific and research services.

All this points to the fact that the urban land reform has created a class of better-off employees, especially in the private sector, and this new middle-class group will consolidate the demand for better housing, which is an important factor in the success of the urban land reform programme. The improvement in the living standard of average citizens has also resulted in an increase in personal savings, and given the limited choice of capital

Table 4.8 Average yearly wages in the 'private sector', 1992–96 (yuan)

	National average	Farming, forestry, fishery, etc.	Percentage of national average	Wholesale, retail and catering	Percentage of national average	Manu-facturing	Percentage of national average	Financial services and insurance	Percentage of national average	Real estate activities	Percentage of national average	Construc-tion	Percentage of national average
19	3 966	4 069	102.60	4 368	110.14	4 154	104.51	9 761	246.12	5 561	140.22	5 061	125.61
19	4 966	3 905	78.63	4 975	100.18	4 874	98.15	6 073	122.29	4 940	99.48	4 464	89.89
19	6 303	5 394	85.58	6 460	97.57	6 096	96.72	10 400	165.00	9 610	152.47	5 766	91.48
19	7 463	6 992	93.69	7 190	96.34	7 245	97.01	12 949	173.51	10 746	143.99	6 798	91.10
19	8 261	7 389	89.44	7 862	95.17	7 945	96.17	15 818	191.48	11 801	142.85	6 937	83.97

Source: China Statistical Yearbook (1995, 1996, 1997).

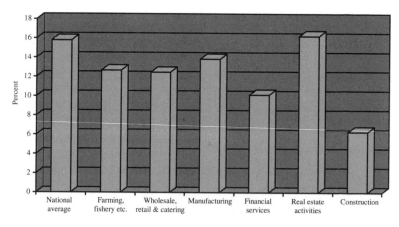

Figure 4.1   Average annual growth of wages in the 'private sector', 1992–96

market investment vehicles, investment in real estate has become an important way of diversifying risk, especially the risk of inflation (particularly during the period 1992–1995).

CREATING A PRICE MECHANISM FOR URBAN LAND

One of the most distinct features of the urban land reform in China, as in other transitional economies, is the revival of the price mechanism for urban land as land had no 'price tag' of any description during the strictly communist era. However the Chinese reform programme is unique in that the state is not attempting to superimpose a purely market system onto the existing one. Instead the intention is to establish a framework that will facilitate a compromise between China's socialist ideology and the market mechanism. Consequently the authorities have attempted to develop guidelines for a land pricing system that reflects the official view with regard to land pricing behaviour and the allocation of land for various uses (Li, 1996a).

The opening up of the land market to investors meant that the government had to establish land prices in the virtual absence of benchmark data. The authorities decided that a market reference point for average land prices in each city should be compiled so that the local authorities would have a set of guidelines to hand when selling land to investors. This led to the formulation of a benchmark price (BMP) for various land grades and different land uses. The BMP table serves as a rudimentary guide for local governments, but as the state has the monopoly over the supply of land,

Table 4.9 Changes in the number of employees, by sector, 1978–96 (10000 persons)

	Total			Farming, forestry, fishery, etc.			Transport, storage and communications			Manufacturing			Financial services and insurance		
	Employees[1]	Staff[2]	State enterprises[3]	Employees	Staff	State enterprises	Employees	Staff	State enterprises	Employees	Staff	State enterprises	Employees	Staff	State enterprises
1978	40152	9499	7451	28318	830	774	750	669	465	5332	3595	2449	76	65	42
1980	42361	10444	8019	29122	788	740	805	714	498	5899	3947	2601	99	89	63
1985	49873	12358	8990	31130	777	726	1279	823	585	7412	4620	2975	138	126	93
1986	51282	12809	9333	31254	748	736	1376	846	604	8019	4820	3096	152	138	101
1987	52783	13241	9654	31663	792	744	1453	860	618	8359	4988	3209	170	154	113
1988	54334	13608	9983	32249	789	743	1521	874	636	8652	5149	3327	194	174	128
1989	55329	13742	10109	33225	782	736	1522	874	640	8547	5206	3344	205	184	136
1990	63909	14059	10346	34117	780	737	1566	895	660	8624	5304	3395	218	195	145
1991	64799	14508	10664	34956	769	727	1617	916	682	8839	5443	3482	234	208	154
1992	65554	14792	10889	34795	758	717	1674	921	693	9106	5508	3526	248	223	166
1993	66373	14849	10920	33966	708	672	1688	826	664	9295	5469	3444	270	239	182
1994	67199	14849	10890	33386	680	653	1864	835	677	9613	5434	3321	264	261	196
1995	67947	14908	10955	33018	660	634	1942	824	677	9803	5439	3326	276	273	203
1996	68850	14845	10949	32910	617	592	2013	830	684	9763	5293	3218	292	288	208
Average annual increase (%)	3	2	2	1	−2	−1	5	1	2	3	2	1	7	8	9

Table 4.9 (Continued.)

	Wholesale, retail trade and catering			Social services			Scientific research services			Real estate activities			Construction		
	Employees	Staff	State enter-prises	Employees	Staff	State enter-prises	Employees	Staff	State enter-prises	Employees	Staff	State enter-prises	Employees	Staff	State enter-prises
1978	1140	1079	907	179	166	107	92	92	91	31	31	28	854	623	447
1980	1363	1239	1005	276	218	130	113	105	104	37	37	33	993	710	475
1985	2306	1518	800	401	271	181	144	131	129	36	36	32	2035	900	545
1986	2413	1544	824	466	289	193	152	137	135	38	38	34	2236	922	557
1987	2576	1578	851	501	304	203	158	142	140	39	39	34	2384	946	566
1988	2743	1643	900	534	318	214	161	144	142	42	42	37	2491	955	568
1989	2770	1675	923	550	327	221	165	147	144	43	43	38	2407	900	541
1990	2839	1715	947	594	344	236	173	152	148	44	44	40	2424	896	538
1991	2998	1786	993	604	369	251	179	156	151	48	48	43	2482	940	557
1992	3209	1844	1037	643	386	269	183	159	153	54	54	48	2660	995	577
1993	3459	1796	1014	543	422	293	173	166	153	66	66	55	3050	1153	663
1994	3921	1833	1054	626	447	308	178	174	165	74	72	59	3188	1072	629
1995	4292	1828	1061	703	449	315	182	178	167	80	77	61	3322	1053	605
1996	4511	1807	1055	747	458	329	183	176	166	84	82	63	3408	1035	595
Average annual increase (%)	8	3	1	8	5	6	4	3	3	5	5	4	8	3	2

Notes:
1. 'Employees' are those who receive remuneration from the business/unit to which they supply their labour. This is the broadest definition of workforce and includes the following groups: (a) normal staff, (b) reemployed retirees, (c) employees and employers in private enterprises, (d) individual entrepreneurs, (e) employees in collective enterprises, (f) others such as civil servants within and outside the nation.
2. 'Staff' refers to persons who work for state-owned and collectively owned enterprises, joint venture companies, shareholding companies and companies owned by overseas Chinese and Chinese from Hong Kong, Macau and Taiwan.
3. 'State enterprise' refers to persons on the payroll of state-owned economic units and their affiliated units.
Source: China Statistical Yearbook (1995, 1996, 1997).

Table 4.10 Changes in the estimated number of 'private sector' staff, 1978–96 (10000 persons)

	Total		Farming Forestry, Fishery, etc.		Manufacturing		Wholesale, retail trade and catering		Transport storage and communications	
	Staff	Annual change per cent	Staff	Annual change per cent	Staff	Annual change per cent	Staff	Annual change per cent	Staff	Annual change per cent
1978	2048	–	56	–	1146	–	172	–	204	–
1980	2425	9	48.7	–	1346	8	234	17	216	6
1985	3368	7	51	1	1645	4	718	25	238	2
1986	3476	3.2	12	−76.50	1724	4.80	720	0.28	242	1.68
1987	3587	3.2	48	300.00	1779	3.19	727	0.97	242	0.00
1988	3625	1.1	46	−4.17	1822	2.42	743	2.20	238	−1.65
1989	3633	0.2	46	0.00	1862	2.20	752	1.21	234	−1.68
1990	3713	2.2	43	−6.52	1909	2.52	768	2.13	235	0.43
1991	3844	3.5	42	−2.33	1961	2.72	793	3.26	234	−0.43
1992	3903	1.5	41	−2.38	1982	1.07	807	1.77	228	−2.56
1993	3929	0.7	36	−12.2	2025	2.17	782	−3.10	162	−28.9
1994	3959	0.8	27	−25.00	2113	4.35	779	−0.38	158	−2.47
1995	3953	−0.2	26	−3.70	2113	0.00	767	−1.54	147	−6.96
1996	3896	−1.4	25	−3.85	2075	−1.80	752	−1.96	146	−0.68
Average annual change		3.6		−4.4		3.4		8.5		−2.00

Table 4.10 (Continued.)

	Financial services and insurance		Real estate activities		Construction		Scientific research service		Social services	
	Staff	Annual change per cent	Staff	Annual change per cent	Staff	Annual change per cent	Staff	Annual change per cent	Staff	Annual change per cent
1978	23	–	3	–	176	–	1	–	59	–
1980	26	6	4	15	235	16	1	0	88	22
1985	33	5	4	0	355	9	2	15	90	0.5
1986	37	12.12	4	0	365	2.82	2	0.0	96	6.67
1987	41	10.81	5	25.0	380	4.11	2	0.0	101	5.21
1988	46	12.20	5	0.0	387	1.84	2	0.0	104	2.97
1989	48	4.35	5	0.0	359	-7.24	3	50.0	106	1.92
1990	50	4.17	4	-20.0	358	-0.28	4	33.3	108	1.89
1991	54	8.00	5	25.0	383	6.98	5	25.0	118	9.26
1992	57	5.56	6	20.0	418	9.14	6	20.0	117	-0.85
1993	57	0.00	11	83.3	490	17.22	13	116.7	129	10.26
1994	65	14.04	13	18.18	443	-9.59	9	-30.8	139	7.75
1995	70	7.69	16	23.08	448	1.13	11	22.22	134	-3.60
1996	80	14.29	19	18.75	440	-1.79	10	-9.09	129	-3.73
Average annual change		7.2		10.8		5.2		13.6		4.40

Source: China Statistical Yearbook (1995, 1996, 1997).

pricing policy is naturally subject to state appraisal. BMPs allow local governments both to estimate the average price of different grades of urban land, usually based on location, and to make adjustments for other site-specific factors when estimating the price of individual development sites. However in some cases BMPs are based on residual land value, that is, the income derived from a piece of land after accounting for the various production costs and the land user's profit margin. In essence, this involves a calculation of what can be earned from the economic activities carried out on the land and the expenses incurred in carrying out such activities. Hence we can say that land value is based on property value, so the higher the price of the property the higher the residual value and the more the developer can expect to pay for the land. This is not explicitly found in the official BMPs of many cities in China. For instance the BMP table for Beijing (Table 4.11) is used to calculate the price of particular land grades for particular uses according to the following formula:

BMP/sq. m = (1) × plot ratio factor + [(2) + (3)] × plot ratio + (4) × adjustment factor + (5) or (6)

Where the adjustment factor (resettlement of the current occupier) is 2 when the current occupier is a state enterprise and 4 when it is a commercial or special land user, and the plot ratio is the ratio of gross floor area to site area. The plot ratio factor is obtained from the following table, and numbers (1) to (6) are explained in the notes to Table 4.11.

Plot ratio	1 or less	2	3	4	5	6	7	8	9	10
Plot ratio factor	1	1.91	2.74	3.5	4.2	4.9	5.6	6.3	7	7.7

For instance an average site of Grade 1 land for commercial use with a plot ratio of 7 where the existing tenant is a state enterprise has an average base land price of

US$540 × 5.6 + (US$84 + US$35) × 7 + US$860 × 2
= US$ 5577.00/square metre

This can be compared with the actual market prices in the same period in Beijing (Table 4.12).

In the BMP equation for Beijing there is a fixed cost that is the same for all grades and all kinds of land use. This is the summation of the land development fee. Taking the average of this fee, and assuming the adjustment factor is 2, then the BMP equation will always include a fixed cost of US$1720 per square metre, which is higher than the unit land price of

Table 4.11 Benchmark price table for Beijing city in 1993 (in US$/sq. m)*

Land grade	Conveyance fee				Infrastructure fee		Land development fee		
	Com. (1)	Apt. (1)	Res. (1)	Ind. (1)	(2)	(3)	(4)	(5)	(6)
1	400–680	380–580	250–340	40–70	68–100	20–50	740–980	20–56	—
2	300–400	280–380	200–250	30–40	68–100	20–50	740–980	20–56	—
3	250–300	230–280	125–200	25–30	68–100	20–50	740–980	20–56	—
4	190–250	180–230	100–125	20–25	68–100	20–50	740–980	20–56	—
5	125–190	125–180	75–100	15–20	68–100	20–50	740–980	20–56	—
6	65–125	65–125	50–75	10–15	68–100	20–50	740–980	20–56	10–23
7	50–65	40–65	20–50	5–10	68–100	20–50	740–980	20–56	10–23
8	10–50	10–40	8–20	4–5	68–100	20–50	—	—	10–23
9	8–10	5–10	4–8	3–4	68–100	20–50	—	—	10–23
10	5–8	4–5	3–4	2–3	68–100	20–50	—	—	10–23

Notes:
*The exchange rate between the US dollar and the Chinese yuan before the reform of the exchange rate system on 1 January 1994 was US$1 per 10 yuan.
(1) Land uses – commercial, apartment, residential and industrial.
(2) Fee charged for urban services and the connection of public utilities – gas etc.
(3) Fee charged for neighbourhood infrastructure.
(4) Resettlement fee in urban areas.
(5) Resettlement fee in urban fringe areas.
(6) Resettlement fee in rural areas.
Source: Beijing City Government document no. 34, 1993.

Table 4.12   Land sales in Beijing, 1994

Location	Lot size (sq. m)	Plot ratio	Use	Price (US$10 000)	Unit land price (US$/sq. m)
Wangfujing Street	19 045	8.40	Office	6049.5	3176.5
Chaoyang District	12 200	3.93	Mixed	691.8	567.1
Chungwen District	21 691	1.08	Residential	359.8	165.9
Haidien District	10 600	2.83	Commercial	370.6	349.6
Xicheng District	5 740	2.09	Mixed	440.7	767.8
Chungwen District	19 000	6.37	Mixed	1852.4	974.9
Dongcheng District	618	13.77	Office	224.1	3625.9
Dongcheng District	2 650	11.00	Mixed	1047.8	3953.8
Haidien District	20 000	0.50	Residential	252.9	126.5
Haidien District	18 000	1.25	Residential	272.0	151.1
Dongcheng District	9 600	3.65	Mixed	881.5	918.4
Chungwai Main Street	10 000	2.22	Mixed	611.8	281.1
Xicheng District	13 900	5.52	Office	1354.7	974.6
Xuanwu District	11 364	4.31	Mixed	734.9	646.8
Chaoyang District	5 179	5.12	Office	467.6	902.9

Note: The exchange rate between the Chinese yuan and the US dollar in 1994 was about US$1 per 8.5 yuan.
Source: Wang and Wang (1995).

some of the sites shown in Table 4.12. As no information is available on the relevant grades of the various sites in the table it is difficult to evaluate the differentials between the official BMPs and the market prices.

Tianjin city is a potential second-tier real estate market. A comparison of BMPs and actual transaction prices in Tianjin is presented in Table 4.13, and it can be seen that, as in the case of Beijing, there are large discrepancies between the sales prices and the BMP valuations carried out by the local government. Obviously the benchmark pricing model, which relies heavily on the cost approach, makes no allowance for investors' perception of land values. So while the BMP is useful as a point of reference for local governments with little experience of the land market, refinement of the methodology is required when enough market data becomes available. The BMP model aims to recoup the various production costs incurred (in particular resettlement costs) when making the land available for sale, but a price arrived at in this way takes no account of a developer's view of the value of the land to him.

A comparison of Tables 4.14 to 4.19 provides some interesting observations about the official land price guidance system. In the case of Xiamen

Table 4.13   Land sales in Tianjin, 1993–94

Lot size (sq. m)	Plot ratio	Use	Price (US$/sq. m)	BMP range for use type grade 1–grade 7 (US$ sq. m)
4995	8.8	Mixed	1410.381	88–647
77027	4.8	Mixed	729.431	88–647
4108	6.6	Mixed	823.525	88–647
34796	7.0	Mixed	1462.341	88–647
19925	2.6	Apartment	593.320	27–354
38744	7.0	Mixed	830.118	88–647
42393	5.5	Mixed	841.177	88–647
7381	7.0	Mixed	1514.141	88–647
36022	3.5	Residential	698.641	27–354
10572	6.5	Commercial	994.118	80–649
6491	6.0	Mixed	952.941	88–647
1577	10.0	Mixed	2083.059	88–647
7891	5.8	Mixed	740.684	88–647
18001	8.0	Mixed	1342.682	88–647
19166	5.3	Mixed	779.412	88–647
15808	6.0	Mixed	945.177	88–647
20007	7.0	Mixed	1462.341	88–647
9219	10.8	Mixed	1531.373	88–647
3933	13.0	Commercial	2704.918	80–649

Note: The exchange rate between the Chinese yuan and the US$ in 1994 was about US$1 per 8.5 yuan.
Source: Wang and Wang (1995).

(Table 4.14), the 1990 BMPs were in accord with the market-determined land values. Most of the LURs sold that year were within the range of the official BMP, and even the lot that fetched the lowest price was still above the lowest BMP guideline for commercial use. However once the market got started the BMPs ceased to function effectively through want of updating. It is obvious from the 1991–93 transactions that BMPs became less and less aligned to the market trend, and in 1993 the market price of urban land rose to almost eight times the average BMP. It was not until the national economy began to slow down in the second half of 1994 that market prices fell back to the BMP level.

A similar situation prevailed in Dalian and Jinzhou (Tables 4.16–4.18), where the official BMPs bore little relation to the market prices. However the situation was different in Shantou (Table 4.15), where market activities started before the first set of BMPs was compiled. Shantou, a prosperous

Table 4.14   Land sales in Xiamen, 1990–94

Date	Lot size (sq. m)	Unit price (yuan/sq. m)	BMP range for commercial use (yuan/sq. m)
15.6.90	3340	2015.57	582–2478
22.6.90	4032	1899.96	582–2478
30.7.90	5081	2399.18	582–2478
18.6.90	2347	2049.49	582–2478
4.5.90	6584	2000.30	582–2478
4.5.90	3292	1998.78	582–2478
9.9.90	3289	3649.03	582–2478
9.9.90	6351	2598.02	582–2478
9.9.90	4728	1797.86	582–2478
9.9.90	4948	1717.92	582–2478
9.9.90	3614	1660.23	582–2478
9.9.90	3702	1485.70	582–2478
10.9.90	4005	586.78	582–2478
Average		1856.99	1530
10.9.91	4660	3300.43	582–2478
10.9.91	3306	2518.99	582–2478
10.9.91	3786	1912.00	582–2478
10.9.91	3117	2807.25	582–2478
Average		2634.66	1530
3.3.92	4728	2250.00	582–2478
27.4.92	2502	2250.00	582–2478
11.5.92	8073	2700.00	582–2478
30.4.92	11 739	2450.00	582–2478
5.6.92	5822	3000.00	582–2478
10.9.92	3831	8111.00	582–2478
10.9.92	3790	7258.00	582–2478
10.9.92	2112	3100.00	582–2478
Average		3889.87	1530
8.5.93	6838	13011.00	582–2478
8.5.93	5050	12000.00	582–2478
8.5.93	5711	12010.00	582–2478
Average		12340.00	1530
12.9.94	6379	960.00	582–2478
8.10.94	3318	800.00	582–2478
8.10.94	3750	533.33	582–2478
8.10.94	3690	533.33	582–2478
12.9.94	4498	3250.00	582–2478
30.12.94	5474	1800.00	582–2478
30.12.94	4398	1800.00	582–2478
Average		1382.38	1530

Note: All are commercial plots.
Source: Wang and Wang (1995).

Table 4.15   Land sales in Shantou, 1990–91

Date	Lot size (sq. m)	Use	Unit price (yuan/sq. ft)	1992 BMP range (yuan/sq. m)
Sept. 1990	8431	Commercial	367.49	420–815
Oct. 1990	717	Commercial	289.97	420–815
	6158	Residential	289.97	420–815
	717	Commercial	747.89	350–725
	14064	Industrial	270.00	250–376
Nov. 1990	6779	Commercial	720.02	420–815
	4835	Commercial	330.00	420–815
	1239	Commercial	420.18	420–815
	4727	Residential	351.18	350–725
	2495	Residential	21.00	350–725
	1807	Residential	329.95	350–725
	6830	Industrial	269.99	250–376
	2000	Industrial	247.50	250–376
	11865	Industrial	198.00	250–376
	6250	Industrial	270.00	250–376
Dec. 1990	3575	Commercial	344.97	420–815
	10146	Commercial	599.98	420–815
	7602	Commercial	896.98	420–815
	11856	Commercial	600.00	420–815
	4116	Commercial	434.57	420–815
	5652	Commercial	418.76	420–815
	74260	Commercial	187.50	420–815
	13566	Commercial	600.00	420–815
	7844	Industrial	220.50	250–376
	5979	Industrial	198.00	250–376
	6931	Industrial	304.34	250–376
	5664	Industrial	269.99	250–376
	7517	Industrial	270.00	250–376
Jan. 1991	4384	Industrial	270.00	250–376
	7782	Industrial	220.50	250–376
Feb. 1991	4983	Industrial	270.00	250–376
March 1991	4679	Industrial	247.51	250–376
	4406	Industrial	270.00	250–376
April 1991	13227	Industrial	306.61	250–376
	13040	Industrial	270.00	250–376
May 1991	3553	Commercial	480.00	420–815
	4652	Industrial	247.57	250–376
	6125	Industrial	270.00	250–376
	4306	Industrial	240.00	250–376
June 1991	5906	Industrial	270.00	250–376
	24005	Residential	289.49	350–725

Source: Wang and Wang (1995).

Table 4.16 Residential land sales in Dalian, 1993

Lot size (sq. m)	Unit price (yuan/sq. m)	Grade 1	Grade 2	Grade 3	Grade 4	Grade 5	Grade 6	Grade 7	Grade 8	Grade 9
							1992 BMP range for residential land (yuan/sq. m)			
8 858	303.00	819	702	585	468	351	234	210	187	164
10 630	296.00	819	702	585	468	351	234	210	187	164
3 380	379.00	819	702	585	468	351	234	210	187	164
4 526	319.00	819	702	585	468	351	234	210	187	164
8 195	255.00	819	702	585	468	351	234	210	187	164
35 293	218.00	819	702	585	468	351	234	210	187	164
14 943	369.00	819	702	585	468	351	234	210	187	164
3 528	852.90	819	702	585	468	351	234	210	187	164
1 100	949.70	819	702	585	468	351	234	210	187	164
3 159	1138.20	819	702	585	468	351	234	210	187	164
2 040	377.90	819	702	585	468	351	234	210	187	164
800	666.46	819	702	585	468	351	234	210	187	164
8 650	857.00	819	702	585	468	351	234	210	187	164
795	351.00	819	702	585	468	351	234	210	187	164
14 463	545.45	819	702	585	468	351	234	210	187	164
2 001	276.00	819	702	585	468	351	234	210	187	164
6 300	799.75	819	702	585	468	351	234	210	187	164
630	492.80	819	702	585	468	351	234	210	187	164
1 200	468.00	819	702	585	468	351	234	210	187	164
1 100	892.06	819	702	585	468	351	234	210	187	164
6 700	484.00	819	702	585	468	351	234	210	187	164
6 680	526.50	819	702	585	468	351	234	210	187	164
5 500	1267.60	819	702	585	468	351	234	210	187	164
2 697	226.75	819	702	585	468	351	234	210	187	164

Table 4.16 (continued)

Lot size (sq. m)	Unit price (yuan/sq. m)	Grade 1	Grade 2	Grade 3	Grade 4	Grade 5	Grade 6	Grade 7	Grade 8	Grade 9
						1992 BMP range for residential land (yuan/sq. m)				
2697	226.75	819	702	585	468	351	234	210	187	164
3718	586.89	819	702	585	468	351	234	210	187	164
320	357.00	819	702	585	468	351	234	210	187	164
1764	1205.00	819	702	585	468	351	234	210	187	164
4385	185.00	819	702	585	468	351	234	210	187	164
5522	580.00	819	702	585	468	351	234	210	187	164
771.5	453.00	819	702	585	468	351	234	210	187	164
6977	422.04	819	702	585	468	351	234	210	187	164
2100	234.00	819	702	585	468	351	234	210	187	164
5774	612.20	819	702	585	468	351	234	210	187	164
7000	634.70	819	702	585	468	351	234	210	187	164
4200	849.40	819	702	585	468	351	234	210	187	164
3000	311.87	819	702	585	468	351	234	210	187	164
2800	116.14	819	702	585	468	351	234	210	187	164
17400	315.90	819	702	585	468	351	234	210	187	164
1785	234.00	819	702	585	468	351	234	210	187	164
5017	847.58	819	702	585	468	351	234	210	187	164
2827	685.10	819	702	585	468	351	234	210	187	164
9717	491.40	819	702	585	468	351	234	210	187	164
965	261.00	819	702	585	468	351	234	210	187	164
37327	150.00	819	702	585	468	351	234	210	187	164
3757	280.81	819	702	585	468	351	234	210	187	164
1382	205.90	819	702	585	468	351	234	210	187	164
2470	456.68	819	702	585	468	351	234	210	187	164
1840	100.05	819	702	585	468	351	234	210	187	164
600	609.30	819	702	585	468	351	234	210	187	164

Source: Wang and Wang (1995).

Table 4.17 Commercial land sales in Dalian, 1993

Lot size (sq. m)	Unit price (yuan/sq. m)	1992 BMP range for commercial land (yuan/sq. m)								
		Grade 1	Grade 2	Grade 3	Grade 4	Grade 5	Grade 6	Grade 7	Grade 8	Grade 9
3 213	580.00	990	891	693	594	495	396	297	238	218
2 680	1501.80	990	891	693	594	495	396	297	238	218
850	1141.80	990	891	693	594	495	396	297	238	218
2 610	263.00	990	891	693	594	495	396	297	238	218
2 810	2272.00	990	891	693	594	495	396	297	238	218
1 238	2246.83	990	891	693	594	495	396	297	238	218
3 024	1082.67	990	891	693	594	495	396	297	238	218
885	304.00	990	891	693	594	495	396	297	238	218
3 291	1748.00	990	891	693	594	495	396	297	238	218
1 286	2298.00	990	891	693	594	495	396	297	238	218
2 142	1846.43	990	891	693	594	495	396	297	238	218
6 750	811.85	990	891	693	594	495	396	297	238	218
3 130	2137.80	990	891	693	594	495	396	297	238	218
3 950	1441.00	990	891	693	594	495	396	297	238	218
7 394	1683.76	990	891	693	594	495	396	297	238	218
6 689	1202.00	990	891	693	594	495	396	297	238	218
7 784	1734.84	990	891	693	594	495	396	297	238	218

Source: Wang and Wang (1995).

Table 4.18   Land sales in Jinzhou, 1992

Lot size (sq. m)	Land use	Unit price (yuan/sq. m)	1992 BMP range for the relevant use of land for different grades (yuan/sq. m)						
			Grade 1	Grade 2	Grade 3	Grade 4	Grade 5	Grade 6	Grade 7
3 300	Commercial	9363.30	2930	1956	1499	1298	1231	569	314
3 150	Residential	323.40	348	292	260	235	217	120	75
10 197	Residential	86.90	348	292	260	235	217	120	75
1 500	Residential	666.66	348	292	260	235	217	120	75
66 927*	Industrial	0.54	481	297	252	136	109	96	70
6 355*	Commercial	6.70	2930	1956	1499	1298	1231	569	314
22 977*	Industrial	1.10	481	297	252	136	109	96	70
15 331*	Industrial	0.87	481	297	252	136	109	96	70
25 907*	Industrial	2.00	481	297	252	136	109	96	70

* Agricultural land.
Source: Wang and Wang (1995).

city in Guangdong province, was the first city to attract the attention of foreign investors, particularly investors from Hong Kong and Macau, when the open-door economic policy was introduced in the 1970s. These market activities provided a concrete basis for the compilation of the BMP table, and hence the 1992 table largely reflected the market trend. The case of Chongqing (Table 4.19) seems to confirm the relevance of BMPs as market guidelines as long as the information upon which they are based is regularly updated.

Hence it is important to set up an official appraisal system at the beginning of any urban land reform in order to provide land price guidelines for the state, private landlords and prospective purchasers. But to be effective the data must be frequently updated since most emerging markets are very dynamic. In the following section we examine urban land as an investment asset and the associated pricing mechanism.

Land as a Financial Asset

In 1994 a policy document titled 'Regulations on the Appraisal of Land Value in the Audit of State Assets' was jointly issued by the Ministry of Finance, the Ministry of Construction, the State Land Administration Bureau and the SAAB. The main purpose of these regulations was to establish baseline prices for land belonging to state enterprises, including those using their land as capital in joint-venture activities and those changing themselves into share-capital firms. Similar regulations exist for assets brought in by foreign investors, that is, the Administration Procedures of the Appraisal of Assets Invested by Foreign Investors, 1994. Part Three of these procedures describes the appraisal methods, as follows:

Article 10: The appraisal of foreign investment assets must be conducted in accordance with the appraisal methods and relevant provisions set forth in these Appraisal Procedures and on the basis of the current state, degree of wear, indications of performance, technical parameters, replacement cost, profitability, etc. of the assets.

Article 11: The methods of appraising foreign investment assets shall include on-site inspection, technical tests and value appraisal, of which value appraisal shall include:

(1) the market-based method,
(2) the cost-based method,
(3) the profit-based method and
(4) other methods prescribed by the Ministry of Finance or the State Administration for Commodity Inspection.

Table 4.19 Land sales in Chongqing, 1992

Lot size (sq. m.)	Land use	Unit price (yuan/sq. m)	1992 BMP range for relevant use of land for different grades (yuan/sq. m)											
			1	2	3	4	5	6	7	8	9	10	11	12
16 000	Com.	131.3	516	407	349	292	264	230	192	169	133	110	87	43
12 900	Com.	165.0	516	407	349	292	264	230	192	169	133	110	87	43
233 000	Com.	131.5	516	407	349	292	264	230	192	169	133	110	87	43
1 477 000	Com.	139.0	516	407	349	292	264	230	192	169	133	110	87	43
12 000	Com.	83.3	516	407	349	292	264	230	192	169	133	110	87	43
1 143	Ind.	227.5	24	23	22	19	16	15	14	13	11	8	7	6
22 306	Com.	3000.0	516	407	349	292	264	230	192	169	133	110	87	43
298	Res.	151.0	38	34	31	27	24	22	18	16	13	11	9	7
2 437	Com.	310.0	516	407	349	292	264	230	192	169	133	110	87	43
212	Com.	377.0	516	407	349	292	264	230	192	169	133	110	87	43

Source: Wang and Wang (1995).

Article 12: Where the market-based method is used to appraise the value of foreign investment assets, reference shall be made to the current market price of identical or similar assets.

Article 13: Where the cost-based method is used to appraise the value of foreign investment assets, the reestimated value shall be determined on the basis of the replacement cost of the assets being appraised as brand-new assets less the cumulative depreciation calculated on the basis of the replacement cost with respect to factors such as changes in productivity, percentage of newness, etc. Alternatively, the reestimated value of the assets may be obtained by determining their percentage of newness on the basis of the current state and useful life of the assets being appraised with regard to factors such as changes in function, etc.

Article 14: Where the profit-based method is used to appraise the value of foreign investment assets, the current value of the assets being appraised shall be calculated on the basis of the reasonably expected profitability of such assets at a suitable discount rate.

Article 15: The appraisal of foreign investment assets shall be conducted in accordance with the following procedures:

(1) the applicant files an application for appraisal,
(2) the appraisal authorities accept the application following preliminary examination of information,
(3) appraisal personnel draft an appraisal plan,
(4) receipts, certificates and information provided by the applicant are examined and verified and market surveys are conducted inside and outside China,
(5) an on-site inspection is conducted,
(6) a suitable appraisal method is selected for the appraisal and
(7) a Certificate of Appraisal is issued.

Article 16: Applicants applying for the appraisal of foreign investment assets shall fill out an application form, clearly stating the purpose and objects of and requirements for appraisal, and shall also provide ... a list of property items, Customs declaration list, contract, receipts, insurance policy, a list of maintenance expenses, technical documentation concerning equipment, etc.

According to Regulation 7 of the 1994 'Regulations on the Appraisal of Land Value in the Audit of State Assets', local authorities that have compiled BMPs can base their appraisal of land values on the published benchmark prices in accordance with the 'Provisional Regulations of the

People's Republic of China on Granting and Transferring the Rights to the Use of State-owned Land in Cities and Towns' (1991) and the 'Provisional Procedures for the Administration of Appraisal Practice in the Urban Real Estate Market' (1992) (Li, 1995). Theoretically, therefore, local governments and developers should have a common reference point when assessing the development potential of urban sites.

Regulation 10 recommends that the method used for asset valuation should be one of the following: market comparison; the investment method or the cost approach. Regulation 13 requires state enterprises to form an asset valuation committee to oversee the valuation work, which should take the following into account:

• Historical background of the ownership and use of the land.
• Locational advantages and quality of the land.
• Benchmark prices and other adjustments in the locality.
• Data on the local property market.
• Other relevant factors that will affect the value of the land.

In the early stages of the LUR reform, some cities and provinces in China tried to attract foreign investors to their regions. One way of doing this was to set land prices at a low level and offer special rates for investors, especially in coastal cities and towns in the Pearl River Delta region (Li, 1996a). This created unhealthy competition and resulted in a substantial loss of income from the uncontrolled granting of LURs. In 1986 the newly established State Land Administration Bureau (SLAB) attempted to make the appraisal of land assets relatively more unified and systematic. The SLAB was charged with establishing a market system for land, so the appraisal of land was at the top of the agenda. However the SLAB was not able to establish a market appraisal system overnight, and there remained a conflict between the ideological definition of 'value' and the market approach (Li, 1995).

The SLAB is not the only authority to deal with appraisal. Currently the State Asset Administration Bureau (SAAB) is responsible for assessing and approving the asset value of all companies listed on the Shanghai and Shenzhen stock exchanges. These companies' public shares take the form 'A shares', which are yuan-denominated ordinary shares, or 'B shares' which are yuan-denominated special shares that are fully convertible to Hong Kong dollars. By the end of 1997 there were more than 250 A-share companies listed on the two stock exchanges and 100 B-share companies. These numbers are expected to increase substantially as the reform of the state sector proceeds. In addition, 40 mainland enterprises are listed on the Hong Kong stock exchange. These companies are normally called

'H-share' companies and are among the most competitive state enterprises in China. The speed of this development has created an urgent need for trained professionals to give objective advice to accountants when formulating their companies' balance sheets and company reports. Most Chinese companies that wish to value their land assets appoint a professional surveyor from Hong Kong as well as local valuers. However it is always the SAAB that determines the final value.

Appraisal Criteria

Chinese state enterprises that wish to raise funds usually choose to list their firms on the local stock exchange in the form of B shares or in Hong Kong in the form of H shares. Valuation of their assets is required to be undertaken by Hong Kong valuers or surveyors, and the following points have to be borne in mind:[1]

1. Chinese enterprises wishing to achieve B-share or H-share listing have to submit valuations of their property and land interests in accordance with the law and regulations of the securities commissions in Shanghai and Shenzhen. Hong Kong listing is governed by Hong Kong company law.
2. Foreign parties or investors entering into a Sino-foreign joint venture should obtain an independent valuation of all property that is to act as the Chinese partner's capital contribution.
3. Foreign developers should conduct a feasibility study of and market research into any property development project they intend to undertake in China. In the case of large development projects, a separate in-house team should be set up to conduct the valuation work.
4. Chinese enterprises have to raise funds through bank loans, mortgages or private loans.

Under the current law in China, the maximum duration of LURs is 70 years for residential land, 50 years for industrial land and 40 years for commercial and social land. Appraisers and valuers are required to ascertain how long LURs have to run and take this into consideration when making their valuation.

In China, land and buildings valuations are always conducted separately because of the twofold registration system for land and buildings. Most enterprises and other commmercial entities in China still have separate LUR certificates and property ownership certificates. The value of these assets, however, is recorded as a single amount.

The immaturity of the property market in China means that little data is available to valuers and appraisers for purposes of comparision, particularly with regard to industrial property with purpose-built structures. Some information on market transactions can be obtained from government agencies or local valuation consultancy centres, but the volume of data is usually inadequate and substantial adjustments have to be made, which affects the accuracy of the valuation.

Since early 1995 the SLAB has insisted that allocated land must be converted into market land by means of a land premium payment before it can be used as a capital contribution to a joint venture. This policy retrospectively affected joint-venture enterprises that had already been established. Such enterprises are required to show evidence of how and from whom they have obtained the land upon which their premises are built. Certain documents have to be submitted to the SLAB for examination and a land premium may be required. The SLAB also stipulates that an independent, certified land valuer must be appointed to determine the value of the land, taking account of the land grant fee, the development cost and the annual land use fee. The BMP table discussed above is widely used by local valuers in many major cities when they carry out valuations. Most rely on the tables provided by provincial, municipal or county government rather than base their valuations on actual market transactions. Hence foreign investors are often concerned about the accuracy of the valuation and may seek the assistance of an external or international valuation firm to review the valuation reports prepared by Chinese valuers.

When the Chinese partner in a joint venture is a state enterprise, an asset valuation report on the land, buildings and structures in question must be presented to the SAAB for approval. The SAAB presently allows foreign valuation firms to collaborate with local valuers in determining a fair market value for a property, but each must prepare an independent report for submission to the SAAB. In the event of a marked difference between the two valuations the SAAB decides which is the more accurate. Sometimes legal advisers specialising in Chinese law are consulted to provide their opinion on the legal title of the land – a large amount of land is held by Chinese state enterprises as allocated land, and the dual-track system of land tenure fosters black market activities in the transfer of LURs, hampers the legal transfer of LURs, distorts the accuracy of information and data on property market transactions and complicates the valuation process.

To investigate the process of valuation in practice and illustrate some of the valuation methods discussed in previous sections, two case studies are presented below. In both cases Hong Kong valuers were involved in the process and carried out their valuations independently of the local valuers.

Case Study One

In this analysis we examine a joint-venture project in Beijing, and compare the market approach to land valuation and the benchmark land price set by the government when negotiating with foreign investors. The project in question, which commenced in August 1993, is located in the Chaoyang District on the south-east fringe of Beijing city. The details of the site are as follows:

- Site area: 37 233 square metres.
- Use: commercial (25 per cent)/residential (75 per cent) mixed development.
- Building height: not exceeding 99.6 metres.
- Plot ratio: not exceeding 5.99.
- Duration of land use rights: 70 years for residential and 40 years for commercial.

The site in this case study is ranked as Grade 4 land, and the price of the land should lie between the lower-end and upper-end figures in the Grade 4 section of the 1993 BMP table for Beijing. The formula for the lower end (land in a non-prime location) is as follows:

$$US\$180 \times 4.2 + (US\$68 + US\$20) \times 5.99 + US\$740 \times 2$$
$$+ US\$20 = US\$2783.12 \text{ per square metre}$$

This represents Grade 4 land for apartment use – in China, mixed office and residential buildings are normally referred as apartment buildings. Hence the lower-end BMP for this site is US\$2783.12 × 37 233 sq. m = US\$103.6 million (or 880 million yuan at the exchange rate of US\$1 = 8.5 yuan).

If on the other hand the site is situtated in a prime location in the neighbourhood, the average land price becomes:

$$US\$230 \times 4.2 + (US\$100 + US\$50) \times 5.99 + US\$980 \times 2$$
$$+ US\$56 = US\$ 3880.5 \text{ per square metre}$$

Hence the upper-end BMP for this site is US\$3880.5 × 37 233 sq. m. = US\$144.5 million (or 1228 million yuan).

However in the professional valuation report dated commissioned by the foreign partner in this project, the transfer fee, which is the agreed land price to be paid to the local government, amounted to US\$16.8 million (or 142 million yuan) – substantially less than even the lower-end official BMP. This is not an isolated example. Table 4.20 shows the divergence between the market price for real estate in Beijing and the official BMP.

Table 4.20 Comparison of market prices and BMP prices in Beijing, 1994

Location	Lot size (sq.m)	Plot ratio	Use	Unit price (US$ sq. m)	BMP¹ (US$/sq. m)	Market price BMP¹	BMP² (US$/sq. m)	Market price BMP²
Wangfujing Street	19 045	8.40	Office	3176.5	6159.6	0.52	4143.6	0.76
Chaoyang District	12 200	3.93	Mixed	567.1	3540.9	0.16	2787.4	0.20
Chungwen District	21 691	1.08	Resid.	165.9	2181.5	0.08	2000.0	0.08
Haidien District	10 600	2.83	Comm.	349.6	3126.0	0.11	2515.0	0.14
Xicheng District	5 740	2.09	Mixed	767.8	2923.5	0.26	2398.0	0.32
Chungwen District	19 000	6.37	Mixed	974.9	4868.0	0.20	3520.5	0.28
Dongcheng District	618	13.77	Office	3625.9	7754.6	0.47	5091.0	0.71
Dongcheng District	2 650	11.00	Mixed	3953.8	6763.0	0.58	4646.0	0.85
Haidien District	20 000	0.50	Resid.	126.5	2112.5	0.06	1930.0	0.07
Haidien District	18 000	1.25	Resid.	151.1	2201.8	0.07	2019.0	0.07
Dongcheng District	9 600	3.65	Mixed	918.4	3507.6	0.26	2754.0	0.33
Chungwai Main Street	10 000	2.22	Mixed	281.1	5312.6	0.05	2583.8	0.11
Xicheng District	13 900	5.52	Office	974.6	4682.9	0.21	3338.9	0.29
Xuanwu District	11 364	4.31	Mixed	646.8	3950.9	0.16	2988.4	0.22
Chaoyang District	5 179	5.12	Office	902.9	4635.3	0.19	3291.3	0.27

Note: The exchange rate in 1994 was about 1US$ = 8.5 yuan. BMP¹ represents the estimated BMP on grade one land in each district with averaged figures. BMP² represents the estimated BMP on grade four land in each district with averaged figures. Mixed refers to mixed commercial and residential development. Col. 6 refers to market price divided by BMP¹ and col. 8 refers to market price divided by BMP².

Source: Wang and Wang (1995).

We can see that in 1994 the market land prices fell below the official BMPs in the major districts of Beijing. For instance, assuming that the first lot in Table 4.20 is an average Grade 1 commercial site (Wangfujing Street is the main shopping and business street in Beijing) and the existing tenant is a state enterprise, then the average base price of this site should lie between the lower end of the BMP table:

$$US\$400 \times 6.3 + (US\$68 + US\$20) \times 8.4 + US\$740 \times 2 = US\$4739.2$$
per square metre

and the upper end of the table:

$$US\$680 \times 6.3 + (US\$100 + US\$50) \times 8.4 + US\$980 \times 2 = US\$7504.4$$
per square metre

However the actual market transaction price was US\$3716.5 per square metre, which is 22 per cent below the minimum BMP and 50 per cent lower than the maximum figures in the BMP table.

To take another example, the last transaction in Table 4.20 is a Chaoyang District development and according to the BMP table the price should fall between:

$$US\$400 \times 4.2 + (US\$68 + US\$20) \times 5.12 + US\$740 \times 2 = US\$3611$$
per square metre

and

$$US\$680 \times 4.2 + (US\$100 + US\$50) \times 5.12 + US\$980 \times 2 = US\$5584$$
per square metre

The actual market transaction price for this site was just US\$903 per square metre. There is, however, a possible explanation for this. That is, the Chinese partner took financial responsibility for the conversion of administratively allocated land into market land, while the foreign partner made the required payment to the development fund, including the land premium and the infrastructure and resettlement fees. Hence we can divide the financial burden of the venture into two parts, namely the land premium and the 'preparation fees,' which distorts the residual nature of the land value. Hence we can apply only the first section of the official BMP formula, (that is BMP/sq. m = (1) × plot ratio factor + [(2) + (3)] × plot ratio) to the compilation of BMP prices (Table 4.21).

From Table 4.21 we can begin to see a relatively logical function of the BMPs. The ratios between the actual market land prices and the corresponding BMPs show that in most cases BMPs can serve as a reference point for both the developer and the local authority. This is especially

Table 4.21 Comparison of market prices and recompiled BMPs, Beijing, 1994

Location	Lot size (sq. m)	Plot ratio	Use	Unit price (US$ /sq. m)	BMP¹ (US$ /sq. m)	Market price BMP¹	BMP² (US$ /sq. m)	Market price BMP²
Wangfujing Street	19 045	8.40	Office	3 176.5	4 401.6	0.72	2 385.6	1.33
Chaoyang District	12 200	3.93	Mixed	567.1	1 782.9	0.32	1 029	0.55
Chungwen District	21 691	1.08	Resid.	165.9	423.5	0.39	241.0	0.69
Haidien District	10 600	2.83	Comm.	349.6	1 368.2	0.26	757.0	0.46
Xicheng District	5 740	2.09	Mixed	767.8	1 165.5	0.66	640.3	1.20
Chungwen District	19 000	6.37	Mixed	974.9	3 110.0	0.31	1 762.5	0.55
Dongcheng District	618	13.77	Office	3 625.9	5 796.6	0.63	3 332.6	1.09
Dongcheng District	2 650	11.00	Mixed	3 953.8	5 005.0	0.79	2 887.5	1.37
Haidien District	20 000	0.50	Resid.	126.5	354.5	0.36	172.0	0.73
Haidien District	18 000	1.25	Resid.	151.1	443.8	0.34	261.3	0.58
Dongcheng District	9 600	3.65	Mixed	918.4	1 749.6	0.52	996.1	0.92
Chungwai Main Street	10 000	2.22	Mixed	281.1	1 178.6	0.24	825.9	0.34
Xicheng District	13 900	5.52	Office	974.6	2 924.9	0.33	1 580.9	0.61
Xuanwu District	11 364	4.31	Mixed	646.8	2 192.9	0.29	1 230.4	0.53
Chaoyang District	5 179	5.12	Office	902.9	2 877.3	0.31	1 533.3	0.59

Note: The exchange rate in 1994 was about 1US$ = 8.5 yuan. BMP¹ represents the recompiled BMP on grade one land in each district with averaged figures. BMP² represents the recompiled BMP on grade four land in each district with averaged figures. Col.6 refers to market price divided by BMP¹ and col. 8 refers to market price divided by BMP².
Source: Wang and Wang (1995).

obvious with Grade 4 land, where BMPs can serve as the minimum price, or the starting price in the case of auctions, with the final bid price exceeding the BMP.

For new players in this market the only official information available on land prices is the BMP table. This is supposed to serve as a reference for both the local authority, which has power to sell LURs, and the developer until a real market mechanism has been established. However BMPs include several elements that are unfamiliar to developers from market economies, such as the LUR conveyance fee (the first component of the Beijing BMP formula), a payment for infrastructural development in the neighbourhood in question and compensation for sitting tenants. Hence if a proper development analysis is to be carried out in this market, foreign developers have to be very careful when interpreting information. Here we shall utilise market information and the official BMP in order to analyse the development potential of the project in the case study.

1. Land cost: US$75 per square metre of floor area. This is calculated by dividing the conveyance fee of US$16 803 840 paid to the State Land Administration Bureau in Beijing City by the total floor area, that is, the site area (37 233 square metres) multiplied by the plot ratio (5.99).
2. Construction Cost: US$210 per square metre. As this is a mixed development, the average construction cost of residential projects for local residents (average construction standard, US$118 per square metre) and the average cost of office development (US$307 per square metre) are taken together. Assuming this project is of a higher standard, the residential component is estimated to be US$177 per square metre (or 50 per cent higher than the local housing construction cost). Given a residential/commercial ratio of 75 : 25, a construction cost of US$210 per square metre is assumed for the whole development.
3. Preparation fees: US$486.5 per square metre of floor area. Preparation fees include all the infrastructural and resettlement fees.
4. Total cost: US$771.5 per square metre of floor area.
5. Selling price: US$2100 per square metre of floor area. This is the average price of properties in mixed developments for sale in the open market in Chaoyang District.

Thus the total development cost (that is, land costs plus construction costs and preparation fees) is about 772 yuan per square metre, which converts into a unit cost of about 4624 yuan per square metre of the site area. This figure falls within the BMP range for this site (3611–5584 yuan), as estimated above. Consequently the official BMP table does provide useful information for the developer in terms of gaining a clearer understanding of the total costs that will be incurred, but not in terms of land value, as the table implies. Nonetheless the financial feasibility of the project can be deduced from the estimated development costs.

This case study illustrates the difficulty of carrying out a development analysis for real estate projects in China, which is mainly the consequence of the different meaning given to 'value' in a socialist economy (Li, 1996a). Furthermore the reference prices provided by the state must be checked for possible double-counting of the various costs.

Case Study Two

The main business of a state enterprise owned by the Chongqing Government was the production of motor vehicles, automotive components and a variety of medium-duty trucks. In 1994 the enterprise was reorganised and formed into a Sino-Hong Kong joint venture company producing a full range of vehicles with the aid of modern technology. The company's facilities included an assembly plant, a stamping plant, a casting plant and a foundary, located in an area of 468 180 square metres in a rural part of Chongqing. In order to meet the requirements of State Assets Administration Bureau, a valuation report was prepared by foreign valuers.

During the initial negotiations the site had planning approval for industrial use and numerous structures were erected on the site, with a total gross floor area of about 165 719 square metres. However only the land was to be valued, not the structures and facilities erected on it. Industrial LURs were granted for a term of 50 years, commencing on 4 April 1994. The valuation date was set for 31 May 1994. The land was originally allocated land, but for the purposes of H-share listing the state enterprise converted it into granted land before entering into the joint venture.

Chinese Valuation
The benchmark land price adjustment method was employed by the Chinese valuer when valuing the land, with reference to the BMP table and adjustment tables released in 1992 by the Chongqing government. The land was classified as Grade 10 and the BMP for industrial use Grade 10 was 8.1 yuan per square metre. The average land price for Grade 10 was calculated according to the following formula:

$$\frac{8.1 \times 1.15}{r} \left(1 - \frac{1}{(1+r)^n}\right)$$

where $r = 0.076$, as specified by the Chongqing government in its Land Administration document, n is the duration of the LURs, 1.15 is the adjustment factor and 8.1 is BMP for Grade 10 industrial land. The adjustment factors in the 1992 Chongqing BMP table, which were used when calculating the transaction price, totaled 1.55. Since the location of the site was better than the standard Grade 10, an upward adjustment of 1.3 was required to reflect this factor. The unit land price, using the above formula and making the necessary adjustments, was determined as follows:

$$\frac{8.1 \times 1.15}{r} \left(1 - \frac{1}{(1+r)^{50}}\right) \times 1.3 \times 1.55 = 240.63 \text{ yuan per square metre}$$

The land value of the site was $241 \times 468\,180 = 112\,831\,380$ yuan.

Thus the Chinese valuer employed the BMP to calculate the unit land price and made adjustments in accordance with the regulations and locational and other factors to arrive at a land value of about $112\,800\,000$ yuan. The Hong Kong valuer, on the other hand, used the direct comparison method to work out the land value. Based on the 'compare like with like' principle, four comparables were selected for adjustment. The adjusted unit land price was then multiplied by the site area, giving a valuation of $116\,100\,000$ yuan. Both valuation figures were submitted to the State Assets Administration Bureau, and eventually the SAAB accepted the valuation prepared by the Hong Kong valuer.

CONCLUSIONS

The introduction of urban land valuation has provided state enterprises with the oppurtunity to become financially more efficient as their land assets can now be transferred into share capital, and in some cases the substantial land assets of state enterprises have attracted foreign joint-venture investors. However, continued success in this area depends on the establishment of a proper system that reflects the true value of urban land. This is not easily achieved in an emerging economy as an active market is needed before a proper appraisal system can be set in place. The guideline appraisal system set up in some Chinese cities has provided a short-term solution in that it has allowed a land market to be developed quickly; too quickly in fact for the BMP pricing information to be kept up to date.

Urban land reform in China is a bold experiment as it has to work within the prevailing socialist ideology and the Chinese people's resistance to change is more than just lip service. Notable changes have taken place not only in the urban land market, but also in the other sectors of the economy. Since urban land is both an asset and factor of production, the multiplier effects of releasing the latent value of urban land have been substantial.

However, as with other major reforms, problems have arisen during the learning process. One problem is establishing a proper balance between the old and new systems. As China is not completely abandoning its socialist system, the privatisation programme is strongly influenced by socialist principles. This is reflected in land pricing behaviour, and as Li (1996a) shows, the cost approach has dominated pricing behaviour in Shanghai. The determination of the official benchmarking pricing model described above shows the influence of cost approach and the 'component structure' (Li, 1996b) when determining market prices of LURs under the privatisation programme.

A further problem is the different pace at which the various sectors are pursuing privatisation. This can be seen in the revenue earned from the real estate market since the start of privatisation. Revenues from the sale of commodity housing have increased substantially over the entire period while revenues from land transfers only started to increase after 1992. In particular, revenues from rented real estate have remained very low throughout. This is mainly due to widespread sensitivity to the need to provide low-cost housing in the socialist economic system. If the market mechanism is to work in the rented housing market, the entire system will have to be overhauled. However, wages and rents in socialist economies have always been treated with great care due to their social implications, which will have to be considered if rented housing is to be privatised.[2]

Problems can also be observed in the legal system with respect to privatisation. The 1995 Real Estate Law was enacted with the hope of consolidating all existing legislation in the real estate market and providing guidance for policy makers. However there are some legal grey areas, such as:

- The overlapping of functions between administrative departments at both central and local level.
- The relative inexperience of the legal system, especially with regard to land tenure.
- The coexistence of state land and collectively owned land. Most collective land is used for agricultural purposes and there is no real estate market in rural areas. The Real Estate Law does not make specific reference to the administration of collectively owned land, other

than stating that LURs for collectively owned land must first be requisitioned in accordance with the law and turned into state land before it can be granted to others by the local authority.

In the old land use system, all land was transferred administratively. This created a situation where some users obtained their land free of charge but the land had limited transfer value, while other users purchased their land with a certain set of rights attached. If a real market is to be developed a single supply mechanism must be created, that is, the price mechanism.

In the course of relocating individuals and enterprises occupying privatasied land a few negative factors have emerged that must not be overlooked. Relocation has gone ahead with little publicity and this lack of 'transparency' has allowed avoidable contradictions and problems to recur. To eliminate the problems that arise during relocation it is important to protect the legitimate rights and interests of those who are relocated. It is vital for the government to promote fairness and present a clean and honest image. To prevent the possibility of corruption the relocation of residents should be handled by the government, not by real estate development companies, some of which have pocketed the compensation money that should have been given to the former to residents.

5 Urban Land Reform in Shanghai: the Socialist Experience of a Capitalist Land System

HISTORY OF THE SHANGHAI LAND MARKET

Land markets or rather the so-called 'leased boundaries', started to develop in Shanghai after 1914 when foreign powers began to establish a sphere of influence in the city. To a certain extent this foreign involvement in the land market changed the architectural face of what is today the central business district.

The rising urban land values in Shanghai from 1865 to the presocialist era are shown in Table 5.1. As we can see, the price of land rose 25 fold

Table 5.1 Changes in urban land prices, Shanghai, 1865–1933

	Total area valued (mu)*	Unit price (taels of silver per mu)	Accumulative growth rate (%)
1865	4 310	1 318	—
1875	4 725	1 459	110
1903	13 126	4 603	249
1907	15 643	9 656	633
1911	17 094	8 281	528
1916	18 451	8 819	569
1920	19 461	10 476	695
1922	20 038	12 102	818
1924	20 776	16 207	1130
1927	21 441	18 652	1315
1930	22 131	26 909	1942
1933	22 330	33 877	2470

*A mu is an old Chinese measurement unit: one mu is approximately equal to 43 560 square feet.
Source: Z. Pu, (1990) 'Shanghai Real Estate Market before Liberation', in *Essential Economic Situation* (Shanghai City Planning Commission, 20 August 1990) (in Chinese).

Table 5.2   Total foreign investment in Shanghai by 1995

	Number of contracts signed	Agreed investment (US$10 000)	Actual investment (US$10 000)
Australia	200	5.36	0.58
Hong Kong	5950	169.84	56.12
Taiwan	1923	17.84	5.74
Japan	1640	32.64	9.83
Korea	93	4.29	0.40
Singapore	500	19.06	2.74
USA	1686	31.15	16.77
Canada	270	4.48	1.35
UK	203	17.31	3.00
Germany	130	8.53	3.04
France	67	1.06	0.94

Source: *Shanghai Real Estate Market 1996* (Shanghai: China Statistical Bureau).

over the period, with the highest increases taking place in the final 20 years.

For the first 30 years of the socialist economic system there was no economic growth in Shaghai. Land was confiscated by the state and both foreign and local firms fled, mostly to Hong Kong. As land ceased to have a value because none was allowed to be sold, the real estate market foudered. Nevertheless, economically Shanghai remained the most important city in the socialist regime.

The miraculous recovery of the Shanghai economy started with the national economic reforms. During the first half of 1994 Shanghai exported US$3.7 billion worth of products. This represented an annual increase of 28.5 per cent and its total foreign trade reached US$4.1 billion, an increase of 24.5 per cent. This rapid growth led to increased incomes among both urban and rural citizens and hence to higher savings and rising living standards. Per capita GDP in Shanghai was 3.4 times the national average in 1993, and the growth rates were 15 per cent, 24 per cent and 42 per cent in real terms in 1991, 1992 and 1993 respectively. The attractiveness of Shanghai to foreign investors can be observed in Table 5.2.

URBAN LAND REFORM IN SHANGHAI

The participation of Shanghai in the overall reform of land use rights (LURs) started in December 1985 when a pilot study on land values was carried out by the Shanghai Urban Economics Society, sponsored by the Shanghai City Planned Economy Research Institute (Li, 1995). The researchers looked at a sample of 1161 enterprises in the major commercial zones (including general retailing, hardware, cigarettes, confectionary, clothing, trading and so on), and based on these enterprise' profits between 1982 and 1984 an average profit of 12 per cent was calculated. The differential profit was then regressed as:

$$Rn = 254.68 * (1 + 0.435)n - 254.68$$

Where $n =$ the grade of the land zone.

The study area was then divided into seven zones, zone R7 being the most profitable location. From the above, the differential land profit of each zone became:

- R7 = 2936.55 yuan/sq. m
- R6 = 1969.17 yuan/sq. m
- R5 = 1295.04 yuan/sq. m
- R4 = 825.27 yuan/sq. m.
- R3 = 497.7 yuan/sq. m
- R2 = 269.76 yuan/sq. m
- R1 = 110.79 yuan/sq. m

This study provided the benchmark for subsequent research on land values in China (Li, 1997a).

The Current Land Market in Shanghai

Despite this early interest in the LUR reform (which actually started much sooner than the amendment of the constitution in 1987), it was not until 1992, when Deng Xiaoping stressed that reform must continue in China, that Shanghai became a major hot spot for land development. Before 1992 the urban land use distribution had been rather haphazard. This was reflected in the local government's preference for the sale of LURs in urban and suburban areas (Li, 1997c).

From 1988 to 1996 over 600 pieces of land (or land leases) were sold for various uses. While most of the land sold in the earlier years was designated for residential and mixed use (that is, high-class residences and offices), the amount of land granted for industrial use, especially in the counties (*xians*), increased substantially when the oversupply of offices became evident.[1] This reflects a gradual learning curve on the part of the local government in terms of overall land policy.

Table 5.3 shows the importance of analysing the actual supply of floor space for various uses instead of land areas only. Although the land sold for mixed development was less than that sold for residential use, the actual supply of developed properties in this category was much higher. This prompted the reorganisation of the planning department in Shanghai. In 1995 the new Planning Commission was formed to take care of all planning issues (this refers to land use rather than economic planning, as traditionally interpreted in China). The Planning Commission now parallels the Construction Commission, the traditional supreme local government body in charge of all land, housing and construction issues.

The rise of the Shanghai real estate market in the wake of the urban land reform has not only brought in substantial revenue for the local government, but has also led to a change in the city landscape and improved living conditions. Table 5.3 shows that the amount of slum housing has reduced quite significantly due to the increase in government income and the greater availability of decent housing. In fact the improvement of living conditions has been at the top of the agenda and the Shanghai government has even cooperated with real estate developers to clear slum areas. In return the developers have been promised development rights over the cleared sites. A similar situation has been happening with regard to old residential blocks.

In all urban districts there has been a substantial increase in office floor space, and between 1991 and 1996 the amount almost doubled. This reflects developers' interest in this major city. However it is clear that some districts are more favoured by developers than others. For instance office floor space in Changning district, which is in the middle of Shanghai, more than doubled in the period 1991–96 while in Yangpu district there was only a slight increase. The fact that there was only a small increase in office floor space in Huangpu district, the traditional business district of Shanghai, was mainly due to the existence of preservation orders on old buildings with architectural value along the Huangpu River.

The redesignation of land use in some districts has gone some way towards alleviating the unreasonably high concentration of industry in the city centre. For example, the amount of industrial floor space in Huangpu district was reduced more than eight-fold between 1991 and 1996 (Table 5.3). The interesting aspect of this is that the contraction of industrial floor space in Huangpu has not been matched by corresponding increase in other districts. This implies that the high concentration of industrial land in the city centre was due to the inefficient allocation of land (Li, 1996a).

Table 5.4 allows us to look further at the overall changes in the built-up areas of Shanghai. First of all, the proportion of residential floor space

Table 5.3 Changes in the distribution of various types of building in urban Shanghai, 1991–97 (10 000 sq. m)

	Slum housing					Old residential blocks					Office buildings					Retail shops					Factories				
	1991	1993	1995	1996	1997	1991	1993	1995	1996	1997	1991	1993	1995	1996	1997	1991	1993	1995	1996	1997	1991	1993	1995	1996	1997
All urban districts	119	100	84	6.3	57	923	901	798	790	749	650	766	955	1127	1491	419	485	562	656	755	4878	5489	5573	5513	5566
Huangpu	11	0	0	0	0	211	200	155	148	146	139	122	132	145	148	83	63	58	65	66	174	33	22	20	19
Nanshi	14	12	9	7	7	109	106	98	100	75	23	15	18	35	56	38	20	24	28	30	315	123	114	131	107
Luwan	6	4	3	2	2	126	120	111	111	108	32	42	47	53	88	26	28	40	40	50	216	199	202	202	205
Xuhui	7	6	6	3	1	22	23	22	22	22	106	100	130	137	160	28	29	48	48	42	471	473	493	492	296
Jingan	6	4	3	1	0	126	125	104	93	88	50	53	56	55	96	27	28	28	26	38	204	203	178	171	168
Putuo	11	9	8	8	8	13	10	9	8	8	66	67	77	92	105	38	39	46	50	66	458	462	450	450	443
Changning	4	3	2	3	2	4	4	2	2	2	50	60	69	119	163	32	33	36	44	48	321	333	337	338	322
Hongkou	19	16	13	11	11	176	169	160	159	155	67	68	72	90	97	34	38	43	57	66	383	388	394	392	393
Yangpu	37	29	24	22	20	53	53	51	56	55	33	31	36	39	45	44	42	47	48	48	1054	992	1004	1006	1000
Zhabei	4	3	1	1	0	82	81	80	79	78	36	35	54	73	77	27	29	32	42	52	426	430	443	450	449
Pudong	–	–	15	4	4	–	5	3	–	10	–	55	102	95	213	–	53	53	48	48	–	561	552	424	424

Table 5.4   Changes in urban buildings by type, 1980–97 (10 000 sq. m)

	1980	1990	1994	1995	1996	1997
Housing						
Detached houses	134	158	174	179	188	185
Apartments	92	118	110	111	119	151
Staff quarters	1402	4 884	7 006	7 998	9 420	11 622
Improved housing blocks	434	474	463	454	447	448
Old housing blocks	1822	3 067	3 131	3 004	2 823	2 582
Slum housing	437	123	90	85	63	57
Rebuilt from non-dwellings	82	77	75	75	75	71
Subtotal: housing	4403	8 901	11 049	11 906	13 135	15 116
Non-housing						
Factory buildings	2646	4 822	5 511	5 573	5 513	5 566
Office buildings	336	599	813	955	1 127	1 491
Retail shops	243	403	515	562	656	755
Warehouses	365	472	561	574	585	591
Hotels	54	237	271	280	288	296
Public buildings	647	1 130	1 379	1 406	1 391	1403
Places of entertainment	22	34	42	41	40	40
Others	418	658	760	797	858	890
Subtotal: non-housing	4731	8 355	9 852	10 188	10 458	11 032
Total	9134	17 256	20 901	22 094	23 593	26 148

Source: *Shanghai Statistical Yearbook* (1992, 1993, 1994, 1995, 1996, 1997, 1998).

increased from 48.2 per cent to 55.7 per cent between 1980 and 1996. Of this, staff quarters represented the largest jump in floor space – a 6.7-fold increase. This reflects the obligation of state enterprises to provide housing for their employees and the reliance of most citizens on the public provision of housing, although since the commercialisation of the housing market a large number of enterprises have purchased large residential blocks instead of building the quarters themselves, as was customary in the past. Slum housing represented the largest contraction in this period – a 700 per cent drop in terms of the entire built-up area. Finally, the total floor area for detached houses and apartments remained fairly constant over the years, reflecting the lack of demand for this high end of the housing market due to the welfare housing system.

Table 5.5   Changes in high-rise development, 1991–97

	Buildings of more than 8 floors (10 000 sq. m) & (no. of buildings)					Buildings of more than 30 floors (10 000 sq. m) & (no. of buildings)				
	1991	1993	1995	1996	1997	1991	1993	1995	1996	1997
All urban	1081.1	1478.6	2029	2740	3719	101.4	126.8	231	312	446
districts	(862)	(1171)	(1484)	(1904)	(2437)	(18)	(27)	(53)	(72)	(105)
Huangpu	147.1	103.9	142	162	170	3	7.2	10	17	17
	(119)	(80)	(99)	(103)	(107)	(1)	(2)	(3)	(4)	(4)
Nanshi	37.4	32.2	69	103	146	–	3.6	24	27	27
	(35)	(30)	(52)	(84)	(102)		(2)	(12)	(14)	(14)
Luwan	59.8	80.4	129	173	237	11.2	13.7	57	56	84
	(36)	(47)	(56)	(72)	(97)	(2)	(3)	(8)	(8)	(16)
Xuhui	192	248.3	317	418	619	5.9	9.4	9	11	24
	(168)	(207)	(252)	(322)	(429)	(2)	(4)	(4)	(5)	(9)
Jingan	87.7	106.4	136	197	263	35.4	35.4	45	62	77
	(44)	(58)	(75)	(112)	(149)	(4)	(4)	(8)	(14)	(16)
Putuo	100.3	129.5	152	220	380	10.5	15.2	15	15	38
	(88)	(110)	(129)	(182)	(279)	(2)	(3)	(3)	(3)	(10)
Changning	126.7	189.1	231	341	429	26.1	32.8	43	63	75
	(88)	(132)	(152)	(192)	(246)	(4)	(6)	(8)	(12)	(15)
Hongkou	133.6	187.8	233	283	319	4.8	4.8	10	16	16
	(109)	(157)	(181)	(207)	(222)	(1)	(1)	(2)	(3)	(3)
Yangpu	80.5	121.2	152	223	284	4.7	4.7	4.7	12	22
	(59)	(99)	(124)	(172)	(204)	(2)	(2)	(2)	(3)	(6)
Zhabei	70.1	102.4	144	198	238	–	–	4	18	18
	(63)	(78)	(104)	(140)	(166)			(1)	(3)	(3)
Pudong	–	113.1	231	306	439	–	–	9	15	45
		(98)	(163)	(204)	(257)			(2)	(3)	(8)

Source: *Shanghai Statistical Yearbook* (1992, 1993, 1994, 1995, 1996, 1997, 1998).

During this period Shanghai also witnessed a large increase in the number of high-rise buildings (Table 5.5). On average the number of high-rise buildings increased four-fold between 1991 and 1996 and three-fold in terms of total floor area. In some districts the increase was even higher. This reflects the rising land values in the city centre and the consequent maximisation of land-use efficiency.

Figure 5.1 shows that the land reform is expanding into the urban fringes of Shanghai after four years of expansion of the urban market. In 1996 only 19 per cent of the land sold was urban, the majority being sold in the *xian* districts (suburban counties). Nowadays, in most of the *xians* in China there is considerable industrial activity, and most of the Shanghai land sold in 1996 was for industrial use. This accords with the earlier analysis of changes in floor space usage, where it was shown that industrial floor space has diminished in the core urban districts over the years. The relocation of industry to suburban areas is a much more rational approach to land use. Figure 5.2 shows the original nature of the land sold in 1996.

Development Procedures

The Shanghai land market is one of the most flexible markets in China. In mid 1991 there were about 94 development companies in Shanghai, with an average residential property output of one million square metres a year. Now there are more than 3000 such companies, of which about 400 are foreign or joint venture companies. In 1996 a total of 60 billion yuan was invested in the real estate market by local and overseas developers/investors.

Overseas developers are required to apply to the Commerce and Industry Administration Bureau for a business licence, and must have capital of US$500 000 unless they intend to concentrate on property management

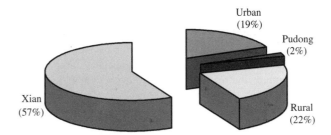

Figure 5.1   Distribution of land area sold, 1996

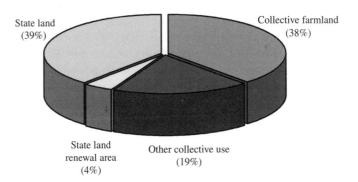

Figure 5.2   Original nature of the land sold in 1996

alone. Once developers have obtained their licence they have to liaise with the Shanghai Housing and Land Administration Bureau (SHLAB) with regard to site availability and land grant conditions, unless they are seeking a joint venture with a sitting tenant of a site. Developers also have liaize with the Planning Department (now directly under the newly formed Shanghai Urban Planning Bureau) with regard to layout, design and plot ratio. Once their plans are approved the developers require presale permission from the SHLAB.

The city government has just completed the first phase of the demolition of old and dangerous housing. Currently 1.6 million square metres of such housing is waiting to be demolished, and once this is done some of the cleared sites will be put to green belt purposes. The remainder will be available for real estate development. Developers can sign an advance contract with the government for particular sites, which are then reserved for future development by them. In return the developers have to pay some of the demolition and resettlement costs. With regard to the latter, developers often employ the services of specialised companies to resettle sitting tenants.

In order to encourage overseas developers to participate in the renewal process the city government is offering them preferential treatment. This includes a guaranteed 15 per cent return on projects, larger plots and exemption from various administration fees, such as the infrastructure fee (270 yuan a square metre) and the air-raid protection fee (100 yuan a square metre).

URBAN PLANNING IN SHANGHAI

The Shanghai Urban Planning Management Bureau (SUPMB) is responsible for urban planning in the macro level throughout Shanghai. All counties and districts authorities have their rights and responsibilities to implement local plans. The Shanghai city government has made public the process of planning application and related planning issues, construction proposals and the licensing of construction engineering planning and supervision of works. This has increased transparency in the urban planning system, which in turn has increased market efficiency.

Criteria for Site Selection and Development Projects

According to Article 30 of the Urban Planning Law of the PRC and Section 24 of the Urban Planning Regulations of Shanghai, site selection and the design of development and construction projects must comply with particular urban planning criteria. Developers must submit a 'Site Selection Proposal for Development Projects' (SSPDP) for the following types of development:

1. New projects and resettlement projects.
2. Extension of the current land use on an established site (including resettlement).
3. Change of land use on the existing site.

Applicants should also submit the following documents:

1. Application form and the relevant site plans.
2. Environmental impact assessment report, where necessary.
3. Legal documents proving ownership of the land and property.

There is a performance pledge that the approval process will be completed within 40 days from the date of submission.

Planning Permit for Construction Land (PPCL)

According to Article 31 of the Urban Planning Law and Section 24 of the Urban Planning Regulations of Shanghai, where construction and development activities require use of land, the applicant must have possessed the relevant approval documents for the construction activites. The applicant should then apply to the urban planning department for the PPCL in addition to the permission to use the land, the delineation of the boundary of the site, design criteria of the project. Upon possessing the PPCL, the applicant can then apply to the local government at or above county level for the actual use of the land.

In addition, according to Article 39 of the Urban Planning Law, if an applicant fails to obtain a PPCL the land shall be returned to the local government and the approval document becomes void. The purpose of the PPCL is therefore to ensure that land use complies with the urban planning criteria and to protect those construction units that do comply with the legal requirements. PPCLs are required for the following:

1. New development projects and resettlement projects.
2. Extension of the current land use (including resettlement).
3. Change of land use.
4. Temporary use of land due to development, land exchange or other purposes.
5. Construction projects on granted or transferred state land.

Planning Permit for Construction Projects (PPCPs)

Under Article 32 of the Urban Planning Law and Section 32 of the Urban Planning Regulations of Shanghai, PPCPs should be obtained from the urban planning department for new development projects, the extension of existing buildings and the redevelopment of existing buildings, as well as for roads, pipelines and other engineering works. Once the PPCP has been obtained the construction works can commence. The purpose of PPCPs is to protect the legal status of construction units and the relevant activities. PPCPs are required for the following:

1. New development projects and resettlement projects.
2. Preservation of buildings of historical interest or architectural worth.
3. When structural changes are needed in order to reinforce the load-bearing capacity.
4. Construction of statues in city squares.

Supervision of Urban Planning Requirements

According to the Urban Planning Law of the PRC, the city urban planning departments are required to monitor adherence to the urban planning requirements. In the case of major construction projects, the urban planning departments are also involved in approving completed projects. The main supervisory activities of the Shanghai Urban Planning Department are as follows:

1. Assessing illegal use of land and construction activities.
2. Ensuring the validity and checking details of the PPCL.
3. Ensuring the validity of the PPCP and adherence to the planning requirements.
4. Assessing the planning criteria for built-up areas and conservation areas.
5. Monitoring construction projects.
6. Approving construction projects.
7. Examining the proposed use of buildings and structures.

Since the urban land reform is government-led, the authority's directives exert a certain degree of influence over the market. One such directive – the Directive on Developing the Secondary Real Estate Market in Shanghai, 1996, jointly issued by the SHLAB, the Shanghai Police Department, the Shanghai City Finance Office, the Shanghai City Inland Revenue Department and the Shanghai City Housing Reform Office – was aimed at revitalising the secondary real estate market. First, in the past commodity housing could only be bought by registered Shanghai citizens, but after August 1996 the right to buy was extended to state enterprises, administrative units, all citizens with valid identity papers, Chinese nationals working or studying abroad, and registered joint venture companies that wished to purchase flats for their employees. Second, the transaction taxes were lowered.

Third, the rented housing sector was restructured by introducing a registration system for leaseholds, and all leasing agreements had to be registered with the local SHLAB offices. The parties in question were then issued with a Housing Lease Registration Certificate and enjoyed undisputed landlord and tenant rights. In addition the taxation on rental income was simplified to 21 per cent tax on income in excess of 2000 yuan and 21 per cent on income of less than 2000 yuan.

To coordinate with the private rental market the rents on public sector properties were adjusted. This applied both to domestic and to non-domestic properties. The tenants of most public housing units faced a 50 per cent rent increase after September 1996, but concessions were granted when the new rent accounted for more than 7 per cent of the household's average monthly income. For non-domestic public sector buildings, the rent increase ranged from 75 per cent to 150 per cent, depending on the location of the building.

The directive also included measures to control the activities of real estate developers and agents and improve construction quality; the establishment of a Real Estate Transaction Centre, which acts as a central listing centre for real estate transactions and a source of market information; and the expansion of mortgage financing.

LEGAL DEVELOPMENTS WITH REGARD TO LAND USE RIGHTS

The legal framework for the introduction of urban land reform in Shanghai was established in 1987 with the promulgation of the Regulations on the Transfer of Land Use Rights with Monetary Compensation (the 1987 regulations). This provided the legal basis for the city government to begin to commercialise LURs for urban land and establish a market system for urban land based on the price mechanism. (In fact this activity started in 1991 under the Provisional Regulations on the Conveyance, Granting and Transferring of the State Land's Use Rights in Cities and Towns 1991 – the 1987 regulations merely legalised the transfer of urban LURs for a limited term within the market system.) The 1987 regulations also covered the procedure for granting (by the city authorities to the land user) and transfer (among land users) of urban LURs, the mortgaging of LURs, the expiry of LURs and transfer tax. While there is a degree of similarity between the 1987 Shanghai regulations and the national regulations, the differences reflect the fact that, given China's vast size, the national legal framework can only be finalised when all the local requirements have been sorted out.

Since the urban land market also incorporates the housing market, the Shanghai authorities further developed the legal environment for the market transfer of built structures on urban land by issuing the 1988 Implementation Procedures for the Management of Market Transfer of Real Estate with the Urban Land Use Rights, which regulates the sale, preselling and leasing of real estate built on land where the LURs have been granted or transferred through the market channel.

Another set of regulations, the 1992 Regulations on the Management of Construction Land in Shanghai, mainly deals with infrastructural development on administratively allocated state land, collective land and requisitioned collective land. The regulations specify the situations in which the Shanghai authorities can requisition state or collective land, including land used for military purposes, to regenerate old districts or establish new development zones, for example that in Pudong. Regulations 27–34 lay down the criteria for compensating sitting tenants and outline the resettlement procedures.

The above provisions illustrate the efforts made by the Shanghai authorities to launch a system of property rights in line with the urban land reform. In 1995 the city government started to take steps to protect property rights and related legislation was incorporated into the 1995 Shanghai City Property Rights Registration Regulations. Since then all officially granted or administratively allocated LURs have had to be registered, as have properties (old and new) on transferred state land and non-agricultural collective land. In cases where LURs and/or property rights are not properly registered, no other rights relating to the real estate may be registered. This provides legal protection of ownership rights over urban land and built properties.

In addition, given China's dual-track land tenure system, it was essential for the Shanghai government to formulate a comprehensive set of regulations that would cover the transfer of real estate in all circumstances. Consequently the Regulations on the Transfer of Real Estate in Shanghai, 1997, were promulgated on 30 April 1997. These regulations are administered by the Shanghai Housing and Land Administration Bureau (SHLAB). Section six of the regulations includes the principle that, in most circumstances, real estate can be sold, exchanged, given as gift, mortgaged or used as share capital. Property rights are inheritable, and transferable upon the merger of companies.

Chapter two of the regulations sets out the rules for the transfer of real estate under different types of land ownership. Section 11 states that real estate built on state land that has been legally granted may be transferred when the LURs for that land are being transferred. Section 12 regulates the transfer of real estate on administratively allocated land. When real estate built on such land is transferred, the recepient must pay the city government an amount equivalent to the market value of the LURs, and when such compensation is not applicable, the sale proceeds from the transfer of the real estate belong to the state.

With regard to the transfer of real estate on collective land, section 13 states that the transfer must comply with the following conditions:

1. The ownership rights over the property and the LURs for the land upon which the property sits must have been properly registered and a certificate of property rights obtained.
2. The recipient of transferred residential real estate must be a qualified applicant for housing development in the relevant county or village. The recipient of non-domestic real estate must be a qualified collective economic unit or an individual business operator in the relevant county or village.
3. The transfer of residential real estate must be approved by the relevant county or village authority.

If the recipient does not conform to the provisions in (1) above, the land upon which the property sits has to be requisitioned and turned into state land before the transfer can go ahead.

The above two sets of regulations have provided the private sector housing market with a more comprehensive legal foundation. However a large proportion of the housing stock is in the public sector, especially the so-called 'employee' housing', which is provided to employees of state enterprises as part of a welfare package. The 1997 Regulations on the Exchange of Public Housing Units Purchased by State Enterprise Employees allow employees who have purchased their housing to exchange their properties for other privatised housing units. In those counties in Shanghai that have not yet formulated a market mechanism for the resale of privatised public housing units, this provides a way for the owners of such units to relocate for reasons of location or quality.

According to the 1997 regulations, when the exchange involves public housing units only, the sales price can be based on the price at which the owner purchased the property from the state enterprise or the market price of similar units. However, when the exchange involves a private housing unit the sales price must be based on the market price. In addition the owner of this unit must be in possession of the proper property ownership rights and there should be no ongoing dispute over the title. When conducting the exchange, the owner of the privatised state enterprise unit should apply to the local Real Estate Exchange Centre (REEC) in the relevant district or county. The two parties have to produce such documents as the ownership certificate and/or proof of purchase from the state enterprise. Upon receipt of REEC approval and endorsement by the SHLAB, the parties may exchange their ownership titles and household registration. When both properties are situated in the same district or county the exchange can be processed by the same REEC, but when they are situated in different counties or districts the exchange should be processed by the REEC in the county or district where the higher-priced unit is situated. An exchange contract is signed when all legal requirements have been satisfied.

When the exchange is based on the purchase price of the public housing unit, the exchange price registered in the exchange contract should be the same as the purchase price. When the exchange is based on the market price and the price registered in the exchange contract is substantially lower than the market price, the local REEC will insist on a qualified appraisal firm reappraising the exchange price. This is important as tax is involved. According to Regulation 9 of the regulations, all parties who exchange their properties for higher-priced units must pay the difference to the other party, plus 0.5 per cent of the difference to the REEC as an administration charge and 6 per cent of the difference as deed tax. The other party has to pay 5 per cent of the difference as integrated tax.

Because the land reform in China involves leasehold tenure rather than outright ownership the question of sensitive foreign ownership of land is less of a problem than elsewhere. The 1996 Regulations on the Management of Land Use by Foreign Investors and Enterprises in Shanghai apply only to foreign investors investing in enterprises situated on or planning to use state or collective land. Hence the normal granting of state land in the open market to foreign investors for real estate development is excluded from this set of regulations.

Under regulation 4 the Chinese partner in a joint Chinese–foreign venture can use his LURs as share capital in the venture, even if the land in question is administratively allocated state land or requisitioned collective land. Furthermore, when a foreign investor purchases a state enterprise the LURs are transferred to the investor. In this way foreign investors can participate in the urban land market without going through the LUR granting system. This is an efficient way of attracting foreign investment in urban renewal, which is an important resource in most emerging economies. However some investors seek to purchase state enterprises simply in order to gain possession of the land. This kind of asset stripping is not desirable so the state is trying to encourage joint ventures rather than purchases. Joint ventures also help rescue inefficient state enterprises as new technology is often introduced by the foreign partner.

THE REJUVENATION OF OLD SHANGHAI

Most of the buildings in the central districts of Shanghai (for example Huangpu, Nanshi, Huwan and Jingan) were built between the beginning of the century and the 1930s. Many of these are structurally simple, sometimes crude or even unsafe. There are also a large number of shack dwellings with very poor sanitary facilities. In 1993 these old structures accounted for more than 40 per cent of total residential housing (Table 5.6).

The living conditions and environment in these central districts are poor and the population density is more than twice the national average. On average, nearly 60 000 people inhabit each street, and in extreme cases there may be more than 100 000 inhabitants. The per capita living area is therefore unacceptably low (Table 5.7), much less than the national minimum desirable standard of 16 square metres. This means that the need to restructure the old central area is more urgent than in other cities.

According to statistics compiled by the Municipal Construction Committee, unsafe buildings, shack dwellings and other crude dwellings covered an area of close to 3 650 000 square metres in 1991. Added to this was substandard older housing amounting to approximately 15 000 000 square metres. The extent and laborious nature of the reconstruction task

Table 5.6   Residential space in four central districts of Shanghai, 1993

District	Total residential floor area (10 000 sq. m)	Total old residential floor area (10 000 sq. m)	% of total residential area occupied by old housing
Huangpu	770	352	45.71
Jingan	510	205	40.20
Huwan	453	193	42.60
Nanshi	950	401	42.21

Source: *Shanghai Land*, Issue 4, 1993, p. 10.

Table 5.7   Living conditions in urban Shanghai

District	Area (sq. km)	Total population (10 000)	Population density (10 000/sq. km)	Dwellings per sq. km	Per capita living area (sq. m.)
Huangpu	4.54	24.88	5.48	1.52	6.11
Nanshi	7.87	53.13	6.75	2.99	5.63
Huwan	8.05	42.87	5.33	2.63	6.13
Jingan	7.62	44.15	5.79	3.39	7.68
Average	28.08	165.03	5.88	10.53	6.38

prove to be an onerous responsibility for the authorities (there are ten urban districts and other county authorities, in addition to the various Pudong local district authorities in Shanghai).

In the last few decades the municipal government has devoted a great deal of attention to urban renewal in an attempt to improve the living conditions of the residents. Between the 1960s and the 1980s the districts of Fan Gua Lane, Yuan Ming village, Cao Xi North Road and other areas underwent extensive renewal and rebuilding. Later the authorities drew up plans for the 23 slum areas and began to raise funds for the regeneration process. Yao Shui Alley in Putuo District, Shi Min Village in Xuhui District, Xi Ling Jia Zhai in Nanshi District and Jiu Geng Li in Hongkou District were just some of the older areas that became subject to urban renewal.

In a twelve-year period (1979–90) a total of 4 000 000 square metres of dangerous shack dwellings and substandard houses were torn down across the city. On average 330 000 square metres were cleared each year and 10 000 households were relocated. This led to a comparative improvement in the living conditions of a large number of people and the quality of the environment was improved enormously. However, due to the extent of the overcrowding a substantial number of residents had to be relocated and the alternative housing was usually of a low standard. This, combined with resistance from sitting tenants to the renewal process, made it very difficult to raise money locally to fund the renewal and private real estate development companies showed interest in participating in the project.

This problem persists and requires a prompt solution if Shanghai's urban inhabitants are to benefit from the economic prosperity of the city. As the urban land reform system becomes more complex, LURs will be treated as a market commodity and the revenue from LURs can be used to finance the construction of public facilities and housing, and the further renovation of old districts. The treatment of land as a commodity will provide impetus to the urban renewal process and the development of new residential areas. In addition the urban land market created by the reform will provide the means to accelerate the replacement of dangerous shack dwellings with new housing.

Between January 1992 and December 1994, 2 289 500 square metres of housing were torn down across Shanghai and the areas cleared were converted into leasehold land for other uses. Of this cleared area, shack dwellings had occupied 1 088 600 square metres or 47.55 per cent. The aim is to complete the urban renewal programme by the end of the year 2000, and already 29.8 per cent of the target has been reached. The destruction of dangerous old dwellings is said to be proceeding at the rate of approximately 10 per cent. One example of the use of the leasehold land tenure system to accelerate urban renewal in the old districts is that of Xie San Ji Di in Luwan district. Xie San Ji Di, which is about 19 790 square metres in area, comprised a few factories intermingled with the residential accommodation, with shack dwellings accounting for 80 per cent of all structures and covering 26 000 square metres of floor area. There were about 1060 households and 16 factories, which was fairly typical of the old districts of Shanghai. The district authorities were keen to start the restructuring process but were handicapped by insufficient funding.

Then on 25 January 1992 a Hong Kong real estate development company paid $US23 000 000 in conveyance fees for LURs in Xie San Ji Di in order to construct four 31-storey residential blocks, to be sold to foreigners (mainly from Hong Kong and Taiwan). The Luwan district authorities used the proceeds from the sale of this leasehold interest to resettle former residents and companies in a more desirable location with adequate facilities. Thus the residents' and companies' circumstances substantially improved. The experience of Luwan district provided inspiration for other districts, and soon afterwards all district authorities pledged their support for the leasehold system and urban renewal in the interests of the local economy and environment.

Also in 1992, nearly one hundred leasehold plots were offered for sale in the Puxi area. Sixty per cent of this land was occupied by unsafe dwellings, or 715 400 square metres of the total area of 1 251 600 square metres. When cleared, some of the land was given over to comprehensive urban developments such as the Everbright City programme in Zha Bei district, a private development funded mainly by a Hong Kong/Malaysian company. The project involved about 6.35 hectares of leasehold land and 107 400 square metres of housing were demolished, of which slum dwellings accounted for 67 500 square metres, or 62.85 per cent. Huangpu,

Nanshi, Xuhui, Yangpu, Jingan and Hongkou districts subsequently promoted similar development projects due to the following findings:

1. The use of foreign capital for regeneration projects sparked new rounds
   of urban renewal in the old districts. This was a self-perpetuating
   process as private investment, especially from outside the country,
   increased when the investment environment became positive as a result
   of the success of the initial foreign investment.
2. Relocation made it possible for the former occupiers of substandard
   housing to achieve a better standard of living at a cost the local authorities could bear.
3. Relocation also enabled the restructuring of land use. In the past, most
   of the central area had been occupied by industrial enterprises, and the
   relocation of factories outside the residential areas freed the land for
   more appropriate uses.
4. Foreign investors tended to favour mixed development that was well-
   planned in terms of layout, facilities and design. Thus foreign investment would enable Shanghai to take on a smarter appearance.

Notwithstanding these benefits, many problems and difficulties have arisen
during the process of urban regeneration. In recent years the scale of urban
renewal has grown ever larger, and with it the number of people who cannot be rehoused in the original area and have to be relocated elsewhere. For
example in 1993 and 1994 some 213 400 households had to be relocated,
and as each family was deemed to need 60 square metres of living space,
the housing requirement for these years alone amounted to more than
12 800 000 square metres. The current annual state production of housing
stock in Shanghai is about 7–8 million square metres, but after deducting
that allocated to accomodation for employees and new suburban housing
the supply available for relocation purposes amounts to less than one third
of the requirement. Hence the relocation rate is not very satisfactory – less
than 30 per cent in the higher-income districts and about 10 per cent in
the low-income districts. In some districts temporary accommodations had
to be provided for some 80 000 households.

For private investors, rate of return is the main consideration, and consequently, only prime locations are selected for development, usually at
the highend of the property market for rich purchasers from China and
abroad.

A look at the statistics reveals that the rate of demolition of dangerous shack dwellings on leasehold plots fluctuates widely. In 1992 this
accounted for 57.15 per cent of total housing demolition. In 1993 the
proportion dropped to 23 per cent, and from January to May 1994 it rose

to 54 per cent. The private housing provision of 3 000 000 square metres was scattered across the city, mainly in the Pudong, Changning, Zhabei and Baoshan districts, where the services to housing ratio was highly inadequate. In some cases only 13–15 per cent of the land area was devoted to the provision of facilities, which led to further problems for the relocation and urban renewal programme in terms of schools, childcare, hospitals, shopping facilities and traffic problems.

Property Rights

The ongoing macroeconomic reform in China created a class of private property users for commercial purposes. Most retail and commercial property users preferred to conduct their business in the old districts where the population was densest. Resettling this group of occupiers proved problematical as they required more than just the usual compensation. This matter was addressed in the 1997 Compensation Regulations on the Resettlement of Individual Commercial Occupiers of Properties in Shanghai, which are modelled on the national Resettlement of Urban Properties Ordinance, with local elements added. According to the regulations, commercial users of fixed property must be compensated when resettlement becomes necessary as a result of infrastructural and other development. Regulation 3 lays down four basic resettlement rules:

1. When a user occupies a street-level property for his trade, a similar street-level or a suitable non-street-level property should be found for him.
2. When a user occupies a non-street-level property for his trade, a similar non-street-level property must be provided.
3. If the above two provisions cannot be fulfilled, the resettlement agent should seek approval from the relevant district or county authority to construct a commercial centre and use surplus housing of similar size for resettlement.
4. If necessary a lump-sum cash compensation may be paid to the occupier as a housing gratuity payment and he will be relocated to another property of similar size.

In the case of clause (3) above, the resettlement agent must sign a contract with the relevant local authority and pay the local authority 30–50 000 yuan per household relocated. This sum will be used to develop a central commercial centre for the resettled occupiers.

When there is domestic element to the original premises, the occupier can choose to have combined accomodation or separate domestic and commercial premises. In addition, when resettlement involves moving to a less desirable location the user is compensated by being allocated extra space, as shown in Table 5.8.

For example an individual commercial user who occupies a Grade 1 location and is resettled in a Grade 5 location receives an extra 40 per cent floor space as compensation. However this may not be adequate compensation for the loss of a prime trading location, so the 1997 compensation regulations provide extra compensation for temporary or permanent loss of business. For permanent loss of business, the occupier receives double the amount of his previous three years' business taxes.

Additional Problems

In the course of urban renewal, each district has been regarded as a single unit, thus indicating an apparent lack of overall planning. Furthermore some districts do not have an adequate stock of alternative housing and have to purchase commodity housing in order to relocate those being made homeless. Quite frequently the demolition of old buildings and the relocation of former residents are conducted in accordance with a timetable, with complete neglect of the suitability of the alternative housing arrangements.

Urban renewal, the demolition of old housing and the relocation of residents is supposed to be a government function, and to gain the people's confidence the district authorities should have devised a comprehensive plan for the appropriate relocation of residents. In particular, special attention should have been paid to those who were to be moved a considerable distance from their former neighbourhood. Instead, what has actually happened in some districts is that the work of relocation has been contracted out to private real estate development companies, so what should be the

Table 5.8 Extra space awarded as compensation, by grade

Grade of original location	Grade of new location and relevant compensation (%)					
	1	2	3	4	5	6
1	Nil	Nil	Nil	20	40	80
2	Nil	Nil	Nil	20	40	80
3	Nil	Nil	Nil	20	40	80
4	Nil	Nil	Nil	Nil	20	40
5	Nil	Nil	Nil	Nil	Nil	20

responsibility of the government has become the profit-seeking activity of development companies.

If a private developer is involved in the regeneration process the local authority requires the developer to pay the LUR charges and resettlement fee separately. The resettlement fee is then paid to a specialist resettlement company, which negotiates with the sitting tenants on details such as compensation and the timing of resettlement. Of course it is the interests of such companies to set the compensation as low as possible so as to increase their own profits. This has seriously damaged the government's image and created extreme discontent among a massive number of residents.

CONCLUSIONS

Throughout most of its modern history Shanghai has been the most energetic and forward-looking city in China. Whilst not a forerunner in the urban land reform, when it did get started the speed of take-off was very rapid.

The socialist bureaucratic structure at the heart of the new capitalist land system has manifested itself in certain requirements for a proper land management system. Nonetheless, one of the main reasons for the launch of the urban land reform was to boost state revenues, and this has been used to justify the privatisation of the LURs. A sound local economy will attract not only foreign investors, but also local investors from other cities and provinces. The more participants in the market, the larger the need for a proper market framework so that the players' interests can be protected.

For a market to continue to attract internal and international interest the government's policy on the land market should be as transparent as possible, but from the start of the boom market in 1991 in Shanghai the government has provided no clear indication of its future land sale plans or overall development programme. The consequence of this is that developers have forged ahead while the going is good, with a resulting oversupply of some types of property. The obvious example of this is the office sector. In the early 1990s there was an acute shortage of suitable offices for international companies, so when the land market began to develop, office floor space was the most attractive proposition for developers. Hence the provision of more information on policies and plans for development is vital, particularly as it is the government that is providing the land in China's leasehold system. Furthermore a well-informed market makes for a more stable market, which in the long term will produce the maximum possible land revenues for the local authorities.

Finally, the question of property rights tends to be overlooked in the process of urban land reform in transitional economies. Under the socialist system, sitting tenants were regarded as having common property rights as all land belonged to the state on behalf of the people and accomodation was guaranteed. The privatisation of urban land has severely disturbed this system and the problems of resettlement have been considerable. In this respect the government should take a much direct and active role in the redistribution of LURs so that a balance between social and economic interests can be struck.

6 The Urban Land Market in Hong Kong: the Capitalist Experience of a Socialist Land System

Hong Kong had been a British colony for more than 100 years when it was returned to China on 30 June 1997. Despite the fact that both private and public land ownership systems had coexisted in Britain for many years, one of the first tasks of the British administrators upon arrival in Hong Kong was to establish a crown land system. Despite this Hong Kong became one of the freest and most capitalist economic entities in the world with the least government intervention in the market. The land leasehold system created in Hong Kong brought in a substantial income for the government and enabled it to keep down taxes while maintaining tight control over planning and development. When the urban land reform in China first started Hong Kong acted as an important model for the reform officials, and Hong Kong's long-term leasehold system provided the perfect solution to Chinese reformists wishing to resolve the conflict between socialist ideology and market reform.

It is therefore interesting to look at the evolution of the land market in Hong Kong, particularly as the establishment of the new regional government in July 1997 heralded a move away from the colonial urban land policy towards greater government involvement in the market mechanism, which was not necessarily a desirable move. In the following section the changes in the urban land market system in Hong Kong will be discussed as the development trend in Hong Kong can provide invaluable lessons for mainland China. Likewise the way the urban land market on the mainland is evolving may have important implications for policy makers in Hong Kong when formulating their long-term land supply and control policies. Such policies and related actions in the early months of 1998 have recently been criticised as counterproductive to the market mechanism (a brief description of the current state of affairs will be given below).

The real estate market in Hong Kong is one of the most dynamic markets in the world. The annual volume of transactions has always been substantial and because of this property prices have tended to fluctuate, which

151

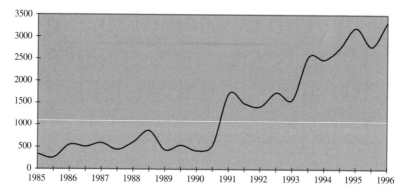

Figure 6.1   Land price trends in Hong Kong, 1985–97 (year-end figures)
Source: Wong Mau On, unpublished BSc dissertation, Department of Real Estate and Construction, University of Hong Kong, 1998.

has also led to fluctuating land prices. Between 1985 and 1997, land prices underwent many upturns and downturns (Figure 6.1).

Due to the pegged exchange rate system, interest rates in Hong Kong have largely followed the US trend, and when the inflation rate has exceeded the bank rate, which happened in the early 1990s, the purchase of properties had been the most efficient way for investors to hedge against inflation. It was under such circumstances that property prices rose substantially between 1991 and 1995, in some cases by more than 200 per cent. This huge increase resulted in government intervention, and in June 1994 the colonial government implemented a series of measures to curb property speculation. These measures included the tightening of mortgages, a shorter preselling period and punitive stamp duties. This had a temporary cooling effect on the market, but it did not last for long, as in 1995 the commercial banks cut their mortgage rates to attract more business. Property prices rose again, but at the end of 1997 the ever-booming property market came to a sudden halt.

In retrospect, it seems that the soaring property prices had more to do with the housing shortage than organised speculation, which was the convenient charge levelled by the politicians. The government's interventionalism, which was in direct contradiction to its free economy policy, did send out a warning signal to the overheated market, but due to the acute imbalance between supply and demand the price rise did not stop. This was especially so in the luxury sector, where prices began to accelerate in 1992/93 and reached nearly HK$18 000 (or US$2314) per square foot in 1996. This sector was particularly undersupplied as the Sino-British Joint Declaration and the Land Commission required the colonial government to release land for high-density development, that is, for the lower-to middle-class residential market.

It is interesting to note that when the government of the Hong Kong Special Administrative Region (SAR) came to power in July 1997 there were rumours that it would introduce severe measures to halt the rising property prices. In particular C.Y. Leung, the Executive Council member in charge of housing and land matters, publicly stated that various options were being considered, including capital gains tax. This had a cooling effect on the market as people were expecting a more intervenionist approach in land management. However, when the chief executive of the SAR made a speech in October 1997 on the government's long-term policies, much to everyone's surprise he made no mention of administrative measures to control the land and property market. There was only a goal to supply property units at the rate of 85 000 per year, although this goal was greeted with scepticism in the market. As a result, business went on as usual and property prices did not fall as expected. It was not until the financial crisis in the South-Eastern Asian countries that demand suddenly fell, and prices dropped by more than 30 per cent between November 1997 and June 1998.

The dramatic volatility of land and property prices in Hong Kong between 1996 and 1998 provided an interesting revelation. During the time of the colonial government land policy was very much its private domain, and all strategic questions such as the total area of land to be granted each year and the total floor area to be built were decided by the government. As a consequence most politicians blamed the government for the ever increasing land and property prices. However the signing in 1994 of the Sino-British Joint Declaration on the future of Hong Kong changed this environment, especially with the establishment of the Land Commission to supervise the sale of government land.

The establishment of the new state prompted a rethink of the role of the government. The image of Hong Kong being ruled by the people for the people was to be maintained so that public involvement in the market, especially the property market, would protect the welfare of ordinary citizens. However, as we shall see below, the balance between allowing the market to operate and flexing the 'invisible hand' of government is so delicate that the market as well as government staff may not be able to adjust. Before discussing this we shall examine the urban land system and land price policies under the colonial government.

THE URBAN LAND SYSTEM IN HONG KONG

Currently Hong Kong accommodates more than six million people in just 1095 square kilometres.[1] With a projected population of 8.1 million by the year 2011, the population density is almost the highest in the world. Therefore land policy and the allocation of this precious resource is both an economic and a political issue.

Only about 16 per cent (175 square kilometres) of Hong Kong's total land area is developed. Most of the built-up urban land was originally created by land reclamation, especially along the shores of Victoria Harbour. Since the end of the Second World War, Hong Kong has reclaimed 3600 hectares of land from the sea, almost the combined area of Kowloon and New Kowloon.[2] Housing accounts for 58 square kilometres or 33 per cent of the developed area (Figure 6.2). The government is the principal lease-holder of all the land and is responsible for the supply of land.

Evolution of the Colonial Leasehold System

At the very beginning of British rule in Hong Kong, there was no firm long-term land policy. Originally the British allowed the freehold sale of land, subject to government approval. However in 1843, when the Treaty of Nanking was ratified, the British changed their minds. In a the despatch from the Earl of Aberdeen to Sir Henry Pottinger[3] it was stated that 'Her Majesty's Government would ... caution you against the permanent

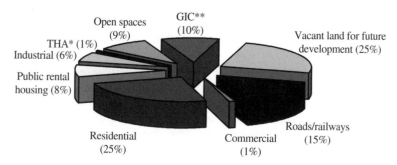

Figure 6.2   Distribution of developed land and development land in Hong Kong
*Temporary housing area for families on the waiting list for public housing. This is supposed to be a transitional arrangement but many families have lived there for more than 10 years.
**Government/institutional and community land use.
Source: Liu *et al.* (1997).

alienation of any portion of the land, and they would prefer that parties should hold land under leases from the Crown'.

On 1 July 1898 the British acquired a 99-year lease for the New Territories under the Second Treaty of Peking. Basically, the colonial government retained its freehold interest[4] over all the land in Hong Kong[5] under three unfair treaties. Instead of buying land outright, purchasers of land in Hong Kong could only obtain leases of set duration. Therefore when we speak of selling land in Hong Kong we are speaking of the sale of fixed-term leaseholds (known as crown leases before July 1997). This system is in fact the same as the sale of land use rights in mainland China.

The leasing system differed between Hong Kong/Kowloon and the New Territories. For all land on Hong Kong Island and the Kowloon Peninsula, crown leases were granted for 75 years, initially without the option to renew. In 1849 the term was extended to 999 years and most of the valuable sites in the city centre were granted that term. However the 999-year leases were discontinued in 1898 and from then onwards 75-year renewable leases were granted. Renewable 99-year leases were granted for land in the Praya East Reclamation in the 1920s.

In the New Territories (land leased to the British Empire), where the inhabitants held land titles dating from the Qing Dynasty (the last empire before the birth of the Republic in 1911), the colonial Hong Kong government adopted a 'block crown lease' system[6] to replace the existing titles. On 1 August 1905 the New Territories Land Ordinance was enacted, whereby all leases, including the block crown leases, were deemed to run for 75 years from 1 July 1898, renewable at a reassessed crown rent for a further 24 years minus the last three days before 30 June 1997. After 1959, all leases were deemed as running for 99 years from 1 July 1898 minus three days.

The system continued until the Sino-British Joint Declaration on the future of Hong Kong, which was signed in 1984 and came into force on 27 May 1985. In early 1984 the British government announced that British sovereignty over Hong Kong would end in 1997. Annex III of the Joint Declaration was drafted to resolve any disputes that might arise with respect to land leases. Under the Joint Declaration, the existing leasehold system would continue after the handover. All non-renewable leases (except short-term tenancies and leases for special purposes) that were due to expire before 30 June 1997 would be extended to 2047 at no premium. However leaseholders would be subject to an annual land rent of 3 per cent of the rateable value of the property at the time of extension. Leases expiring after 30 June 1997 would be dealt with under the new law, of the

Hong Kong SAR. Moreover the term 'crown lease' would be changed to 'government lease'.

Land Disposal Mechanisms under the Leasehold System

There have been three methods of dispensing new land to the public in Hong Kong: public auction, tender and private grants.

Auctions

Soon after taking possession of Hong Kong Island the British held their first land auction and such auctions became a normal business activity in Hong Kong.[7] Between 1985 and 1997, more land was sold through public auction than by tender. However in 1992–93, when the land market was less active, the government tended to put more land out to market tender so that market sentiment would not be affected immediately. This was because the whole bidding process in an auction was open to the public and the lack of interest was observable immediately. Tenders were usually used by the government to resell land that had been withdrawn from auction as the bidding was too low.

In addition, due to urban–rural land price differentials, the government favoured the use of public auctions for urban land. When Hong Kong was mainly an industrial city, industrial land attracted more attention and auctions generated higher prices. The trend switched to residential land when the population increased and the local economy took off (Table 6.1).

Nevertheless auctions have not always resulted in the highest prices. In May 1994, when the market sensed that the government intended to impose measures to cool down the property market, more than 10 developers bid together in collusion. Consequently two pieces of land were sold at prices that were just 6.25 per cent and 13.33 per cent higher, respectively, than the government reservation prices. This can be compared with the situation at a previous auction when three sites were sold at approximately 40 per cent higher than the reservation price. The action at the May 1994 auction was regarded as a protest by major developers against government intervention, which was seen as violating the non-interventionist market approach that was expected of the Hong Kong government.

Tenders

Land has been sold by tender when: (1) its use was strictly defined and the sale was unlikely to attract general interest, or (2) the government wished to examine detailed proposals for the development of a particular lot with an unusual user restriction in order to ensure that the best type of

Table 6.1   Sale of land for different uses (number of sites)

	Industrial use		Non-industrial use		Residential use	
	Auction	Tender	Auction	Tender	Auction	Tender
1985–86	7	2	4	12	6	4
1986–87	4	0	11	16	5	16
1987–88	12	1	4	6	10	14
1988–89	11	1	5	14	9	10
1989–90	14	1	3	6	12	12
1990–91	12	0	5	7	10	7
1991–92	8	0	3	6	17	5
1992–93	11	0	7	8	10	7
1993–94	8	0	4	3	8	2
1994–95	2	0	4	3	20	1
1995–96	1	3	5	7	6	4
1996–97	0	4	5	5	8	4
Total	90	12	60	93	121	86

Source: Liu *et al.* (1997).

development would take place and that the development would meet all the government's requirements. Land that was usually put out to tender was that which was destined for the construction of petrol filling stations, kerosene stores in public housing estates, profit-making private schools, cinemas and multistorey carparks, and land with a sea frontage. However, during some period of time, the rationale for tendering, as listed above may not create the maximum private or public interests. This is observed from two extreme tendering results in the history of Hong Kong. Both the highest and the lowest land prices (in real terms) in colonial Hong Kong were fetched by tender. In February 1982 the site of the Exchange Square development in the central district of Hong Kong was sold, making it the most expensive site ever. Conversely in March 1988, the government sold a piece of land in Ma On Shan, the latest generation of new towns in Hong Kong, at approximately HK$200 per square foot when residential flats in the district were selling at an average of HK$4500 per square foot. It is obvious that the tendering system is not a perfect substitute for public auctions in an open market system and care must be taken with the selection criteria for the winning bid.

Private Grants
In the early colonial days, agricultural land in the New Territories and land for non-residential use (usually special industry) in urban areas was

granted to private individuals upon application (Lai, 1993) in order to promote commercial and industrial development. Most private land grants went to public service providers who could afford the high land costs, for example universities, hospitals, and public utility companies, in return for an annual land rent determined by the government.

PLANNING CONTROLS AND SUPPLY MECHANISMS FOR URBAN LAND

Planning Control

The leasehold system in Hong Kong provides for leaseholders to apply for a change of land use as circumstances require (Section 16 of the Town Planning Ordinance). Applications are lodged with the Town Planning Board (TPB), which is composed of government officials and professional advisers. It is the task of the TPB to consider all applications and to issue a rejection, approval or approval subject to certain condtions. Should an applicant wish to appeal against a rejection or an imposed condition, he or she may apply through Section 17 of the same Ordinance. The irony is that the appeal is heard by the same group of people in the TPB.

Since land in Hong Kong is leased out by the goverbment rather than sold, the government is able to impose constraints on development. In all auctions, conditions are attached to each lot, for example restrictions on uses, floor area and so on.

Section 16 of the Town Planning Ordinance applies both to private developers and to the landlord, that is, the Lands Department on behalf of the government. When an outline zoning Plan for a particular district or region has been formally introduced by the Town Planning Board and the Lands Department intends to dispose of any land, it has to take account of the zoning controls set out in the plan. The Lands Department may apply for a Section 16 change of use before putting the land to auction so as to generate maximum interest for the site. However it does not necessarily follow that such internal applications are smooth or efficient. For example on 22 October 1994 the District Land Officer applied for the designation of a lot in Kowloon to be changed from 'road' to 'commercial'. On 18 January 1995 the application was rejected.

The lack of coordination between the government bodies responsible for land use and land supply, respectively, can be illustrated by an incident that began on 20 August 1994. The Lands Department applied for a change of site use from 'commercial' to 'commercial/residential' and simultaneously invited applications for tender. The change-of-use application was eventually approved by the TPB on 10 November 1994, 14 days after the tender had closed. There might have been prior discussions between the two bodies, but it still seems to have been an improper procedure and could have proved unfair to the purchaser of the lease.

Supply Mechanisms

Hong Kong aims to 'provide sufficient land, in a timely fashion, for additional new homes, offices, factories, a growing range of community services, and the necessary supporting infrastructural facilities' (Territorial Development Strategy Review, 1996). The process of land supply can be divided into the planning process and the development process. The planning process is undertaken within the framework of the Territorial Development Strategy. The related departments (the Planning Department for planning issues, the Development Department for overall land use, the Civil Engineering Department for infrastructural development and so on) carry out planning studies and engineering feasibility studies for specific areas before preparing outline plans. Such studies involve a detailed examination of various aspects of the development, including geotechnical, environmental and infrastructural considerations.

A detailed outline plan encompassies road and drainage systems, the disposition land usage, the permitted scale of building developments and so on. Based on this an outline zoning plan (OZP) is prepared for the area concerned. The OZP is a statutory document that must be made available for public inspection. Any objection to the plan is heard by the Town Planning Board and amendments are incorporated into the plan if necessary. When the final plans are approved the development may proceed.

There are two main types of site, namely reclamation-based and land-based, and the latter include areas earmarked for demolition and redevelopment. After the formation of developable sites the Territory Development Department and the Civil Engineering Department record the new supply in an annual report entitled 'Assessment of Future Land Supply'. This report, together with an assessment of new land supplies in all districts by the District Land Offices, is then delivered to the Land and Building Advisory Committee (LBAC) and the Committee on Planning and Land Development (CPLD) so that they can prepare their land disposal programme. This disposal programme also takes into consideration the various constraints set out in Annex III of the Sino-British Joint Declaration.

The above process may seem a reasonable one, but due to the number of departments involved and the amount of coordination required, it is usually very time-consuming. Consequently it is not sufficiently responsive to the short- to medium-term demand for different types of land. This contributes to fluctuations in the real estate market as it also affects the supply of properties. In the worst possible case it may take 19 years for the process to be completed (Table 6.2).

In addition, according to the Planning Department land supply does not equate with land that is available for disposal in the market. Accordingly there are two categories of land supply: (1) land whose availability is

Table 6.2   The land conversion process in Hong Kong (months)

Procedures	Shortest possible time	Longest possible time
Outline planning studies/ engineering feasibility studies	18	24
Preparation of departmental plans	6	18
Preparation of outline zoning plans	12 (no objections)	36 (no objections)
Submission of planning application/amendment to outline zoning plans	n.a.	22
Preparation of planning brief	n.a.	12
Total time taken	36	112

	Reclamation-based		Land-based	
	Shortest	Longest	Shortest	Longest
Planning process	36	112	36	112
Clearance/resumption		n.a.	48	
Commissioned for engineering works		12	12	
Reclamation works		24	n.a.	
Land formation		n.a.	24	
Building and infrastructural work		36	36	
Total time taken	108	184	156	232

Source: Liu *et al*.

certain and (2) land whose availability is less certain. The first of these is further subdivided into:

1. Vacant government land that is available for immediate disposal.
2. Government land currently in temporary use but expected to be available shortly.
3. Land to be made vacant under a development and production programme.

Land whose availability is less certain is that without priority status in the resource allocation system (the resource allocation system is the system used by the government to plan capital works expenditure on a five-year basis, including public works projects in new town/development areas). The director of the Territory Development Department, advised and assisted by the Development Coordinating Committee, is responsible for formulating five-year resource allocation programmes for capital works projects. These are submitted to the Finance Branch and the Chief Secretary's Committee for consideration. Subject to the endorsement of the latter, the programmes form the funding basis for public works projects in new town/development areas. Therefore land that is not subject to a definite development programme requires further considerations, and hence its release may not take place in the short to medium term.

THE BUREAUCRATIC LAND POLICY STRUCTURE

Until the 1970s, there was no single body or government department solely responsible for the formulation of land policy in Hong Kong. In those days land policies for the New Territories were decided by the New Territories District Office and the commissioner of New Territories Administration, while those for Hong Kong Island and Kowloon were decided by the Crown Lands and Survey Office.

In 1977 the government recognised the need for a proper land policy system, and hence the Special Committee on Land Production was established. On 1 June this committee was renamed the Special Committee on Land Supply in recognition of its responsibility for not only the formulation of land production programmes, but also the disposal of land to ensure the optimum use of existing land resources. The colonial government had a special system of advisory committees outside the government structure to help formulate policies. This was a perfect way of involving local people in government policy making. One such committee was the

Special Committee on Land Supply, whose task was to assist the government in regulating market forces.

On 1 June 1985 the Land and Building Advisory Committee was established, combining the Special Committee on Land Supply and the Building Development Committee. The committee was given the following tasks:

1. To inspect and evaluate policy and procedures relating to design, land and the building and construction industry.
2. To allocate and resume land, and to review land use in the light of demand.
3. To consider the correct development of land and to assist the government with land policy formulation.

Of course this committee, as its name implies, merely acted in an advisory capacity. Before 1989 overall land policy was the domain of the government's Public Works and Land Branch, together with the Land Development Policy Committee (LDPC) and the Development Progress Committee (DPC). The LDPC was the higher of the two latter bodies and comprised a chief secretary and a number of officials. Their duty was to draft and review long-term development, plus land production and land disposal programmes. The LDPC and DPC were combined in 1995 to form the Committee on Planning and Land Development, chaired by secretary for planning, environment and lands.

The hierarchy of land policy formulation in Hong Kong is as follows:

1. The Executive Council (decision making) and the Legislative Council (legislation).
2. The Committee on Planning and Land Development (policy formulation).
3. The Land and Building Advisory Committee (policy consultation).

In 1989 the Public Works and Land Branch was split into the Planning, Environment and Land Branch and the Works Branch. The formulation of land policy became the responsibility of the Planning, Environment and Land Branch (in July 1997 the word Branch was replaced by Bureau). There are four major operational departments within the PELB:

1. The Lands Department, which is responsible for:
   - the disposal of all government land;
   - land management, which includes the prevention of illegal occupation (government land) and the enforcement of lease provisions in the case of noncompliance (private land);
   - valuations for government land transactions and changes to lease conditions.

2. The Buildings Department, which is responsible for:
   - controlling all developments on private land and ensuring that the standards laid down in the Buildings Ordinance are upheld;
   - ensuring compliance with statutory standards on safety, health and the environment in private buildings and building works.
3. The Planning Department, which is responsible for:
   - formulating, monitoring and reviewing urban, rural and marine-related planning and associated programmes to provide a framework for the physical development of Hong Kong;
   - dealing with all types of planning at the territorial, subregional and district levels.
4. The Environment Protection Department, which is responsible for:
   - all issues relating to the environmental protection;
   - monitoring compliance with environment protection standards in urban and rural developments.

We have seen above that there are times when coordination between the various departments is difficult, and this problem could be even worse in the event of a general revision of the current land policy.

The Court of Appeal's decision on Attorney General v. Melhado Investments Ltd in 1981 was regarded as sounding the death knell on development control in the New Territories as the government lost its action to prevent land in rural areas being used for container storage and car parks. It was not until 1992 that the government announced designated 'Development permission areas' to rectify this problem, but no retrospective legislative powers.

THE TRANSITIONAL URBAN LAND MARKET

The Joint Declaration, which came into force in 1985, stipulated that after the deduction of costs, all income from the land sale programme (Table 6.3) should be equally shared between the colonial government and the future SAR government. The latter's share would be placed in a land fund[8] for investment. The fund would be overseen by a body of trustees in order to protect it from erosion by inflation and ensure that it did not destabilise the monetary system in Hong Kong.

The 50 hectares was supposedly calculated on the basis of previous land transactions. However this figure had more to do with politics than reality. The Chinese government had been very suspicious about the British government's handling of the wealth of the Hong Kong people during the

Table 6.3   Urban land revenue, 1985–97

Financial Year	Land area disposed of by the land Commission (ha.)	Government revenue from land sales (HK$ million)	Total revenue (HK$ million)	% of land revenue in colonial government's total revenue
1985–86	58.00	423	41 240	1.0
1986–87	55.00	1 863	43 869	4.2
1987–88	74.10	2 920	55 641	5.2
1988–89	155.40	5 681	65 780	8.6
1989–90	78.26	6 354	74 365	8.5
1990–91	134.33	2 761	82 674	3.3
1991–92	87.55	7 394	1 01 456	7.2
1992–93	164.30	7 459	1 20 780	6.1
1993–94	127.80	16 804	1 43 899	11.6
1994–95	1410.73	16 150	1 51 052	10.7
1995–96	204.93	16 838	1 53 194	11.0
1996–97	310.17	23 468	1 73 857	13.5
Average				7.6

Source: Annual Report, Accounts Department, Hong Kong Government; various Hong Kong reports.

remaining years of their rule, and the 50-hectare constraint was a mechanism to control the sale of land resources before the formation of the SAR government. In 1993, Governor Chris Pattern's constitutional reform programme caused the Sino-British relationship to fall to a low point and the Land Commission was halted. No auction was held for three months.

Under the Joint Sino–British Declaration on the Future of Hong Kong 1984, in order to leave the future SAR government with a sizeable land area for urban development as well as to preserve the value of the land asset in future, there was a maximum control over the land area to be sold in the open market of 50 hectares each year. As mentioned earlier, because of this 50-hectare constraint, whenever possible the colonial government sold land by land area rather than by floor area. This affected the property market in that urban high-intensity development land (which was mainly for lower- to middle-class housing) was sold in larger quantites than lower-intensity development land for luxury accomodation.

In 1992–93 the Land Commission authorised the disposal of 27.96 hectares for commercial, residential and industrial use, compared with 22 hectares in 1991–92. Of the 27.96 hectares 23 hectares were solely for commercial and residential use. Table 6.4 shows that despite the Land

Table 6.4   Land supply and disposal, 1992–97

Land commission quota for commericial and residential land (sq. ft)	Actual disposal of residential land (sq. ft) (%)	Actual disposal of non-industrial land (sq. ft) (%)	Quota remaining (sq. ft) (%)
1992–93	2 475 700	1 090 384 (44)	1 258 301 (51)	127 014 (5)
1993–94	1 978 406	1 338 158 (67)	267 450 (13)	372 798 (18)
1994–95	2 731 880	1 856 893 (68)	671 077 (24)	203 910 (7.4)
1995–96	4 648 932	798 445 (17)	872 619 (18)	2 977 868 (64)
1996–97	4 736 120	1 198 039 (25)	268 249 (5.7)	3 269 832 (69)

Source: Wong Mau On, unpublished BSc dissertation, Department of Real Estate and Construction, University of Hong Kong, 1998.

Commission's supposed supply constraint the colonial government was not able to utilise all its allocation. A political excuse can be found in the 1994 Report of the Task Force on Land Supply and Property Prices, prepared by the Planning, Environment and Lands Branch: it was the government's intention 'to establish a land reserve of up to 50 hectares ... if necessary, to meet further demand'. This plan, if it was aimed at producing a supply of land to circumvent the constraints set the Land Commission, was contrary to the objective of the Task Force, which aimed at resolving the demand and supply imbalance. However establishing a land reserve seems not to have been an excuse for the unusual fall in land disposal in 1996–97, when land prices were rising sharply. The real reason for this may never be known, but the effects on the urban land mechanism can be observed.

THE SAR URBAN LAND SYSTEM

When the chief executive of the Hong Kong SAR was elected in early 1997 he pledged to look into the problem of rising property prices and housing shortages. Earlier, the chief executive's advisor on housing and land matters had publicly stated that the government would look at all options for curbing speculation, including taxation and other administrative measures. To the relief of many, in his first policy address the chief executive did not announce such measures but did promise to ensure the provision of about 85 000 new housing units a year and to increase home ownership to 70 per cent. This represented a substantial increase in new housing, given that the previous supply from the private sector had averaged about 25 000 units, with a similar supply from the public sector. This promise was made on the basis of continuing economic growth and full cooperation from the private sector.

The problem with achieving the chief executive's goal was that even if the government were to sell land at a much greater rate, a constant supply of newly built housing could not be guaranteed, despite the fact that government leases normally specify the completion date. This was because the government normally contributes no more than 30 per cent of the annual supply of new housing units (Table 6.5). The majority come from urban renewal by the private sector, where there is no time limit on project completion. In economically sluggish times, developers tend to slow or even stop their on-site construction work. This was what happened in late 1997, when the Asian economy was seriously damaged by financial turmoil in some of the countries in the region.

Nevertheless the objective of 85 000 new units a year remained government policy and represented a very obvious change of policy from that of the colonial government. A further change was the proposed increase in home ownership. In November 1997 the government announced the 'Tenants Purchase Scheme' to privatise the public housing stock. Similar schemes had been tried before but without success. However this scheme was a very different one and it received a positive response from public housing tenants because the prices were set extremely low – about 5–10 per cent of similar sized private accomodation. In addition, while the average home owner in the private sector could only borrow up to 70 per cent

Table 6.5   Government-supplied housing, 1991–96

	Completed floor space (1000 sq. m)	Floor area available for housing development from land auctions (1000 sq. m)	% of auctioned land in total supply
1991	1 831	365.64	20.0
1992	947	316.64	33.4
1993	1514	400.47	26.5
1994	1255	222.18	17.7
1995	1089	370.16	34.0
1996	769	219.00	28.5
Average			26.68

Source: *Hong Kong Annual Digest of Statistics*, various issues.

of the property price, public housing tenants could borrow up to 100 per cent from the major banks.

However the scheme was launched at a time when the overall economy and the property market were experiencing a downturn, and by March 1998 property prices had fallen by 30 per cent. Some people started to criticise the government for selling public housing at such a low price and thus further devastating the market, forgetting that one year previously they had been protesting against the colonial government's inability to curb rising property prices and provide affordable housing!

What people tend to forget is that the creation of a privatised public housing sector with control on reselling should not affect the private market as the clientele are completely different. Evidence of this is provided by the Home Ownership Scheme in the early 1980s, when the government built and sold housing units to 'sandwich' class people who were not eligible for public housing units and could not afford private sector housing, even at a 40 per cent discount on the market price. That scheme did not affect the prosperity of the private housing market, and neither would a privatised public housing sector.

In terms of land policy, the new SAR government took steps to put the land administration mechanism into the public domain. The proposed land supply programme up to 1999 was put on the government web site for public inspection and was regarded as a positive step towards increased transparency. However these positive moves did not last long, and faced with the downturn in the property market the government announced its intention to be more flexible about its land sale timetable. In addition it would invite tenders for some pieces of land rather than put them up for public auction so that the consequences of negative market sentiments could be minimised. A prime office site at the heart of the business district with a spectacular view of the harbour was withdrawn from sale and earmarked for government headquarters. This kind of site would have been worth billions twelve months previously, but the lack of confidence in the economy caused the government to make this move, which was regarded as oversensitive as all it needed to do was postpone the sale of the site. Besides, the use of a prime site in the business district for public purposes was a direct contradiction of the sound economic principles that the Hong Kong government formerly exhibited.

In addition, in March 1998 a site for hotel use in Ma On Shan, a new town, was sold by tender at HK$200 per square foot, while similar hotel sites in the urban district had been sold at HK$1700 per square foot. This sale provoked a lot of criticism of the SAR government among property market professionals, as they saw it as potentially leading to a further market crash. The use of tenders was put on public trial when another prime site for residential use was sold at a lower than expected price by tender one week later. Perhaps coincidentally, this residential site was sold to the same developer who had snared the hotel site.

These moves by the government were regarded as confusing and counterproductive to the property market, which is a major sector in the SAR economy. The Provisional Legislative Council, which was set up before the handover of sovereignty to avoid a political vacuum before the election of the first Legislative Council, also queried the government on these policies but did not seem able to persuade the government to take positive action to restore public confidence in its land policy. The government went on to sell a number of government staff quarters at 10–30 per cent below the current price level, which caused a widespread drop in property prices in the district where the quarters were located.

The continuously shrinking property market reached a new low when a major developer undercut its competitors by quoting a lower-than-expected price for a prime residential project above an urban station on the new airport railway. This triggered a cut-throat price war and eventually reduced the mortgage valuation of most residential properties. The chain reaction spiralled downwards when a considerable number of purchasers who had bought their flats on a presale basis a year earlier suddenly found that they had to put up more money for their mortgages due to the substantial devaluation of their properties. A massive forfeiture wave seems inevitable if the property market continues to slump and the war price among the developers goes on. This may seriously damage the banking system in Hong Kong. The general public has blamed the inflexible and overinterventionist approach of the government for all these woes.

THE NEW SAR GOVERNMENT

The first Legislative Council elections were held on 24 May 1998. Contrary to all forecasts, the turnout broke all records for Hong Kong as more than 53 per cent of eligible voters braved heavy rain to cast their votes. There are a total of 60 seats in this legislative body, but not all 60 are directly elected. There are 20 seats for geographical constituencies, 30 seats in the functional category and 10 seats are determined by the election committee.

The 20 seats in the geographical constituencies are filled on the basis of popular elections in five geographical areas, each with a different number of seats. One of the special characteristics of this election the use of

Table 6.6   Allocation of seats in Functional Constituencies in the
Legislative Council in the HKSAR

Urban Council	Regional Council	Heung Yee Kuk*	Agriculture and Fisheries
Insurance	Transport	Education	Legal
Accountancy	Medical	Health Services	Engineering
Architectural, Surveying and Planning	Labour (3 seats)	Social Welfare	Real Estate and Construction
Tourism	Commercial	Commercial	Industrial
Industrial	Finance	Financial Services	Sports, Performing Arts, Culture and Publication
Import and Export	Textiles and Garment	Wholesales and Retail	Information Technology

* *Heung Yee Kuk* is an historical organisation comprising the so-called 'original residents' of Hong Kong. The direct translation of *Heung Yee Kuk* is Council for Village Matters, or local council for villagemen.

proportional representation based on list voting. In this way, more candidates from different political parties can be elected.

The 30 seats in the functional category are held by representatives of the departments shown in Table 6.6 – with the exception of Labour (three seats), all groups were awarded one seat in the 1998 election.

Finally, the 10 legislative councillors are elected internally by the 800-member election committee. The committee members come from three main occupational and political groups:

1. Industrial, commercial and financial.
2. Professional.
3. Members of the Provisional Legislative Council, deputies to the National People's Congress, representatives of the National Committee of the Chinese People's Political Consultative Conference on the mainland and representatives of local district organisations.

The election of these 800 people took place in April 1998. The turnout was extremely low due to the limited number who were eligible to vote. This can be sharply contrasted with the main election on 24 May. The first election of the Legislative Council in the SAR era saw the return of the Democratic Party and its allies. Although there are far fewer Democratic party seats than in colonial times, the inclusion of these 'opposition' members has implications for socioeconomic issues raised in the Council. Dissatisfaction with the SAR government's attempts to rejuvenate the economy is regarded as one of the main reasons for the high turnout for the 24 May elections since people would like to see positive changes. This dissatisfaction will provide the main ammunition for the Democratic Party and its allies in terms of the government's land and housing policies. But even so the opposition will be walking on thin ice because of the need to provide the homeless with cheap housing without jeopardising the income of property owners. As long as the SAR economy is heavily skewed towards real estate and construction and people purchase property for both occupation and investment, this issue will remain a hot potato for the politicians.

SUMMARY

The long-term use of a socialist land system framework (but not policy, as will be discussed below) within this capitalist economy worked to the advantage of the colonial government. It brought in huge revenues, which enabled the government to continue to provide a low-tax environment for businesses. The constant shortage of housing made private investment in housing (and to some extent speculation) an attractive proposition. The state-owned land system worked well in the sense that the government retained high degree of control over land use while property and land owners enjoyed continuous capital gains. So long as the *status quo* was not distrubed, any government action to curb speculation was seen as lip service. This led to a considerable rise in property prices in all sectors from 1992 until the bubble burst at the end of 1997, when the property market went into hibernation.

The transfer of Hong Kong sovereignty from Britain to China coincided with the Asian currency crisis, the effects of which went far beyond what had been expected by the SAR government. Property prices plummeted and dragged down the economy. Within a period of ten months, property prices in Hong Kong, especially in the residential sector, fell by 30–50 per cent. The extremely low price of a new residential development set by the developer in May 1998 for Tsing Yi Island, where the new airport railway link will pass, caused a shrinkage of 50 per cent of the capital value of a nearby development that had been sold a year previously. All this forced the SAR government to tighten its contol over land and housing. Land issues are more than economic and social issues, and the unprecedentedly sluggish market, together with the weakening economy and the desire of the new government to distinguish itself, forced it to take matters into its own hands. Consequently the socialist-style land system has been extended to include a socialist (if not planned) policy on housing. After its inception the new government spoke of delivering 85 000 housing units a year, but this target had to be relaxed when the negative effects of planned intervention in the market began to surface. The government is trapped in the dilemma of being burdened with the political pressure to create affordable housing while stablising a property market battered by economic turmoil. The past policy of non-intervention (or more accurately, unseen intervention) is facing a severe challenge as something must be done to keep property prices low enough to be affordable without damaging the overall economy and the wealth of those with a vested interest in the market. This is a major political burden, unfortunately, for the Tung Chee Hwa government on land and housing issues that the era of 'rule by the people for the people' must itself manifest a fair and rational housing market to distinguish the 'conspiracy theory' behind the alleged high land price policy under British rule.

The capitalist experience of the socialist land mechanism shows the importance of delicate government policy in times of market slump. The sudden downturn of the property market in Hong Kong after November 1997 damaged not only the property sector, but also other sectors in the economy, albeit in an indirect or sometimes invisible way. Owners of small enterprises usually mortgage their properties in order to obtain credit, and a sudden and substantial shrinkage of the property market seriously affects their business as their credit is reduced by the fall in the value of their mortgages. This in turn affects overall economic growth.

Hong Kong's experience with urban land policy illustrates that governments should not be active or visible players in real estate. The planned supply of 85 000 residential units, even though this was repeatedly stressed to be a target rather than a certainity, resulted in the erection of unnecessary psychological and emotional barriers in the market. If the government, for whatever reasons, wishes to continue to be actively involved in the market mechanism it must make its intentions clear and straightforward. Its response to the downturn of the property market – first promising to be flexible about land supply and then underpricing prime sites – sent out confusing messages that failed to please either capitalists or the supporters of a welfare state.

Hence the road to transition has to be progressive – there is scope for the merging of different systems and for trial and error, but once an efficient market mechanism is in place, any backward move is likely to be catastrophic.

7 Conclusion

WHAT HAS THE REFORM CHANGED?

While people criticised the previous state land allocation system in China as wasteful of resources, one should never underestimate the historical importance of the state ownership system. As in other agricultural economies, for centuries land in China was more a political and social matter than an economic one. The state's control over land and power to redistribute ownership and user rights has served as an important social equaliser, especially after changes of regime or government. China has experienced many kinds of land tenure system, encompassing state-owned land, private land ownership and a mixture of both. The lessons drawn from the ancient land reforms show that no one system has absolute advantages over another. The rural land systems that emerged almost immediately after the establishment of each new dynasty were the result of the political need to illustrate the fairness of the new government. However the lack of a proper system to protect property rights and ownership soon led to wide-scale land mergers based on political power and small farmers soon fell victim to the more powerful yet again. Likewise, private urban land ownership and the lack of property rights prevented the establishment a proper urban land system. Furthermore the power of the government over land decreased substantially with the transfer of state land to private ownership through various means.

Meanwhile the government was ill-equipped to manage the land system and could only negotiate with landlords for better management and planning objectives, and this process could be endless when their objectives differed. The last resort for all states to alleviate land problems is normally political actions, but this too is undesirable, as can be seen in China's historical experiences.

Land tenure reform has always played a vital part in Chinese politics. Early in the twentieth century Sun Yat Sen placed great emphasis on land tax principles that he hoped would make the system equitable and provide enough food for everybody. The Kuomingtang government lost the civil war in 1949 because they were seen as having a corrupt relationship with the big landlords and causing a large number of landless farmers to suffer. They eventually took steps to alleviate the suffering, but it was too late. However this experience did help them to set up a proper land reform system in Taiwan. The Communist Party won the civil war because of their promise to equalise property rights, a noble principle that had long been regarded as a mere pipe dream.

However not all went to plan and the partial nationalisation of land failed to eliminate exploitation by large landlords. An administrative allocation mechanism was set up to distribute rights to use the land, but the special characteristics of different types of land were not taken into consideration. For example distribution was not equitable in terms of location and fertility, and as a result applicants tended to apply for more land than they really needed and there was a large wastage of limited resources. A further problem was that land was seen as more than a factor of production, it was also a financial asset in that food could be produced for sale on the black market.

With the coming of the present urban land reform a device called 'land use rights' (LURs) was invented. This separated ownership of the land, which would stay in state hands, from the right to use the land, which would be tradable on the open market. In effect the urban land reform in China created a gigantic leasehold system for all urban land with built-in contractual obligations for subsequent land users. This management tool has also provided the state with an additional source of revenue as fees land are charged for the transfer of LURs, and land users who obtained their user rights through the old socialist mechanism can become leaseholders by compensating the state for the leasehold value of the land. Furthermore the reform has encouraged foreign investment and joint ventures with state enterprises that occupy prime locations.

The urban land reform in China has required a number of systemic reconfigurations. The first of these relates to the government structure and the bureaucratic system. The ideological sensitivity of land, which is deemed to belong to all the people, caused the government to separate the management of land from ownership of the properties built upon it. This was a mistake as land and buildings are not separable. The creation of two bureaucratic branches also complicated the privatisation of LURs as different ownership certificates were required for redevelopment projects. This problem has gradually been remedied in the learning process, and the local land bureaux and real estate administration departments are being merged. The learning process has also resulted in competition among the various local land markets to attract investors.

The second reconfiguration has been to the legal framework. In a country where the concept of property rights has never been particularly strong, this had posed a considerable problem. Due to local differences between widely scattered provinces and cities, in the short term national legislation can only serve as a guideline and in the meantime it has been up to local authorities to draft their own legislation. Naturally this has resulted in marked regional differences. The 1988 national Land Management Law was the first attempt to provide guidelines on urban land reform but it offered very little help with the development of a legal market mechanism. It was not until 1994, when the Urban Real Estate Administration Law was enacted, that a comprehensive piece of legislation was available to give legal effect to the urban land reform process.

The final reconfiguration involves the establishment of a price mechanism for urban land. The pricing of land was a completely new experience for the authorities, and rather than letting the market determine the first set of prices they chose to set up their own benchmark prices for reference purposes. This was necessary as the state was the landlord of all urban land and the granting of urban LURs was a one-way process. Since the authorities did not favour public auctions as a means of establishing land prices they were more or less obliged to set them themselves, especially for the less popular local markets. However, due to their inexperience, the authorities based the benchmark prices on the cost of land, rather than its economic value. The benchmark pricing approach is not mandatory for all cities, and in popular cities where an urban land market is already in place, such as Shanghai, it is not necessary. Nonetheless, even though the benchmark approach may not be the perfect way of establishing a pricing system for urban land, for some cities it is the best available starting point.

The Chinese urban land reform has changed the magnitude of the overall economic reforms. By separating user rights from the ownership of land, LURs have been turned into a commodity while leaving the socialist ideology of state ownership intact. Urban land is now more than just a factor of production, and the introduction of a price mechanism will allow the land market to evolve according to economic principles. Trading activities are taking place in various cities in China, but whether these activities can be regarded as an embryonic market mechanism is a matter of interpretation. However, at least a new urban structure based on efficient land use can start to flourish.

The urban land reform has allowed improvements to be made in other aspects of the socioeconomic structure. For example the commodification of LURs has facilitated a flexible real estate market, which in turn has allowed the much needed urban housing reform to take place as investment in housing provision is now financially feasible for private developers. Furthermore, turning land into a financial asset has allowed some enterprises to use their land as share capital in joint ventures. In some cases, the incorporation of land into the company's assets has allowed the company's total value to be reflected more realistically on the stock market.

WHAT COURSE HAS THE REFORM TAKEN?

The Chinese approach to urban land reform has been top down and gradual. The reform was initiated by the central government with legislation and executive orders for the hierarchy to follow. It did not start off as an attempt to overhaul the urban land system.

Due to inexperience and ideological constraints the government could only proceed step by step, allowing it time to develop a system that would suit both national and local requirements. It should be noted that this gradual approach had nothing to do with *laissez-faire*, and the commercialisation of urban land use rights before the establishment of a proper legal and financial framework was a bold move. As it provides the time to monitor and improve the reform process, the gradual approach is politically and economically efficient.

The gradual approach can be expressed by means of an analogy. When taking off an aeroplane needs to build up speed before it can lift itself from the ground. The acceleration required depends on a number of factors, including the size of the plane, the sophistication of its technology, the capacity of its engines and the external environment. A large plane with relatively simple technology requires a much longer take-off period than a small, high-tech fighter. During this period the plane is horizontal, but accelerating. After take-off its trajectory becomes more vertical and acceleration increases. Hence the rate of change before taking off from the ground varies from plane to plane, but the rate of change after take-off should be similar.

The Chinese model highlights a number of factors that can contribute to the success of any urban land reform. First of all, the desire for reform must be genuine and its purpose must be better urban land use, rather than simply being part of an overall reform that calls for the privatisation of all state-controlled resources. In any sector, privatisation for privatisation's sake will not deliver the best results. What all authorities need to understand when initiating an urban land reform programme is the fact that it involves a network of interlocking subsystems encompassing legislation, property rights, finance, the housing market and urban planning. A thorough understanding of the interaction of these subsystems is vital to any economy emerging from a socialist past as the instantaneous release of the market mechanism makes for an unmanageable situation.

This has been especially problematic in the case of China's economic reforms as the overall socio-political system is to remain unchanged. The only solution that has been acceptable to reformists and ideologues alike has been a step by step experimental reform programme that is in tune with socialist ideology. Starting as it did in the mid 1980s, China's path towards urban land reform may be proving a long one, but compared with other emerging economies it has been a relatively smooth.

Nevertheless the achievements to date would not have been possible without the financial support of overseas Chinese and Chinese citizens living in Hong Kong, Macau and Taiwan. Cultural ties have led to Singaporean Chinese investment in Suzhou, Hong Kong Chinese investment in Guangzhou, Taiwanese investment in Fujian and so. Their strong financial involvement has provided the 'engine' of the reform with the much needed fuel that has not been evident in emerging land markets elsewhere, and made feasible the Chinese approach of 'creating market activities first, market structure afterwards'. Creating trial markets with outside support has proved for more effective than formulating an overall package.

Another cultural factor that has been instrumental in the success of the urban land reform is the Chinese people's inherent desire for property ownership. The demand for urban land is a derived demand, and if the privatisation of urban land is to be successful there must be a substantial demand for buildings to be put on that land. An interesting characteristic of the Chinese is the sense of security they obtain from property ownership. Take Hong Kong and Taiwan as example. There the private rental market is insignificant in comparison with the market in Western societies. This is because, for most Chinese people, home ownership provides security for the whole family and forms the basis of their wealth-building capacity. Furthermore, due to mobility restrictions in most Chinese cities, people are more attached to their locality than is the case in the West. Hence it makes sense to own a piece of local property that can be passed on to future generations. Another factor that is contributing to the popularity of property ownership is the limited choice of investment vehicles. The Chinese stock market is still rudimentary and very risky, and the high inflation that has accompanied the economic reforms has caused people to look for inflation-proof investments.

Since the urban land reform in China is a top-down process, the attitude of the authorities has also been critical to its success. Because China is so vast the balance of power between the central and local governments is different from that in smaller countries, and despite the centralisation of government under socialism, local authorities in China enjoy room to manoeuvre when it comes local interests. In a way the central government is testing the water by allowing local authorities to develop their own reform frameworks before drawing up concrete national guidelines, especially with regard to the legal framework. So in effect the more advanced cities are shaping the blueprint for second-tier cities to follow. The merging of the real estate administration departments and the state land administration bureaux in some coastal cities is now a trend in other cities and makes for a more efficient local government structure.

WHAT COMES NEXT?

While this book has praised the gradual approach to urban land reform in China, some issues require immediate attention by the authorities. The first item on the agenda should be the medium- to long-term adjustment of the reform process. The gradual approach, despite its success, should only be regarded as an initial measure. Once a market structure has been established and the experiences of the various subsystems have been pooled, the process should be accelerated and national policies drafted with a macro view to the overall reform process. Coordination at the centre is now more important as the reform process is growing more and more political. The current proposal to review the Land Management Law of 1988 provides an opportunity to discuss the future direction of urban land reform, especially with regard to the power to grant LURs at the local level and the protection of agricultural land.

Revision is also required in other sectors, particularly the financing and banking system as the mortgage system for urban land and real estate is far from perfect. Although substantial savings have been accrued by individual citizens, the possibility of using this money to purchase urban real estate is still restricted, especially in the major cities where good quality real estate is usually associated with high prices. To make urban real estate a product that is available to ordinary people rather than an additional investment opportunity for rich locals and foreign investors, the mortgage system must be expanded. Currently only 1 per cent of the total loans extended by the Construction Bank, the largest bank for the financing of urban real estate projects, are mortgage loans. There is certainly room for improvement in the complicated application procedure, which currently requires all applicants to find a personal guarantor. Attention should also be given to the high mortgage rate and to extending the loan term, which is currently about 10 years.

Another issue that needs to be tackled is the coordination of urban and rural land development. While some major cities have made huge improvements in the central urban areas, beyond the urban fringe there has been limited improvement. This had pushed the price of urban real estate even higher. Thus an infrastructure-led development programme should be launched by the government to make urban fringe and suburban areas accessible to ordinary people. This should involve massive new town projects and the provision of good communication networks. Due to the substantial discrepancies between the living standards in rural and urban areas, population migration has always been one way, leading to severe overcrowding in cities. Extension of the urban land reform could help alleviate this situation by shifting residents to urban fringes served by a good transportation system. By using urban land income for infrastructural development in suburban areas, local authorities may be able to induce private real estate developors to provide affordable housing for urban employees.

Finally, at the policy level, the so-called 'one-cut solution' (*yi dao ce*) should be avoided. The Yi Dao Ce approach defines the one way direction of reform that the reform movement should advance. This means that the direction of the reform should not always be one-sided and that every element in the reform should move in a single direction. For example it has been suggested that the dual-track system for the supply of urban land (administrative allocation and market granting) be eliminated completely. For a lot of people, the continuation of the old system is a constant reminder of the weakness of the centrally planned economic system and hence should be eliminated. But this has much to do with business enterprises being given land free of charge while more efficient land users are prevented from acquiring the best locations.

The same applies to housing reform. While it is necessary to relieve state enterprises of the burden of housing provision and increase the private production of housing stock, the public housing sector should remain. That is, the reform programme should not just be aimed at the commodification of housing but should also encompass the provision of better-quality public housing for the poor to rent. Hence those responsible for the urban land reform process should study the existing system and try to improve upon it, rather than sweeping away the old system and imposing a completely new one without consideration of the consequences.

Urban land reform can take many forms. The approach discussed in this book suits the particular situation in China. Although still in its initial stage, the reform has already created an active urban real estate market and efficient land users have been able to obtain the best locations. However it should be stressed that China's gradual approach using experimental programmes is not necessarily the solution for other emerging economies as it involves cultural and environmental factors that are unique to China. Nevertheless, an important message from the experience of China is that the urban land system is multilayered and multifaceted, and that the authorities should always start from the existing model and improve up on it, rather than superimpose a completely new system on the old.

Appendix 1

THE COMPREHENSIVE RULES AND REGULATIONS
CONCERNING STATE ASSET VALUATION PROCEDURES
(SAAB, 18 JULY 1992)*

General Provisions

1. These Comprehensive Rules and Regulations have been formulated according to Article #38 of ⟨The Administrative Procedures for the Valuation of State Property⟩ issued by the State Council (henceforth referred to as ⟨The Procedures⟩).

2. The legislation, rules and other regulations referred to in ⟨The Procedures⟩ are based on the relevant Asset Valuation legislation issued by the National People's Congress and other Party Standing Committees, as well as the relevant administrative regulations governing Asset Valuation issued by the State Council.

3. The State Property described in ⟨The Procedures⟩ refers to all forms of investment and investment income or donations, in the form of fixed assets, liquid assets, intangible assets or other types of asset which according to legislation, have been acquired by the State.

4. Those Departments Occupying State Property (henceforth referred to as the Occupying Departments) referred to in Article #3 of ⟨The Procedures⟩ include:

    (a) Government Offices, Armed Forces, social organisations together with other societies occupying State Property
    (b) State enterprises and institutions
    (c) all forms of domestic joint venture and share enterprises
    (d) Chinese–foreign joint ventures or co-operatively managed enterprises
    (e) collectively owned departments that occupy State Property, and
    (f) other departments occupying State Property.

5. When the economic circumstances which require an asset valuation occur, as mentioned in Article #3 of ⟨The Procedures⟩, with the exception of those who have the approval of the Regional Office of the State Asset Administration Bureau (SAAB) not to carry out an Asset Valuation, all must undertake an Asset Valuation.

6. Of the circumstances mentioned in Article #3 of ⟨The Procedures⟩:

    (a) Property Transfer refers to Occupying Department compensation transfers in excess of 1,000,000 Yuan or when economic activity of the incomplete asset portfolio occupies 20% or more of the original value of fixed assets in the whole department.
    (b) Enterprise Acquisition refers to an enterprise receives compensations in the form of assuming debt, purchases, stocks and holdings etc. or receives the

---

* Translated from the original by the author.

179

property rights of other enterprises, causing the company being annexed to lose their corporate qualifications or alter their corporate entity.

(c) Enterprise Sale refers to the whole individual business entity or sections of the enterprise, also the sale of other entire asset portfolios.

(d) Joint Venture Enterprises refers to all forms of joint venture amongst the domestic enterprises and departments, composed of fixed assets, liquid assets, intangible assets, and other assets.

(e) Public Companies refers to enterprises with share control, this includes corporate share holding enterprises, internal workers share holding enterprises, public share non-market exchange enterprises and public share market exchange enterprises.

(f) Liquidation refers to the declaration of bankruptcy and initiation of liquidation procedures according to the regulations of the Enterprise Bankruptcy Legislation of the People's Republic of China; or according to relevant national regulations, the reshuffle, merger, or confiscation of legal qualifications and the liquidation of the assets of the enterprise; or the complete termination of economic activity and enterprise liquidation according to the regulations in the enterprise contract, deed, or agreement.

7. Of those circumstances mentioned in Article #4 of ⟨The Procedures⟩:

(a) Mortgage refers to using the State Assets of the Occupying Department as a material guarantee for the economic actions of another department in return for payment.

(b) Guarantee refers to using the State Assets of the Occupying Department as a guarantee for the economic actions of another department, and undertake joint liability.

(c) Lease of the enterprise refers to the asset portfolio of the Occupying Department or the senior Management Department within a defined period, transfer the usage rights of the entire portfolio or one section of the enterprise to others and in return collect rental payments.

8. Article #4 of ⟨The Procedures⟩ refers to those circumstances where you might undertake an asset valuation. When the circumstances outlined take place, according to the particular situation you may undertake a valuation of the asset or not carry out a valuation. However if the actions are any of the following, you must carry out an asset valuation:

(a) lease the entire asset portfolio of an enterprise

(b) State Property leased to foreign businessmen or departments which aren't state-operated

(c) assets of the National Administrative Affairs Department that have been transferred from non operational to operational assets.

(d) other circumstances under which the Regional Office of the SAAB believe an asset valuation should be carried out.

9. The 'Interested Parties' mentioned in Article #4 of ⟨The Procedures⟩ refers to those involved in the above mentioned economic transactions, the Occupying Departments, Industry Management Departments, Regional Offices of the SAAB along with other departments.

10. In those circumstances there has not been an asset valuation despite the require- ment, or haven't according to ⟨The Procedures⟩ and these Comprehensive Rules, submit a Project Proposal or given confirmation given, the economic conduct is invalid.

11. According to Article #5 of ⟨The Procedures⟩, the procedures for a National valuation of State Property or assets of a specific industry are separately regu- lated by the State Council.

12. The National regulatory standards mentioned in Article #7 of ⟨The Procedures⟩ refers to the relevant technological and economic standards issued by the State and Local People's Governments as well as all departments of the Central authority.

Administrative Organisation

13. The Regional Offices of the SAAB mentioned in Article #8 of ⟨The Procedures⟩ refers to those specific departments at each government level which are responsible for the management of State Property. Central refers to the SAAB, Regional refers to each level of the SAAB or those organisations specially responsible for the management of State Property.

14. The State employs the principles of centralised leadership and separated respon- sibility in the management of Asset Valuation operations. The SAAB is respon- sible for the organisation, management, leadership and supervision of Asset Valuation Organisations nationwide. According to National Government Policy regulations and the regulations of the Senior Offices of the SAAB, Regional Offices of the SAAB are responsible for the administration of Asset Valuation operations at the local level. In the course of administering Asset Valuation Organisations, the Senior Office of the SAAB has the authority to redress the work of the subordinate office if it does not conform to ⟨The Procedures⟩ or the methods of operation outlined in these Comprehensive Rules.

   The management of State Asset Valuations being the responsibility of the Industry Management Department as mentioned in Section #2 of Article #8 of ⟨The Procedures⟩ refers to each government level of the Industry Management Department undertaking first inspection, commentary and signing the results of the asset valuations of the departments under their jurisdiction, as well as being responsible for supervision, encouragement and guidance of asset valua- tions within the industry.

15. The Asset Valuation companies, Accounting Offices, Auditing Offices, Financial Consultancies etc. referred to in Article #9 of ⟨The Procedures⟩ must be enrolled on the Commercial and Industrial Management Administration Departments register, have Corporate qualifications, and hold Asset Valuation Qualifications Credentials issued by the State Council or Provincial, Autonomous Region, or Municipal (including Cities) Office of the SAAB. Only departments who satisfy the above mentioned conditions will be permit- ted to engage in State Asset Valuation operations.

   When the circumstances under which you must carry out an Asset Valuation occur (according to what is outlined in #3 and #4 of ⟨The Procedures⟩ and these Comprehensive Rules) the Occupying Department must contract one of the above mentioned Asset Valuation Organisations who has Asset Valuation Qualification Credentials, to perform the valuation.

16. All departments that are engaged in the occupation of performing Asset Valuations, according to the reporting structure of the organisation, apply to the State Council or Provincial, Autonomous Region or Municipal Regional Office of the SAAB for Asset Valuation Qualifications. After passing through the inspection and approval and acquiring Asset Valuation Qualifications or Temporary Valuation Qualifications they may engage in the valuation of State Property. They may also engage in private valuation operations. SAAB Offices of the cities who are engaged in Asset Valuation operations will have their Asset Valuation Qualifications verified by the Provincial Office of the SAAB and will be issued qualification credentials.

   (a) The Valuation Qualification Credentials are centrally printed, stamped and given a serial number by the National Administrative Bureau of State Property.

   (b) The Valuation Qualification Credentials of the Asset Valuation Organisations under the Central administration (this includes all Asset Valuation Organisations) will be verified and issued by the National Administrative Bureau of State Property.

   (c) The Valuation Qualification Credentials of the local Asset Valuation Organisations (includes those who work independently of Asset Valuation Organisations) will be verified and issued by the Provincial, Autonomous Region and Municipal Offices of the SAAB, and a report filed with the National Administrative Bureau of State Property. With the exception of operational reports which have been filed with the National Administrative Bureau of State Property, the issue of Asset Valuation Qualification Credentials by the City Offices of the SAAB must be filed with the Provincial office of the SAAB.

   (d) The State Council and the Provincial, Autonomous Region and Municipal, and City Offices of the SAAB are responsible for conducting an annual inspection of those Asset Valuation Organisations who have already acquired Asset Valuation Qualification Credentials (in addition to other particular measures).

17. Ordinarily it is the Occupying Department who contracts out the Asset Valuation work; it can also be someone who is permitted by the Occupying Department to contract the work, or another party who has an interest in the Asset Valuation outcome. In principle it is conducted by the person who has applied to have the Asset Valuation performed. Under special circumstances the Regional Office of the SAAB will contract out the work.

    The contractor should sign an agreement to perform the valuation which includes these major contents: the name of those being valued, valuation contents, period of valuation, procedures for the receipt of fees and amount of money, responsibilities if the contract is broken etc.

18. When the parties who have an interest in the valuation dispute about the organisation contracted to perform the valuation, the Regional Office of the SAAB will appoint an Asset Valuation Organisation which is accepted by the two parties.

    When required, the SAAB may directly organise an Asset Valuation Organisation to perform a valuation of all those major assets valued at 100,000,000 Yuan or more or those Chinese–foreign joint ventures or co-operatively managed enterprises who have the approval of the State Economic Planning Commission to conduct a valuation.

19. The Asset Valuation Organisations who have acquired Asset Valuation Qualifications are not subject to district or industry restrictions in taking on valuation work. The organisations may take on the task of valuations in their own locality and their own industry as well as being able to take on projects in other localities, across borders and in other industries. Asset Valuation Organisations who have immediate economic connections with a department that is having a valuation performed, must not be contracted to perform that asset valuation.

20. Everyone whose application for asset valuation is approved, strictly according to fact, must supply all information necessary for the valuation. The Asset Valuation Organisations should safeguard the confidentiality of the information.

    As for State secrets that are involved in the valuation, without exception each party should in strict accordance with the National Security Legislation, implement each of the regulations. When it is necessary, the National Administrative Bureau of State Property will immediately organise an Asset Valuation Organisation to perform a valuation.

21. The determination of the value of Rights of Use over State Land and the value of State Housing Property, both should be brought into the scope of the ⟨State Asset Valuation Administrative Procedures⟩.

    Professional Asset Valuation Organisations engaged in the valuation of the Right of Use over State Land and State Housing Property valuations, according to ⟨The Procedures⟩ and these Comprehensive Rules, must apply for Asset Valuation Qualifications with the National Administrative Bureau of State Property. Only after acquiring these qualifications may they then perform asset valuations.

22. According to Article #11 of ⟨The Procedures⟩ Asset Valuation is a paid service. According to National Regulations for the Receipt of Payments, when the Asset Valuation Organisations accept the contract to perform the valuation they should direct the fees be received by the contractors department. This particular fees receipt procedure needs to be clarified in the valuation contract.

23. Procedures for the collection of Asset Valuation fees are formulated separately by the SAAB in conjunction with the State Bureau of Commodity Prices.

Valuation Procedures

24. When it is learned that the economic circumstances mentioned in Article #3 and #4 of ⟨The Procedures⟩ are to occur, in advance of the said event taking place, according to the bureaucratic hierarchy the Occupying Departments should submit a valuation Project Proposal. According to the principles of centralised leadership and separated administration, the Central Administration has jurisdiction over the approval of valuation Project Proposals for State property and the National Administration of State Property is responsible for management. Each of the Regional governments have jurisdiction over inspection and approval of Project Proposals for State Property valuations, and in principle management is the responsibility of the Regional Offices of the SAAB. Those localities and provinces who don't satisfy the conditions to obtain approval for a valuation may according to ⟨The Procedures⟩ and these Comprehensive Rules be engaged in specific regulations by the Senior Office of the SAAB.

Project Proposals for valuation of major items whose value is in excess of 100,000 Yuan and Chinese–foreign joint ventures or co-operatively managed enterprises which have been approved by the State Economic Planning Commission (includes State Property held by the Central Administration, local State owned enterprises and specific industries), in addition to submitting the Project Proposal to the same level of the SAAB (i.e. provincial to provincial etc.), must still file a report with the National Administrative Bureau of State Property. When required, the National Administrative Bureau of State Property will give direct approval for Project Proposals.

25. In principle the outcome of the asset valuation should be announced by the Occupying Department whose assets were valued.

26. After the relevant Administration Department approves and signs the Project Proposal for the valuation of the Occupying Department's State Assets, a report should be made to the Local Office of the SAAB. The departments of the State or local 'Planned Cities' as well as those departments without a Senior Management Department, the Asset Valuation Project Proposal is directly submitted to the same regional level of the SAAB.

Asset valuation Project Proposals include the following:

(a) names of the assets of the Occupying Department, the department hierarchy and addressees of all
(b) list of items for valuation
(c) the range of asset valuation
(d) reporting date
(e) other contents

The asset valuation application should have the seal of the reporting department and the senior of the Management Department affixed to it, and depending on the particular economic activity, documents of approval from the approving organ and the property rights certification issued by the Regional Office of the SAAB.

Within 10 days of receipt of the application, the Regional Office of the SAAB they should issue notification of the decision to approve or deny the proposal. If the period exceeds 10 days the approval is automatically validated, and the Regional Offices of the SAAB will supply the approval formalities.

27. The Asset Valuation Organisation in accordance with notification of approval to perform the valuation accepts the valuation contract, and according to the limits of these regulations will perform the valuation. When making a valuation of the Occupying Department asset portfolio, on the basis of a comprehensive check of the rights and liabilities of the Occupying Department, undertake a check of the assets, money and goods and operational conditions.

28. In accordance with different valuation aims and objectives, the Asset Valuation Organisation, according to national legislation, regulations and policy, and taking into consideration each factor that influences the value of the asset, will undertake a valuation of the assets of the contracting department. Using scientific valuation methods and appropriate valuation parameters the Asset Valuation Organisation will make an independent, impartial, and equitable assessment of the value of the assets.

29. After the Asset Valuation Organisation has completed the valuation they should submit a report of Asset Valuation Results to the contracting department. The report is made up of two parts, the main body and attachments. The principal contents of the main body:

(a) Name of the valuation organisation
(b) Name of the contracting party
(c) The range of assets being valued, names and a brief description
(d) Standard valuation period
(e) Valuation principles
(f) All legislation, regulations and policy according to which the valuation will be conducted
(g) Valuation methods and assessment standards
(h) A brief description of specific assets for valuation
(i) The outcome of the valuation: includes the value and a written description
(j) Names of the attachments
(k) Start and finish dates for the valuation the date which the report was submitted
(l) A list of names of those of the Valuation Organisation involved in the valuation, a list of their signatures and affix it with the official seal of the valuation organisation
(m) others

Attachments:

(a) asset valuation summary and a detailed breakdown
(b) a description of valuation methods and process of calculation
(c) accounting reports written in accordance with the valuation standard
(d) Asset Valuation Organisations Qualification Credentials documentation and duplicates
(e) Certificates of the valuation of the Occupying Departments and duplicates
(f) other material relevant to valuation

30. After the Occupying Department receives the official asset valuation report they will submit formal confirmation of the valuation results, including a valuation report which has been signed by the Senior Office of the Administration Department together with relevant materials, to the Regional Office of the SAAB for approval.
31. Acknowledgement of the asset valuation results by the Regional Offices of the SAAB is split into two steps; verification and confirmation. Firstly determine whether or not the valuation was impartial and scientifically equitable and afterwards put forward verification of these opinions and circulate a notice of confirmation of the results of the asset valuation.
32. Bearing in mind the following aspects, the Regional office of SAAB makes a check of the asset valuation report:

(a) whether or not the asset valuation process conforms to policy regulations
(b) whether or not the asset valuation organisation has valuation qualifications
(c) whether or not the scope in which the valuation is implemented and the valuation regulations are consistent, and if there is any area that has been overlooked or reduplicated

(d) whether or not the factors that influence asset value are considered comprehensive
(e) whether or not the recommended legislation and regulations and state policy is appropriate
(f) whether or not the recommended materials and data are authentic, equitable and reliable
(g) whether or not the valuation methods applied are scientific
(h) whether or not the given value is equitable
(i) others

33. Every asset valuation report conforms to the requirements of Comprehensive Rules #29, #30 and #32 should be granted confirmation and formal notification of this circulated by the Regional office of the SAAB responsible for examination and approval. Those which do not conform to the requirements, under the different circumstances perform an alteration, reassessment or do not confirm the results in the report.

    In the course of operations or the transfer of property rights in accordance with the Regional Office of the SAAB regard the confirmed valuation results as the base price or evaluated price.

34. If the Occupying Department disagrees with the notified results of the valuation, or a dispute occurs with a party with an interest in the economic circumstances (i.e. guarantor) or a party involved in the asset valuation over the results, if the same level of the SAAB proves ineffective, they may apply to the Senior level of the SAAB for a reconsideration or arbitration of the dispute.

35. Usually the approval of the Project Proposal and the confirmation of valuation results is carried out according to Articles #26 and #33 of these Comprehensive Rules. When the Regional Offices of the SAAB believe it necessary they may contract the Management Department of the Occupying Department or the subordinate office of the SAAB to carry out the functions specified within. In accordance with ⟨The Procedures⟩ and these Comprehensive Rules, the contracted department should carry out examination and approval of the Project Proposal and confirmation of the results. The contracted department must report the results to the Regional Office of the SAAB for their records.

36. Asset Valuation results confirmed by the Regional office of the SAAB, with the exception of their being major changes in National Economic Policy or additional regulations agreed upon by the parties with an interest in the valuation, they are valid for a period of one year from the date of valuation. When there is a change in the number of assets within this period, according to the circumstances it is permissible for the original valuation organisation or the Occupying Department to make appropriate adjustments to the valuation in accordance with the original valuation methods.

Valuation Methods

37. When the Asset Valuation Organisation performs a valuation, they should choose one or more of the valuation methods outlined in Article #23 of ⟨The Procedures⟩ in accordance with their different valuation aims and objectives. If using many methods to undertake the valuation, they should compare the

results from each method and make adjustments in order to obtain an equitable re-estimated value.

38. Current Income method is where the anticipated earnings every year (or month) over the remaining life of the asset are estimated and using an appropriate discount rate, these earnings are accumulated to obtain the valuation standard and in this way estimate the value of the asset.

39. Replacement cost method is performed under current conditions, to estimate the replacement value in the completely new condition by way of asset valuation, deduct from the asset the entity depreciation, operational depreciation and economic depreciation.

 The depreciation of the entity brought about by wear and tear through use and natural wear and tear. Operational depreciation is brought about by comparatively backward technology. Economic depreciation is brought about by changes in the external economic environment.

40. The Current Market Price Method is determined through market analysis. Choose one or more assets that are identical or similar to the asset being valued and make a comparison. Make a comparative analysis of the negotiated value and exchange conditions, undertake an adjustment, calculate out the asset valuation method.

41. In practise the Liquidation Price Method is used in accordance with the regulations outlined in the People's Republic of China Enterprise Bankruptcy Legislation. The valuation of the assets of the enterprise declared bankrupt is carried out through the Supreme Court. During the asset valuation, according to the enterprise liquidation period reassess the value of the assets should they change.

42. When the Asset Valuation Organisation accepts the contract to perform the valuation, the price standard they select to use should abide by National Legislation, and safeguard the legitimate rights and interests of all those with an interest in the economic situation.

 During the asset valuation, according to various asset valuation aims and objectives, should choose different value standards. Can select and use the National planned prices, can also use the National advised prices or domestic market or international market prices.

 Exchange rates, interest rates should be set according to National regulations for listed prices. Free foreign exchange or freely exchanged foreign assets may also use foreign exchange to adjust the value.

 The valuation of assets from all forms of domestic joint ventures (including big corporations) and public companies, should use an identical standard for valuation of the same kind of assets of each investor in the joint venture.

Asset Valuation in Chinese–Foreign Co-operatively Managed Enterprises and Joint Ventures

43. Everyone who together with foreign organisations, enterprises or other economic organisations or individuals starts a Chinese–foreign co-operatively managed enterprise or joint venture within the People's Republic of China, must according to regulations carry out a valuation of the Chinese investors assets, the confirmed value to become the basis for investment evaluations.

When necessary, a valuation of the assets of foreign investors will be carried out subject to their approval.

44. In principle valuation of Chinese–foreign co-operatively managed enterprises and joint ventures should be performed after approval of the proposal and before the approval of the feasible research report or, in particular situations can also be performed before the examination and approval or before the formal signing of the contract or agreement.

    The report of the asset valuation confirmed by the Regional Office of the SAAB functions as the approved feasibility report for the planning department, and the necessary documents for approval of the trade department contract. The asset valuation report confirmed by the Regional Office of the SAAB and the property rights registration provision (this includes an adjusted registration or a new business registration) are the necessary documents to conduct registration with the Commercial and Industrial Management Administration Department.

45. In circumstances where the events outlined in Articles #3 and #4 of ⟨The Procedures⟩ or #8 of these Comprehensive Rules take place, according to regulatory requirements an asset valuation should be carried out by those already established Chinese–foreign joint ventures or co-operative enterprises in which the Chinese investment makes up 50 per cent or more.

46. Before the establishment of a Chinese foreign joint venture or co-operative business operation there should be a valuation of the Chinese investment. In principle they should contract a Chinese Asset Valuation Organisation with valuation qualifications. In particular circumstances, with the agreement of the Regional Office of the SAAB, they may also contract a foreign valuation organisation or Chinese and a foreign Asset Valuation Organisation to conduct a joint valuation. The report must be submitted to the same level of the Regional Office of the SAAB for confirmation.

47. For those Occupying Departments which have gone into a joint venture or co-operative business organisation together with Hong Kong, Macau and Taiwan regions co-operative business, the asset valuation is carried out according to this section of these Comprehensive Rules.

Asset Valuation in 'Share Control Enterprises'

48. Before the Occupying Department is reorganised into a *Share Control Enterprise* (where control is according to your share percentage) (including corporate share holding enterprises, internal workers share holding enterprises, public shares non-market exchange enterprises and public shares market exchange enterprises), according to ⟨The Procedures⟩ and these Comprehensive Rules they should contract an organisation that has asset valuation credentials to perform a valuation.

49. According to regulations, the asset valuation results of the Occupying Department reorganising into a *Share Control Enterprise* must be reported to the Regional Office of the SAAB for verification and confirmation. The Government authorised departments will not carry out the examination and approval procedures for the establishment of a *Share Control Enterprise* for those departments that do not perform a valuation and those who do not confirm their results.

50. The asset value confirmed by the Regional Office of the SAAB acts as the basis for State Asset share divisions and the determined ratio of share ownership.

If after registered accountants have verified the financial affairs and property conditions of those who are preparing to go into *Share Control Enterprises*, the results of this verification and those confirmed by the Regional Offices of the SAAB prove inconsistent, they must obtain the agreement of the organ which confirmed the original asset valuation results in order to make adjustments.

In order for the Occupying Department to reorganise and become a *Public Corporation* they must issue category B shares. If the results of the investigation by foreign registered accountants and those confirmed by the Regional Offices of the SAAB prove inconsistent, they must obtain the agreement of the organ that approved the original asset valuation results in order make adjustments.

51. When the circumstances outlined in Article #3 and #4 of ⟨The Procedures⟩ and Article #9 of these Comprehensive Rules occur, those *Share Control Enterprises* with some State share ownership should perform an asset valuation according to the requirements in these regulations.

According to regulations, the procedures for asset valuations and confirmation of results from the valuations of *Share Control Enterprises* with State shareholdings should be handled by the Regional Office of the SAAB. Asset valuations of those *Share Control Enterprises* without State shareholdings, the asset valuation results approved by the Board of Directors are reported to a higher body for approval and confirmation.

Legal Responsibilities

52. Violate the regulations outlined in Article #3 of ⟨The Procedures⟩ or Comprehensive Rules, in those circumstances where a valuation should be undertaken but has not been carried out, according to Article #31 of ⟨The Procedures⟩ should issue a fine to those parties concerned. In those cases where it has brought about major losses for State Assets, there should be an investigation into the legal responsibilities of the parties concerned.

53. If the Occupying Departments and Asset Valuation Organisations violate the regulations outlined in ⟨The Procedures⟩ and these Comprehensive Rules bringing about valuation results in losses, the Regional Offices of the SAAB has the power declare the valuation results invalid, and according to the extent of the losses, order a correction or re-evaluation be carried out within a designated time period.

The fees for revaluation are to be paid by the department who violated the laws.

54. Asset Valuation Organisations should assume legal responsibility for the objectivity, impartiality and authenticity of the valuation results. Asset Valuation Organisations that violate the regulations outlined in ⟨The Procedures⟩ and these Comprehensive Rules, with the exception of those who are fined according to Article #32 of ⟨The Procedures⟩, the moneys accumulated as a result of such violations will be confiscated, and in accordance with the seriousness of the actions, fines of up to double the amount of the valuation expenses will be imposed on departments and up to three months basic wage for individuals.

In addition a notice of criticism might be circulated or it might be suggested that the relevant department imposes commensurate disciplinary action. A combination of the above mentioned punishments might also be imposed.

55. The Asset Valuation Organisations punished by closure and consolidation of the business, during the period of closure and consolidation must not accept any valuation contracts. The period of cessation of business must not be less than 3 months. After an investigation into the standards the those Asset Valuation Organisations which are forcibly closed by the Regional office of the SAAB which issued the original Asset Valuation Qualification Credentials, the organisation may resume asset valuation operations.

   The Asset Valuation Organisations who have had their Asset Valuation Qualification Credentials revoked may not have credentials re-issued for a period of two years. On completion of the two year period, the organisation must reapply for the credentials according to procedure.

56. Fines imposed on the Occupying Departments and others who bear responsibility are imposed by the same level of the SAAB. Administrative punishments for those responsible suggestions are made by the same level of the SAAB, submit these to the relevant department or that department's senior Management department to be dealt with.

   The issue a written warning, closure and consolidation of the business, or confiscation of State Property Valuation Qualification Credentials and the imposition of a fine on the Asset Valuation Organisation is undertaken by the by the Regional Office of the SAAB that issued the credentials. The punishment for those directly responsible is suggested by the organ that issued the credentials and passed to the relevant department to be dealt with.

57. The Regional Offices of the SAAB and the contracted department are responsible for management of inspection and approval of Project Proposals and confirmation of results. Those staff who violate the regulations outlined in ⟨The Procedures⟩ and these Comprehensive Rules will be dealt with according to Article #34 of ⟨The Procedures⟩.

58. According to National Regulations, any revenue in the form of fines paid to the Regional Offices of the SAAB should be passed on to the National Treasury. Fines imposed on the departments will be deducted from their final budget surplus and foreign funds budget and other allowances. Payment of fines incurred by the individual is borne by that person.

Supplementary Articles

59. The valuation of State Natural Resources should be carried out under the management of the Regional Offices of the SAAB. The implementation of the valuation methods together with these Comprehensive Rules is jointly formulated by the National Administrative Bureau of State Property together with the related departments. Reports are made to the State Council for approval.

60. Asset valuations involving funds fluctuations by the alteration of accounts or alteration of valuation expenses medium of payment for enterprises and departments, are carried out according to the relevant regulations of the Ministry of Finance.

61. Each region may formulate their own particular methods for implementation in accordance with ⟨The Procedures⟩ and these Comprehensive Rules. Should

the previously issued asset valuation regulations contradict 〈The Procedures〉 or these Comprehensive Rules, without exception 〈The Procedures〉 and these Comprehensive Rules will prevail.

62. Collective Asset Valuation enterprises may consult and follow 〈The Procedures〉 and these Comprehensive Rules.

63. Interpretation of these Comprehensive Rules is the responsibility of the National Administrative Bureau of State Property.

64. These Comprehensive Rules are effective from their date of issue.

Appendix 2

URBAN REAL ESTATE ADMINISTRATION LAW, THE PEOPLE'S
REPUBLIC OF CHINA (EFFECTIVE FROM 1 JANUARY 1995)

Part One General

1. This law is enacted ... to enhance the management of urban real estate and
   property; maintain the order of the operation in the property market; protect the
   legitimate rights and benefits of property owners; and strengthen the healthy
   development of the property industry ...
2. This law covers land use rights ... over state-owned land within the urban city
   planning districts of the People's Republic of China (hereafter referred to as
   'state-owned land') for the purposes of real estate development; real estate
   transaction and real estate management.
       'Building' in this Law refers to houses and buildings and built structures
   alike onland.
       'Real estate development' in this Law refers to the construction of building
   and infrastructural facilities on state-owned land granted with proper land use
   rights in accordance with the regulations set out in this Law.
       'Real estate transaction' in this Law includes the transfer, sale and, mortgage
   of real property.
3. This Law excludes the control on land allocated administratively.
4. The State will gradually improve ... residential developments for its citizens
   and hence living standards in line with the overall economic development of
   society.
5. Legal owners of property interests shall observe the Law and executive regulations, and shall pay relevant taxes accordingly. The legitimate rights of ... property interest holders are protected by the Law, no authority and individual can
   violate them.
6. The administrative departments concerning construction activities and land
   management ... under the State Council shall work closely in partnership to regulate all ... activities concerning real estate management .
       The structure, organization and responsibility of real estate management
   activities of the real estate and land management departments above the county
   level will be decided by the respective provincial, self-autonomous region and
   centrally administered municipality governments.

Part Two Real Estate Development Land

Chapter One Sale of Land Use Rights
7. The sale of land use rights means the sale of the land use rights of state-owned
   land (hereafter known as 'LURs') to land users for a particular term of years,

with ... due payment for the transfer of LURs as conveyance fee as consideration to the State.

8. Collectively owned land within a city planning district must be converted into state-owned land according to the relevant ... legislation before the LURs can be sold or transferred.

9. The sale and transfer of LURs must comply with general land use planning, city planning and the yearly construction land plan.

10. With respect to the regulations set by the State Council, when a local government above county level is selling LURs for real estate development, the local government concerned must apply to the provincial government or the State Council according to the annual plan of total supply of LURs for sale with reference to the control instructions issued by the respective provincial government.

11. The sale of LURs shall be progressively planned by the city or county people's government. The sale particulars of each site such as use of land, term of the LURs and other conditions shall be determined and specified by the land management departments in the city or county people's government in consultation with the city planning agency, construction committee and real estate management authorities concerned. Such specifications should be made in accordance with the regulations laid down by the State Council, and after being endorsed by the authorized people's government concerned, shall be enforced by the land management department of the respective city or county people's government.

   In enacting section 11 above, the extent of the power and authority of the county people's government and the related departments in the centrally-administered municipalities shall be stipulated by these municipalities government.

12. The sale of LURs can be achieved by auction, tender or private treaty.

    Land for commercial, tourism, entertainment and luxurious residential use in good location and environment must be sold through auction or tender; if the environmental conditions are not attractive enough, rendering it impossible to adopt auction or tender method, then private treaty grant can be considered. When such private treaty grant is adopted, the conveyance fee of the LURs cannot be lower than the minimum land price set by the State.

13. The maximum term of the LURs to be sold is stipulated by the State Council.

14. The contract for the sale and transfer of LURs must be in writing. Such a contract should be entered into by the land user and the land management department in the city or county people's government.

15. Land users must pay the conveyance fee for the transfer of LURs in compliance with the agreement in the sale contract; any non-compliance with the sale contract to pay the conveyance sale fee will trigger the right of the land management department concerned to repudiate the contract and sue for damages.

16. Provided the land user has paid the conveyance fee for the transfer of LURs in compliance with the sales contract, the land management department of the city or county people's government concerned must convey the land sold following the conditions in the ... contract. Failure to do so will ... trigger the land user's right to repudiate the contract and ask for a refund of the conveyance fee received by the land management department concerned. The land user can, in such cases, sue for breach of contract.

17. Where the land user needs to alter the use of land sold to him from the original one, as stipulated in the sales contract, he needs the approval of the assignor and the city or county people's government city planning department. Upon

approval, an amended sales contract or a new sales contract will have to be signed ..., and where necessary a premium will have to be paid.

18. The Conveyance fee for the sale of LURs must be passed to the State Treasury, and be credited to the budget for city infrastructure construction and land development. The passing of and use of the conveyance fee will be stipulated by the State Council.

19. Under normal circumstances, the LURs so contracted will not be terminated before maturity and land will not be reclaimed by the local government before the end of the term of the LURs. An exception can be made if it is for the benefit of ... society and in the public interest' when the land can be reclaimed before expiry of the LURs, with proper compensation paid to the land user, taking the actual term of the LURs he obtained and the actual situation of the development carried out so far into consideration.

20. LURs will be terminated by natural disasters which cause the piece of land to vanish.

21. ... Application to renew the LUR contract must be made one year in advance. Renewal of the sales contract shall be allowed unless return of the land is deemed necessary for social and public purposes. A new LURs sales contract must be made with the new term of the LUR stipulated. A conveyance fee shall ... be paid for the new contract.

    Upon expiry of the term stated in the ... contract, the land shall be reclaimed by the State with no compensation to the land user if the land user has failed to apply for ... renewal, or if such an application has been rejected.

Chapter Two   Administrative Allocation of Land Use Rights

22. The administrative allocation of LURs refers to the transfer of land to land user upon payment of compensation to the sitting tenant and resettlement claims from a local government above county level, or the granting of the land use right to the land user without any consideration.

    Unless otherwise stated by law or executive orders, LURs granted by ... administrative allocation shall not be subjected to a limited term.

23. LURs, for the following construction ... purposes, once deemed necessary, ... can be granted by a local government above county level through administrative allocation:

    (a) state authority land use and military land use,
    (b) city infrastructural facility use and public or charitable land use,
    (c) national target projects such as power supply, transportation, irrigation etc.,
    (d) other land uses stipulated by law or executive orders.

Part Three   Real Estate Development

24. Real estate development must comply with comprehensive city planning principles in the interests of economic, social and environmental efficiency so that proper land use patterns as well as good infrastructural facilities can be developed.

25. Land users obtaining LURs for real estate development in accordance with the provisions of this Law must comply with the conditions set for the use of land and the deadline for the latest commencement date ... as stated in the LUR sales contract. Failure to ... commence the building and construction works one year after the deadline for commencement ... will trigger the local authority's right to levy a vacant land charge of not more than 20 per cent of the conveyance fees for the LURs paid by the developer. If no construction or building works have started after two years from the deadline, the LURs can be redeemed without compensation by the local authority. However, delay of development commencement due to events beyond the control of the land user, or due to delay caused by the local authority or related departments, or due to excessive preliminary site preparation necessary for the development commencement shall be excluded from this section.

26. The design and construction of the real estate development projects must comply with the relevant standards and provisions of the State.

    At the completion of real estate development project, the building structures are subject to inspection before occupation can be permitted.

27. LURs obtained through proper legal procedures can be transferred into share capital in ... joint-development projects or joint-venture partnership in accordance with the provisions of this Law, related legislation and executive orders.

28. It is the State's objective to encourage and assist residential real estate development for its citizens through such policies as preferential taxes etc.

29. ... Profit-oriented real estate development enterprises should be able to produce evidence of:

    (a) the company name and organization structure,
    (b) a fixed business address,
    (c) registered capital satisfying the provisions set by the State Council,
    (d) an adequate number of professional and technical staff, and
    (e) other criteria stipulated by the legislation and executive orders.

    In establishing a real estate development enterprise, application should be made to the department of industry and commerce for registration. This department shall register and issue business a license to those qualified enterprises complying with the provisions of this Law; and reject the applications of those who are not qualified.

    ... Real estate development enterprises whose business is in the nature of a limited liability company or a joint-stock company must also comply with the regulations contained in the Company Law.

    Within one month of obtaining a business license, a real estate development enterprise should register with the relevant registration office at the local government office at ... county level or above.

30. The ratio of registered capital to investment amount of a real estate development enterprise must comply with the stipulations set by the State.

    In a phased real estate development, the phased investment amount shall be proportional to the project size. The investment should be made intermittently during the ... construction period according to the terms laid down in the LUR sales contract.

Part Four   Real Estate Transactions

Chapter One   General Provisions

31. In the transfer or mortgage of ... real estate, the owners rights to the building as well as the LURs for the land occupied by the building shall be transferred and mortgaged.
32. The benchmark price of land and the guidance price for individual sites as well as the replacement value of buildings shall be estimated and announced by the authority according to the regulations set by the State Council.
33. The establishment of real estate valuation system:
    Property valuation must observe the principles of equality, fairness and openness following the technical standards and valuation procedures provided by the State. Based on the benchmark price of land, the guidance price for individual sites as well as the replacement value of buildings, reference should also be made to the local market transaction price of real estate when carrying out valuation.
34. The registration system of real estate transaction prices:
    The Legal owner of real estate, when transferring the real estate, shall register and record the transaction price with the local government.... Registration must be made in good faith.
35. The assignor and assignee in an assignment of real estate should register their property rights with the local authority in accordance with the provision in Part Five of this Law.

Chapter Two   Transfer of Real Estate

36. 'Transfer of real estate' means the transfer of ... real estate from the legal property owner to another party by way of assignment, gift or other legitimate means.
37. ... Real estate cannot be transferred in the following circumstances:

    (1) land use rights obtained by sale but not in compliance with S.38 of the Law,
    (2) real estate being confiscated by legal or administrative departments according to specific legislation or real estate whose legal rights are limited by some other means,
    (3) land use rights redeemed from the land user lawfully,
    (4) illegal joint tenancy or co-ownership of real estate without written consent,
    (5) property rights in dispute,
    (6) failure to apply for a valid property rights certificate,
    (7) other circumstances where the legislation and executive orders forbid any forms of assignment.

38. Where LURs are obtained with compensation, the transfer of real estate should comply with the following:

    (1) The conveyance fee for the transfer of LURs must be paid according to the agreement in the sales contract and an LUR certificate ... obtained;

(2) ... Building and construction works ... should commence on the date stipulated in the sales contract. In the case of building projects, at least 25 per cent of the total stipulated amount of investment must have been expended. In case of the comprehensive development of a large piece of land, infrastructural development for industrial use or other construction land use must have been completed.

Where buildings have been completed at the time of transfer, a building ownership certificate must be obtained ...

39. Where LURs are obtained through administrative allocation, the transfer must be assessed by an authorized people's government with power of attorney according to the rules set by the State Council. Upon approval, the assignee shall proceed with the LUR transfer procedures and pay the conveyance fees for LURs according to the relevant regulations.

Where LURs are obtained through administrative allocation, the transfer must be assessed by an authorized people's government with power of attorney according to the rules set by the State Council, and the authorised local government has the power to reject the application. In such cases the assignor should pass all the considerations received from the transfer to the State or retain the sum for other spending purposes.

40. The transfer of real estate should take the form of a written contract, which should state the way in which the LURs were originally obtained.

41. All benefits and burdens that accompany the LURs pass to the assignee with the transfer.

42. Where land use rights are obtained with compensation, after the transfer, the new term of the LURs becomes the original length of the term minus the numbers of years used up by the assignor.

43. Where land use rights are obtained with compensation, if after the transfer the assignee wants to change the use of land from the one stipulated in the land sale contract, approval must be obtained from the assignor, and the city planning department in the city or county people's government. A premium is also payable.

44. The pre-sale of commodity property shall comply with the following conditions:

(1) the ... conveyance fee must have been paid in full and an LUR certificate obtained,
(2) construction project planning permit must have been obtained,
(3) based on the amount of the commodity to be pre-sold, at least 25 per cent of the total investment must have been expended, together with a confirmed construction ... schedule and date of completion,
(4) the project must be registered with the people's government at county level or above and a commodity property pre-sale permit obtained.

The developer should also have pre-sale contract registered and recorded with a people's government at county level or above. The proceeds from the pre-sale must be used for the construction ... work.

45. The transfer of the pre-sold commodity property among purchasers will be decided by the State Council.

Chapter 3   Mortgage of Real Estate

46. 'Mortgage of real estate' means the mortgagor's offering of collateral by the real estate he obtained legally to the mortgagee without transferring the occupation mode of the property to the mortgagee. Upon default on the part of the mortgagor, the mortgagee has first ... claim on the proceeds from the auction of the mortgaged property.

47. If the building has been obtained legally, when mortgaging real estate the ... rights over the building as well as the LURs for the land occupied by the building shall be mortgaged. When the LURs have been obtained with compensation, the LURs can be mortgaged.

48. When mortgaging real estate, the LUR certificate and the building ownership certificate should be presented.

49. A written mortgage agreement must be signed between the mortgagor and mortgagee.

50. When the LURs have been obtained by way of administrative allocation, in the case of a forced sale of the real estate the proceeds from the auction should be used to repay to the government a sum equivalent to the conveyance fee for the LURs, before the mortgagor can lodge his claim.

51. Where new structures have been added to the real estate after the signing of the mortgage agreement and in the case of a forced sale, the new portion can be auctioned together with the mortgaged portion. However, the mortgagor has no claims over the proceeds from the new portion.

Chapter Four   Leasing of Real Estate

52. 'Leasing of real estate' refers to a property owner the lesser ... allowing a lessee to use his property ... in return for rent.

53 .In leasing real estate, the lessor and lessee should sign a written ... agreement specifying the terms of the lease ..., the use of the property, the rent level, and the rights and responsibilities of both parties etc. This agreement should ... be registered with the real estate management department.

54. If the real estate is a residential property, the ... terms of the lease should take account of the leasing policy of the local government concerned. If the real estate is for production or business purposes, all the terms as well as the rent ... should be decided by both parties.

55. When the LURs have been obtained through administrative allocation and the real estate built is being leased for commercial profit-earning purposes, the land income portion in the rental income should be passed back to the State. Detailed mechanisms should be devised by the State Council.

Chapter Five   Real Estate Agency Services and Organisations

56. Real estate agency services and organisations include real estate consultancy, real estate valuation and property agencies.

57. Real estate agency services and organisations should have the following:

   (1) a company name and organizational structure,
   (2) a fixed address of conducting business,
   (3) ... basic business capital and assets,
   (4) an adequate number of professional and technical staff, and
   (5) other criteria stipulated by the legislation and executive orders.

When establishing real estate agency services organisation, application should be made to the department of industry and commerce for registration. This departments shall register and issue a business license to those qualified enterprises.
58. The State will initiate a real estate appraisal certifying system.

Part Five Management of Registration of Property Rights

59. The State will initiate the registration of LURs and building ownership rights.
60. LURs obtained with compensation or by way of administration allocation should be registered with ... land management departments at the people's government at county level or above. Once assessed and approved, the same level of the people's government will issue the LUR certificate.

Where buildings are being built on land legally obtained, registration at the county level or above ... and a valid LUR certificate is necessary. Once assessed and approved, a building ownership rights certificate will be issued.

When there is transfer or change in ownership of real estate, an alteration of real estate registration should be presented to the relevant people's government, and an altered building ownership rights certificate will be issued. This altered building ownership rights certificate should then be presented to the land management department in the people's government for an alteration registration. Once approved, a new or altered LUR certificate will be issued.
61. When mortgaging real estate, a mortgage registration should be made at the county level or above. The LUR certificate and the building ownership rights certificate obtained from forfeited mortgaged real estate should also be registered for ... change of ownership.
62. Where a county or higher local government with a combined real estate and land management department ... has been approved by the relevant provincial, self-autonomous regional or centrally-administered municipalities government, it may issue an integrated real estate rights ownership certificate. According to S.60 of this Law, changes in the ownership of a building or LURs shall ... be contained in the integrated real estate ownership certificate.

Part Six Legal Responsibilities

63. Unauthorised approval of the conveyance of LURs or unauthorised conveyance of LURs for real estate development will be deemed a violation of S.10 and S.11 of this Law. Persons liable will be subject to disciplinary punishment by the superior government unit.
64. Any ... real estate development enterprise without a valid business license will be subject to termination ... by the county or higher level of the people's government. In addition, all income earned from the enterprise will be confiscated and a fine may be charged.
65. Failure to comply with S.38 sub-section (1) of the Law when transferring LURs will ... result in confiscation of the income from the transfer by the county or higher level of the people's government in addition to a fine.

66. Failure to comply with S.39 sub-section (1) of this Law when transferring real estate will ... result in confiscation of the income from the transfer by the land management department in the county level or above ... in addition to the repayment of the conveyance fee for the LURs and a fine.
67. Failure to comply with S.40 sub-section (1) of this Law when pre-selling commodity housing will ... result in termination of the pre-sale activities, confiscation of the income from the pre-sale activities by the real estate management department at the county level or above ... and a fine.
68. Any ... real estate agency service organisation without a valid business license will be subject to termination ... by the department of industry and commerce at the county level or above. In addition, all income earned from the business will be confiscated and a fine may be charged.
69. Any charge levied on ... real estate development enterprises that has no legal or regulatory basis will have to be refunded to the enterprises. When the situation is deemed serious, the officials involved will be subject to disciplinary punishment by the superior government unit.
70. Government officials in ... real estate management departments and ... land management departments who are negligent, misuse their powers or commit wrongful act will be subject to criminal charges. Those not indicted will be subject to disciplinary punishment.

    Government officials in ... real estate management departments and ... land management departments who misuse their powers ... to demand bribes from others or accept bribes from others in return for obtaining benefits for them will be subject to criminal charges based on anti-corruption measures. Those not indicted will be subject to disciplinary punishment.

Part Seven   Annex

71. This Law also covers real estate development and transaction activities from the LURs obtained on State-owned land outside the city planning district areas.
72. This Law comes into effect from 1st January 1995.

Appendix 3

REVISED LAND MANAGEMENT LAW, 1998 (DRAFT)

Chapter One   General Principles

1. This law is enacted to enhance the land management system and promote rational land use planning, protect socialist public land ownership and arable land and seek ... sustainable development.
2. The People's Republic of China practices a socialist public land ownership system. All land apart from that legally classified as collective land is state land and is managed by the State Council on the nation's behalf. No individuals or units can merge, sell or illegally transfer land. When it is in the ... public interest, the State can requisition collective land from farmers ... according to legal procedures. A land use system for monetary value is set up based on land use rights. Land use rights are classified into agricultural land use rights and development and construction land use rights.
3. All levels of government must ... work to protect agricultural land and formulate a rational land use policy.
4. The State will set up a land use management system. Accordingly, the State will provide a master land-use plan, in particular to protect agricultural land and control the conversion of agricultural land into urban development and construction land. ... According to the resource allocation principle and the master land-use plan, land is generally classified into three types, namely agricultural land, development and construction land and vacant land.
5. The relevant land administration department under the State Council will coordinate all national land management duties and responsibilities .... All lower levels of local land management ... will be designed by the relevant provincial governments.
6. When investigating violations of the land management legislation, the investigators from the land management departments can inspect all relevant documents.
7. Local governments have the duty to award those who have made achievements in research in scientific land management.

Chapter Two   Land Ownership and Land Use Rights

8. All urban land belongs to the State while land in ... rural districts and villages belongs to ... collectives, excepted classified otherwise by the law.
9. All state land and collective land can be granted to individuals and units for use according to law.
10. Collective land belongs to various farmers' economic units such as farmers' co-operative societies or village committees.

11. The ownership of collective land is recognised, certified and registered by the county governments. The rights of individuals and units using state land will be registered by local governments above county level.

12. All changes of land use and occupation rights must be re-registered.

13. All legal ownership of land and land use rights ... are protected by law.

14. The management rights over state land and collective land can be contracted out to individuals and units for agriculture, forestry, fishery and animal husbandry. Such management rights are protected by law.

15. All disputes over land ownership and use rights among individuals should be settled privately. When this is impossible, the relevant local government will arbitrate. All disputes among units should be settled by governments above county level. When all else fails appeal can be made to the people's court through civil action within 30 days of the judgement by the local government.

Chapter Three   Land Use and Protection

16. The State will establish a land use survey system. Local governments above county level, in association with the relevant land management departments, should carry out proper surveys on land use.

17. Local governments above county level, in association with the relevant land management departments, should, based on the land use survey, ... establish a land grading system.

18. The State will establish a land statistics system. Local governments above county level, in association with the relevant statistics and survey departments, should carry out proper surveys of land use statistics.

19. The State will establish a national land information system.

20. Local governments at all levels shall provide all necessary information, including on the state of the economy, land use distribution and demand analyses, for the national land information system. In addition, the amount of development and construction land set in the master land-use plan for all levels of government cannot exceed the maximum amount set by the relevant immediate superior level of government.

21. The land-use master plan will be devised according to the following ... principles:

    (1) stringent control over the conversion of agricultural land into non-agricultural land,
    (2) increased land-use efficiency,
    (3) macro coordination of land use,
    (4) encourage re-cultivation

22. At the county, village and township levels, the master land-use plan should divide land into land-use zones with specific land-use requirements.

23. The master land-use plans of provinces, autonomous districts and directly-administered cities must be approved by the State Council. All other cities with a population of over one million and ... other specified cities must have their master land-use plans approved by the relevant provincial governments

first then sent to the State Council for registration. All other cities must have their plans approved by the immediate superior governments.

24. The scale of development ... in ... urban areas should coordinate with the standards set by the relevant construction departments within the State Council. The principle is to fully utilise the current development and construction land and minimise the need for conversion of agricultural land.

25. Comprehensive development areas associated with lakes and rivers should coordinate with the development on land.

26. All levels of governments should take control of and plan for the amount of development and construction land. Annual land-use plans for development and construction should be based on the economic development of the nation and national policies on production and land-use planning.

27. Any amendments to approved master land-use plans must be approved by the relevant organisation. When major infrastructure plans approved by the State Council affect the land-use plan, the master land-use plans will be amended accordingly.

Sections 28 to 37 are concerned with agricultural land management.

Chapter Four   Development and Construction Land

38. When land is required for development and construction by individuals and units, application for the granting of state land is required. This does not apply ... to rural development for public purposes and interests .... State land in this case refers to all state land and requisitioned collective land.

39. When development and construction ... involve the merging and conversion of agricultural land ... , government approval at ... or above the provincial level is required. When agricultural land is required for town planning ... purposes and large scale infrastructure projects approved by the State Council ..., State Council approval is required.

40. Requisition of ... the following types of land requires the approval of the State Council:

    (1) basic agricultural land,
    (2) areas in excess of 500 mu in addition to basic agricultural land,
    (3) ... other land in excess of 1000 mu

    The requisition of other land ... requires the approval of the government at ... the provincial, autonomous region or directly-administered city level. Where agricultural land is involved, the conversion of such land is required first according to section 39 of this Law, except when State Council approval for requisition has been obtained ....

41. When the State is requisitioning land and the relevant approval has been obtained, the requisition order will be made public by the government at the county level and above. Holders of a valid LUR certificate for the affected land should then register their interests with the local government land management department.

42. Compensation for ... compulsory purchase is based on the existing use value before the requisition.

43. When large-scale infrastructure, water and electricity facilities are involved, the amount of compensation shall be determined by the State Council.
44. Local land management departments have the duty to scrutinise all feasibility studies on development and construction projects. When approval is sought for development and construction land, comments by the local land management department on the feasibility study ... must be attached.
45. When development and construction projects requiring the use of state land have been approved, the relevant individual or work unit should apply to the government above county level to use this state land.
46. When development and construction projects require the use of state land, the relevant individual or work unit is required to recompense the State ... except in the following circumstances:

    (1) land used for state administrative departments and military facilities,
    (2) land required for basic city facilities and infrastructure or public facilities ...
    (3) developments to do with natural resources, water facilities and transportation ...,
    (4) other purposes prescribed by law.

    The above four types of land use are not subject to monetary compensation, that is, the land is administratively allocated.
47. When individuals or work units purchase state land ... land use fees and other charges must be paid before the land can be used. Starting from the effective date of this Law, 40 per cent of income from ... land use rights must be sent to the central government and the local government may retain 60 per cent for other purposes.
48. When state land has been obtained for development and construction, the land-use conditions laid down in the ... contract must be complied with. Any subsequent changes must been approved by the relevant government departments.
49. When development and construction require the temporary use of state land or collective land, government approval above the county level is required. A temporary land-grant contract is signed with the local government or farmers' collective setting out the conditions and the ... fees to be paid. In general, the temporary ... contract should not last longer than three years. In addition, no permanent structure ... may be built on the temporary site.
50. The following circumstances trigger the withdrawal of LURs from LUR holders:

    (1) the land is required for public purposes,
    (2) the land is required for urban redevelopement,
    (3) the term of the original LUR contract has expired and the holder has not applied for an extension, or such an application has not been approved,
    (4) ... the ... tenant who obtained the land through administrative allocation is moving away,
    (5) the abandonment of highways, railways, airports or mining facilities.

    Compensation is payable when withdrawal involves items (a) and (b).

51. In the case of development for infrastructural or public purposes in villages and townships ... , the local master land-use plan and the annual land-use plan should be observed.

52. When collective economic units (or ... joint ventures with other units or individuals) ... use collective land for their enterprises, government approval above the county level is required.

53. When development for infrastructural or public purposes in villages and townships requires the use of land, government approval above the county level is required. When the conversion of agricultural land is involved, section 39 of this Law should be observed.

54. Each agricultural household can only occupy one housing site. The size of the housing site is prescribed by the relevant province, autonomous region or directly-administered city. If an agricultural household sells or leases their property to another party, application for a new housing site will not be approved.

55. LURs for collective land cannot be ... transferred to non-agricultural activities, except in the case of bankruptcy or merger with other units.

56. ... Structures that do not comply with the master land-use plan cannot be redeveloped or extended.

57. The following circumstances trigger the withdrawal of LURs on collective land:

   (1) the land is required for public purposes ...,
   (2) unauthorised land use,
   (3) ... the ... tenant is moving away.

Compensation is payable when withdrawal involves item (a)

Sections 58–71 deal with legal responsibilities.

Notes and References

1 Evolution of the Land Tenure System in China

1. *Wu Heng Zhi* (Historical Book of Daily Lives), in *Han Shu* (Book of the Han), ch. 27, p. 616.
2. Chronicle of Prime Minister Xiao, in *Si Ji* (Book of History), ch. 53, p. 805.
3. *Research of the Chinese Legal History* (University of Tokyo Press, 1960).
4. W. J. Wang (ed.), *History of the Land System in China* (Taipei: National Printing House, 1965), p. 166.
5. X. Zhong, *Historical Account of Land Theories in China* (Shanghai: Shanghai Academy of Social Sciences, 1995), pp. 168–9.
6. W. J. Wang (ed.), *History of the Land System in China* (Taipei: National Printing House, 1965), p. 373.
7. X. Zhong, *Historical Account of Land Theories in China* (Shanghai: Shanghai Academy of Social Sciences, 1995), pp. 451–2.
8. R. H. Tawney, *Agrarian China: Selected Source Materials from Chinese Authors* (Shanghai: Kelly and Walsh, 1938).
9. Cheng, Han Chang, *Land Systems and Reforms in China* (Beijing: China File Publisher, 1994), pp. 619–29.
10. Li, Ling Hin, *Privatisation of Urban Land in Shanghai* (Hong Kong: Hong Kong University Press, 1996, p. 30.

2 The Process of Urban Land Reform

1. A classic discussion of rent-bidding activities can be found in William Alonso, *Location and Land Use* (Cambridge: East-West Centre, 1964).
2. George S. Tolley, *Urban Housing Reform in China: An Economic Analysis* (Washington, DC: The World Bank, 1991).
3. Guangzhou State Land Administration Bureau.
4. C. Nechemias, 'The Impact of Soviet Housing Policy on Housing Conditions in Soviet Cities: The Uneven Push from Moscow', *Urban Studies*, vol. 18 (1981), p. 1.
5. Zhou Jia Hua, 'Intensify reform, strengthen management and establish a healthy and speedy economic growth', speech by the vice-premier at the 1994 National Meeting on Land Use Rights Reform.
6. Regulation 14 of the 'Regualtions on the Conveyance and Transfer of State-Owned Land in Qingdoa City'.
7. The Land Management Law was adopted at the Sixteenth Meeting of the Standing Committee of the Sixth NPC on 25 June 1986 and revised at the Fifth Meeting of the Standing Committee of the Seventh NPC on 29 December 1988.
8. The Provisional Land Regulations were promulgated by the State Council and became effective on 19 May 1991.
9. C. Hunter, 'Preface', in *PRC Property Series*, vol. v (Hong Kong: Asia Law and Practice, 1995).

10. Article 65, Clause 8 of the Chinese Constitution states that the NPC Standing Committee has the power to revoke all local regulations or decisions made by the organs of state power in provinces, autonomous regions and municipalities directly under the central government that contravene the constitution, national statues or administrative rules and regulations.

11. A real estate development enterprise is defined by the Real Estate Law (Article 29) as an enterprise engaged in developing and managing of real estate in order to make a profit.

12 The requirement for a written contract for different types of real estate transaction is stipulated in Articles 40, 44, 49 and 53 of the Real Estate Law.

13. Ling Hin Li, 'The Official Land Value Appraisal System Under the Land Use Rights Reform in China', *The Appraisal Journal*, vol. LXII, no. 1 (1995).

14. Commodity housing is housing that is built to be traded in the open market, as opposed to housing built by state enterprises for their employees. 'External' commodity housing can be bought by Chinese and foreign citizens, while 'internal' commodity housing is for Chinese citizens only.

15. See C. Hunter, 'The Guide to National Property Law', *The PRC Property Series*, vol. 5 (Asia Law & Practice, 1995), p. 93.

16. The State Land Administration Bureau', an introductory text published by the SLAB.

3 The Housing Market

1. R. J. R. Kirkby, *Urbanization in China: Town and Country in a Developing Economy 1949–2000* (London: Croom Helm, 1985), pp. 256–330.

2. *Yearbook of the People's Republic of China*, 1992/93, vol. 12 (Beijing: PRC, 1993), pp. 540–49.

3. Stephen K. Mayo, 'Housing Policy: Changing the Structure', *Finance & Development*, vol. 31 (March), pp. 44–6.

4. *Yearbook of the People's Republic of China*, op. cit., p. 46.

5. Ibid., pp. 57–60.

6. Y. W. Kwok, pp. 24–5.

7. *Yearbook of the People's Republic of China*, op. cit., p. 425.

8. Peter K. W. Fong, *The Commercialization of Housing in a Socialist State: An Attempt to Solve China's Urban Housing Problem*, pp. 19–21.

9. Kwok, op. cit., p. 30.

10. Mayo, 'Housing Policy', op. cit., p. 46.

11. *Real Estate News* (Hong Kong), 5 January 1986.

12. Ibid., pp. 23–8.

13. Ibid., pp. 45–7.

14. Ibid., p. 50.

15. World Bank, *China: Implementation Options for Urban Housing Reform*. (Washington, DC: World Bank, January 1992). p. 120.

16. Committee of Housing Reform, Proposal of Different Urban Housing Reform Models, pp. 52–5.

17. Ibid., pp. 126–8.

4 Urban Land Reform in China: the Initial Outcomes

1. 'Appraisal concept takes off in PRC real estate market', *China Property Review*, vol. IV, no. 3 (5 May 1995), pp. 1–5.
2. George S. Tolley *Urban Housing Reform in China: An Economic Analysis* (Washington, DC: The World Bank, 1991).

5 Urban Land Reform in Shanghai

1. 'Office Sector Analysis', *Shanghai Real Estate Market 1996* (Shanghai Statistical Bureau).

6 The Urban Land Market in Hong Kong

1. Liu, E. J. Wu and U. Lee (eds), *Land Supply in Hong Kong* (Research and Library Services Division, Legislative Council Secretariat, Hong Kong, 1997).
2. Government information supplied by the Planning, Lands and Environment Bureau.
3. The first British governor of Hong Kong.
4. Reversionary interest in the New Territories.
5. Except St John's Cathedral in central Hong Kong.
6. The details of the lots and original lessee of each lot are set out in a schedule to the block crown lease, together with details of the rental and use of the land.
7. On 14 June 1841, 50 sea-front lots were put on sale. The area of all the lots was nine acres and the reservation price was £10. Twenty three were sold, mainly to British merchant companies such as Jardine.
8. Established by the trustees of the Hong Kong Special Administrative Region Government Land Fund (three Chinese representatives of the Sino-British Land Commission), and duly authorised by the government of the People's Republic of China on 13 August 1986.

Select Bibliography

Abraham-frois, G. and E. Berrebi (1979) *Theory of Value, Prices and Accumulation* (Cambridge: Cambridge University Press), p. 2.

Alonso, W. (1964) *Location and Land Use* (Cambridge: East-West Center Press).

Balchin, P. N. (1988) *Urban Land Economics and Public Policy* (London: Macmillan).

Banuri, Tariq (ed.) (1991) *Economic Liberation: No Panacea* (Oxford: Oxford University Press).

Bardhan, Pranab K. and John E. Roemer (eds) (1993) *Market Socialism: The Current Debate* (Oxford: Oxford University Press).

Bertaud, A. and B. Renaud (1992) *Cities Without Land Markets*, World Bank Discussion Paper No. 227 (Washington, DC: World Bank).

Brabant, Jozef M. V. (1987) *Regional Price Formation in Eastern Europe* (Kluwer Academic Publishers).

Brueggeman, William B. and Jeffrey D. Fisher (1993) *Real Estate Finance and Investments* (Boston Mass.: Irwin).

Cai, Y. L. (1990) 'Land Use and Management in PR China', *Land Use Policy*, vol. 7, no. 4, pp. 337–50.

China Statistical Publishing House, *China Statistical Yearbook*, various issues. Beijing: China.

China Statistical Publishing House, Statistical Yearbook of Shanghai, various issues. Shanghai: China.

Chao, T. (1975) *The Spatial Distribution of Urban Land Value in the City of Taipei, Taiwan*, PhD Thesis (Kentucky: University of Kentucky).

Chau, K. W. and L. W. C. Lai (1995) 'Valuation of Real Estate Assets in China', *Journal of Valuation & Investment*, vol. 13, no. 5.

Cheng, Han Chang (1994) *Land Systems and Reforms in China* (Beijing: China File Publisher).

Conner, Alison, W. (1994) 'Training China's Early Modern Lawyers: Soochow University Law School', *Journal of Chinese Law*.

Corbo, Vittorio, Fabrizio Coricelli and Jan Bossak (eds) (1991) *Reforming Central and Eastern European Economies* (Washington, DC: World Bank).

Dawson, A. H. (1984) *The Land Problem in the Developed Economy* (London: Croom Helm).

Dowall, D. E. (1993) 'Establishing Urban Land Markets in the People's Republic of China', *American Planning Journal*, Spring, pp. 182–92.

Fitzgerald, E. V. K. and M. Wuyts (eds) (1988) *Markets Within Planning* (London: Frank Cass).

Fong, Peter K. W. (1988) 'The Commercialisation of Housing in a Socialist State: An attempt to Solve China's Urban Housing Problem', *Planning Quarterly*, March 1988, pp. 32–6.

Frisbie, J. (1992) 'Housing Local Employees', *The China Business Review*, September–October, pp. 26–7.

Hu, Cun-Zhi (1990) 'On the Development, Methodology and Management of Land Value Appraisal System', internal report, State Land Administration, Beijing (in Chinese).

Institute of Public Administration of New York (1991) *Report on Urban Land Use and Management in China, 1991*, a joint report with the Institute of Finance and Trade Economics, New York: Institute of Public Administration, Beijing.

Kaganova, O. Z. (1993) 'Creating An Urban Real Estate Market in Russia', *Real Estate Issues*, Spring/Summer, pp. 45–8.

Keith, Tom J. (1991) 'Applying Discounted Cash Flow Analyses to Land in Transition', *The Appraisal Journal*, October.

King, Russell (1977) *Land reform* (Boulder, CO: Westview Press).

Kitay, M. G. (1985) *Land Acquisition in Developing Countries* (Washington, DC: Lincoln Institute of Land Policy).

Kwok, Y. W. (1987) 'Urban Housing Provision in China after 1978', Discussion Paper, Centre of Urban Studies and Urban Planning, The University of Hong Kong.

Lai, Rita S. F. (1993) *'Housing Price and Government Land Policies'*, unpublished MSc thesis, University of Hong Kong.

Lehmann, Scott (1995) *Privatizing Public Lands* (Oxford: Oxford University Press).

Li, Ling Hin (1995) 'The Official Land Value Appraisal System under the Land Use Rights Reforms in China', *The Appraisal Journal*, January.

Li, Ling Hin (1996a) *Privatization of Urban Land in Shanghai* (Hong Kong: Hong Kong University Press).

Li, Ling Hin (1996b) 'The Advent of Valuers in China', *Australian Land Economics Review*, vol. 2, no. 1, pp. 33–9.

Li, Ling Hin (1997a) 'Valuation of Land in China', *The Valuer and Land Economist*, vol. 34, no. 5, February 1997, pp. 462–7.

Li, Ling Hin (1997b) 'Privatization of Urban Land Market in Shanghai', *Journal of Real Estate Literature*, vol. 5, pp. 161–8.

Li, Ling Hin (1997c) 'The Political Economy of the Privatization of Urban Land Market in Shanghai', *Urban Studies*, vol. 34, no. 2, February 1997, pp. 321–35.

Lichtenstein, Peter M. (1983) *An Introduction to Post-Keynesian and Marxian Theories of Value and Price* (New York: M. E. Sharpe).

Lin, Y. Y. (1983) *Valuation of Real Estate* (Taipei: Wen Sheng) (in Chinese).

Liu, E., J. Wu and V. Lee (eds) (1997) *Land Supply in Hong Kong* (Research and Library Services Division, Legislative Council Secretariat, Hong Kong.

Liu, W. X. and D. S. Yang (1990) 'China's Land Use Policy Under Change', *Land Use Policy*, vol. 7, no. 3, pp. 198–201.

Montgomery, J. R. (1987) 'The Significance of Public Landownership', *Land Use Policy*, January, pp. 42–50.

Needham, Barrie (1992) 'A Theory of Land Prices When Land is Supplied Publicly: The Case of the Netherlands', *Urban Studies*, vol. 29, no. 5, pp. 669–86.

Ness, V. P. (ed.) (1989) *Market Reforms in Socialist Societies: Comparing China and Hungary* (London: Lynne Rienner).

Pu, Z. (1990) 'Shanghai Real Estate Market before Liberation', *Essential Economic Situation* (Shanghai City Planning Commission) (in Chinese).

Shanghai Land Academy, *Shanghai Land*, various issues (Shanghai).

Shanghai Urban Economics Society (1987) *Research Report on the Model, Methods and Standards of the Charging of Land Use Fees for the use of Urban Land in Shanghai*, 2nd ed (Shanghai: Shanghai Urban Economics Society).

Song, S. F. (1992) 'Policy Issues Involving Housing Commercialization in the People's Republic of China', *Socio-Economic Planning Sciences*, vol. 26, no. 3, pp. 213–22.

SSB (1996) 'Office Sector Analysis', in *Shanghai Real Estate Market 1996* (Shanghai: Shanghai Statistical Bureau).

State Land Administration Publisher Bureau (Beijing) 1995 *Guidebook for the Qualifying Examinations to the China Land Valuer Institute.*

Tang, Y. B. (1989) 'Urban Land Use in China', *Land Use Policy*, vol. 6, no. 1, pp. 53–63.

Tawney, R. H. (1938) *Agrarian China: Selected Source Materials from Chinese Authors* (Shanghai: Kelly and Walsh).

The Investors' Handbook for Hong Kong and China (Hong Kong: Pitman Publishing Asia) 1995.

Tseng Hsiao (1953) *The Theory and Practise of Land Reform in The Republic of China* (Taiwan: Taiwan Research Institute of Land Economics).

Walker, A. (1991) *Land Property and Construction in the People's Republic of China* (Hong Kong: Hong Kong University Press).

Walker, Anthony, Kwong-Wing Chau and Wai-Chung Lai (1995) *Hong Kong in China: Real Estate in the Economy* (Hong Kong: Brooke Hillier Parker).

Walker, A. and L. H. Li (1994) 'Land Use Rights Reform and the Real Estate Market in China', *Journal of Real Estate Literature*, vol. 2, pp. 199–211.

Wang, W. J. (ed) (1965) *History of the Land System in China* (Taipei: National Printing House).

Wang, X. J. and G. X. Wang (1995) *Estate Price of China* (Beijing: China Product Price Publishing).

Wu Heng Zhi (Historical Book of Daily Lives) in the *Han Shu* (Book of the Han).

Yang, C. G. and Liu, W. X. (1991) *Economics Studies on China's Real Estate Market*, (in Chinese) (Henan: Henan People's Publishing Co).

Zhong, X. (1995) *Historical Account of Land Theories in China* (Shanghai: Shanghai Academy of Social Sciences), pp. 451–2.

Zhuan, M., D. Z. Zhang and W. R. Jiang (1993) *Real Estate Market System* (Beijing: Beijing School of Economics Press) (in Chinese), p. 99.

Index